THE SACRED COW AND THE ABOMINABLE PIG

RIDDLES OF FOOD AND CULTURE

•

MARVIN HARRIS

•

ORIGINALLY PUBLISHED AS *GOOD TO EAT*

A TOUCHSTONE BOOK
PUBLISHED BY SIMON & SCHUSTER, INC.
NEW YORK

Published by Simon & Schuster, Inc.
Simon & Schuster Building
Rockefeller Center
1230 Avenue of the Americas
New York, New York 10020
Originally published as *Good to Eat: Riddles of Food and Culture*
TOUCHSTONE and colophon are
registered trademarks of Simon & Schuster, Inc.
Designed by Edith Fowler
Manufactured in the United States of America

10 9 8 7 6 5 4 3 2 1 Pbk.

Library of Congress Cataloging in Publication Data

Harris, Marvin, date.
  The sacred cow and the abominable pig.

  (A Touchstone book)
  "Previously published as: Good to eat."
  Bibliography: p.
  Includes index.
  1. Food habits.   I. Title.
GT2850.H36   1987   394.1'2   86-24853
ISBN 0-671-63308-2 Pbk.

ACKNOWLEDGMENTS

I should like to thank a number of people for the special ways they have contributed to the writing of this book. They are: H. R. Bernard, Eric Charnov, Ronald Corn, Murray Curtin, Phyllis Durell, Daniel Gade, Karen Griffin, Kristen Hawkes, Madeline Harris, Katherine Heath, Delores Jenkins, Ray Jones, Michael Kappy, Karen Lupo, Maxine Margolis, Alice Mayhew, Daniel McGee, Gerald Murray, Kenneth Russell, Otto von Mering, and Janet Westin.

To Remember
HERBERT ARTHUR HARRIS
1923–1982

AUTHOR'S NOTE

Except for its title, this book is exactly the same book as *Good to Eat: Riddles of Food and Culture.* So why change the title? The problem was that too many bookstores and libraries were treating it as if it were a cookbook. Let me set the record straight. This is not a cookbook. It contains no recipes nor does it make recommendations concerning how or what people should eat. It definitely does not belong on the shelf next to books by Julia Child or Craig Claiborne. In fact, if your digestive tract is not especially robust, you will probably derive greater pleasure from some of the chapters if you do not consume the contents shortly before, during, or soon after mealtimes. My mission is strictly to amuse and edify, to change what you think, not what you eat, to explain what others have not been able to explain before: why certain foods are considered good to eat in some cultures but horrible to eat in others and why, among those foods which we find horrible to eat, some are sacred while others are abominated.

CONTENTS

CHAPTER ONE

GOOD TO THINK
OR GOOD TO EAT?

SCIENTIFICALLY SPEAKING, human beings are omnivores—creatures who eat both animal and vegetable foods. Like others of this ilk such as pigs, rats, and cockroaches, we can satisfy our nutritional needs by ingesting a very broad variety of substances. We can eat and digest everything from rancid mammary gland secretions to fungi to rocks (or cheese, mushrooms, and salt if you prefer euphemisms). Like other paragons of omnivory, we do not literally eat everything. In fact if one considers the total range of potential foodstuffs in the world, the dietary inventory of most human groups seems quite narrow.

We pass up some items because they are biologically unsuited to be eaten by our species. For example, the human gut simply cannot cope with large doses of cellulose. So all human groups spurn blades of grass, tree leaves, and wood (except for pith and shoots as in hearts of palm and bamboo). Other biological restrictions explain why we put petroleum in cars and not in our stomachs, or human excrement in sewers and not on our plates (we hope). Yet many of the substances which human beings do not eat are items which are perfectly edible from a biological standpoint. This seems clear enough since somewhere in the world some groups eat, even relish, what other groups spurn and abominate. Genetic variations can account for only a small fraction of this diversity. Even in the case of milk, which I will be ex- amining later on, genetic differences by themselves only supply part of the explanation for why some groups love to drink it and others do not.

When India's Hindus spurn beef, Jews and Moslems abominate pork, and Americans barely avoid retching at the thought of dog stew, one can be sure that something beyond mere digestive physiology is shaping the definition of what's good to eat. That other something is a people's gastronomic traditions, their food culture. If you are born and raised in the United States, you tend to acquire certain American food habits. You learn to enjoy beef and pork, but not goat or horse, or grubs or grasshoppers. And you are definitely not fond of rat stew. Yet horseflesh appeals to the French and Belgians; most Mediterranean people are fond of goat meat; grubs and grasshoppers are widely esteemed as delicacies; and a survey commissioned by the U.S. Quartermaster Corps turned up forty-two different societies in which people eat rats.

Confronted with the diversity of food traditions in their far- flung empire, the ancient Romans shrugged their shoulders and went back to eating their favorite putrid fish sauces. "There's no disputing taste," they said. As an anthropologist, I also subscribe to the cultural relativism of food tastes: food habits are not to be ridiculed or condemned simply because they are different. But that still leaves much to dispute and ponder. Why are human foodways so diverse? Can anthropologists explain why specific food preferences and avoidances are found in one culture and not in another?

I think we can. Perhaps not in every instance, nor down to the most finicky details. But there generally are good and suffi- cient practical reasons for why people do what they do, and food is no exception. I shall not attempt to disguise the fact that this view is currently unpopular. The fashionable premise is that food- ways are accidents of history which express or convey messages derived from essentially arbitrary values or inexplicable religious beliefs. In the words of a French anthropologist: "When surveying the vast realm of symbolism and cultural representations involved in human food habits, one has to accept the fact that most of it is really difficult to ascribe to anything other than an intrinsic coherence which is largely arbitrary." Food, so to speak, must nourish the collective mind before it can enter an empty stomach. To the extent that food preferences and aversions can be explained, their explanation "must be sought not in the nature of the food items" but rather in a "people's underlying thought pattern." Or expressed in a more strident idiom: "Food has little to do with nourishment. We do not eat what we eat because it is convenient or because it is good for us or because it is practical or because it tastes good."

For my part, I do not wish to deny that foods convey messages and have symbolic meanings. But which come first, the messages and meanings or the preferences and aversions? To extend the scope of a famous dictum proposed by Claude Lévi-Strauss, some foods are "good to think," others are "bad to think." But I hold that whether they are good or bad to think depends on whether they are good or bad to eat. Food must nourish the collective stomach before it can feed the collective mind.

Let me express this viewpoint a bit more systematically. Preferred foods (good to eat) are foods that have a more favorable balance of practical benefits over costs than foods that are avoided (bad to eat). Even for an omnivore it makes sense not to eat everything that one can digest. Some foods are hardly worth the effort needed to produce and prepare them; some have cheaper and more nutritious substitutes; some can only be eaten at the expense of giving up more advantageous items. Nutritional costs and benefits form a fundamental part of the balance—preferred foods generally pack more energy, proteins, vitamins, or minerals per serving than avoided foods. But there are other costs and benefits that may override the nutritive value of foods and make them good or bad to eat. Some foods are highly nutritious, but people spurn them because too much time and effort are needed to produce them or because of the adverse effects they have on soils, animal and plant life, and other aspects of the environment.

As I hope to show, major differences in world cuisines can be traced to ecological restraints and opportunities which differ from one region to another. For example, to anticipate things to come, the most carnivorous cuisines are associated with relatively low population densities and lands not needed or unsuitable for planting crops. In contrast, the most herbivorous cuisines are associated with dense populations whose habitat and food production technology cannot support the production of animals for meat without reducing the amount of proteins and calories available for humans. In the case of Hindu India, as we shall see, the ecological impracticality of meat production so far outweighs the nutritional benefits of carnivory that meat is avoided—bad to eat, and therefore bad to think.

An important point to bear in mind is that nutritional and ecological costs and benefits are not always the same as monetary—"dollars-and-cents"—costs and benefits. In market economies such as the United States, good to eat may mean good to sell, regardless of the nutritional consequences. The sale of infant formula as a substitute for mother's milk is a classic instance of profitability taking precedence over both nutrition and ecology. In the Third World, bottle feeding is not good for babies because the formula is often mixed with dirty water. Also, mother's milk should be preferred because it contains substances which make infants immune to many common diseases. Mothers may benefit slightly from substituting bottled milk for breast milk because they can leave their babies in someone else's care while they go off to find a job in a factory. But by cutting short their period of lactation, women also shorten the interval between pregnancies. The only big beneficiaries are the transnational corporations. To sell their product they resort to advertisements that mislead women into believing that formula milk is better for babies than mother's milk. Fortunately, this practice has recently been discontinued as a result of international protests.

As this example shows, bad foods, like ill winds, often bring someone some good. Food preferences and aversions arise out of favorable balances of practical costs and benefits, but I do not say that the favorable balance is shared equally by all members of society. Long before there were kings, capitalists, or dictators, lopsided allocations of costs to women and children and of benefits to men and adults were not uncommon—a point to which I shall return in several of the chapters to come. Also, where classes and castes exist, one group's practical advantage may be another group's practical disadvantage. In such cases the ability of privileged groups to maintain high standards of nutrition without sharing their advantage with the rest of society comes down to their ability to keep their subordinates in check through the exercise of political power.

What all this means is that it is no easy matter to calculate the practical costs and benefits which underlie food preferences and avoidances. Each puzzling food item has to be seen as part of a whole system of food production, a distinction must be made between long- and short-run consequences, and one must not forget that food is often a source of wealth and power for the few as well as of nourishment for the many.

The idea that foodways are arbitrary gains strength from a number of baffling preferences and avoidances which almost everyone believes to be impractical, irrational, useless, or harmful. My strategy in this book is to attack these citadels—to take on the most baffling cases—and to show that they can be explained by nutritional, ecological, or dollars-and-cents choices. Some may suspect that I have elected to attack only those citadels of arbitrariness whose fatal flaws were known to me beforehand. For the record, this is not true. When I began each case I was as baffled as anyone else and had no prior idea of where the solution would be found. In fact, I have chosen precisely those cases which interested me most because they seemed to contradict my basic premises.

Let me be the first to admit that I shall only touch on a small fraction of humankind's puzzling food habits. Since the number of additional puzzles is unknown and completely open-ended, I cannot draw a random sample of cases to prove that in general there are practical reasons for what people eat. Successful solution of a few baffling puzzles does not guarantee success with all the remaining ones. Yet it does suggest that skeptics ought to be more skeptical of their own favorite impractical, irrational, useless, and harmful food practices. If everyone turned back at the first point of bafflement, no solutions to any difficult problems could ever be found. And then everything in the world would appear largely arbitrary, wouldn't it? But on to the first puzzle. Let the proof be in the pudding.

CHAPTER TWO

MEAT HUNGER

PICTURE A LINE of people dressed in shabby raincoats, umbrellas in one hand and an assortment of plastic bags and briefcases in the other. As they shuffle forward in the grey dawn, the ones up front grudgingly make room for women who are pregnant or carrying infants. Those behind grumble and make jokes about pillows stuffed under dresses and babies borrowed for the morning. One woman in a knit cap explains: "Nothing has gone up in price at this stand because there's nothing here anyway." The Polish people are beginning their daily hunt for meat.

Problems with the meat supply endanger the security of Poland's state socialist system. If the butcher shop lines grow longer and the shelves emptier, watch out. In 1981 the government announced a 20 percent cut in subsidized meat rations and then had to declare martial law to restore order. "The patience of the housewife has snapped," a correspondent for *The Economist* reported. "Used to queuing for hours, clutching empty shopping bags and waiting for meat deliveries that sometimes never come, several thousand of them have taken to the streets in noisy banner-waving hunger marches in Kutno, Lodz, Warsaw and other major towns." "Give us meat," the crowds demanded. (Aren't starving masses supposed to ask for bread or rice?) In Poland they get desperate over a shortage of what many nutritionists

19

consider a luxury and others increasingly condemn as bad for your health.

Why are the Poles and other Eastern Europeans haunted by the specter of shelves bereft of ham and sausages? Are they malnourished? Is their diet deficient in calories or proteins? According to the latest recommendation of the Food and Agriculture/World Health Organization, an adult male weighing 176 pounds (80 kilos) needs about sixty grams of protein per day. In 1980 Poles were getting not sixty but over one hundred grams of protein per day. In fact they had sixty-one grams from animal foods alone—meat, fish, poultry, and dairy products—enough to satisfy the recommended daily allowance without counting on proteins from plant foods at all. As for calories, they were consuming over three thousand per capita per day. By way of comparison, the United States's consumption of animal protein in 1980 was sixty-five grams per day per person—only four grams more than Poland's—and calorie consumption was almost exactly even. I admit that per capita averages cover up some painful details. In Poland, the supply of meat and other animal foods is erratic. Shipments to butchers are bought out as soon as they arrive; some people get a lot of it and others get very little. But these problems are partly a consequence of panic buying. They help to make my point: the Poles, in no danger of malnutrition, could eat less meat and easily remain well nourished, yet they are willing to spend a good part of their lives in an exasperating pursuit of more meat and other animal products. Why?

One might suppose that the Polish government would be trying hard to get people to be satisfied with the dietary status quo. Yet rather than argue that the national diet is already adequate and that more meat is unnecessary, the government has met each crisis by promising more meat. At great cost to the rest of the economy, it raised meat, fish, and fowl production by 40 percent between 1970 and 1975. By 1980, the monthly ration of low-cost meat in the state shops was costing the government $2.5 billion in subsidies, about half of the total national food subsidy bill.

Nor is the Polish government alone in this legitimation of the popular demand for meat. Even without the spur of food riots, the Soviet Union, for example, spends huge sums to import about 40 million tons of soybeans, maize, and wheat from abroad. The sole purpose of this massive effort is to provide feed for animals, much of it by freeing low-quality domestic grains for stock raising while using the imports for human consumption. In 1981 the people of the Soviet bloc consumed 126 million tons of grain while their animals consumed 186 million tons. In Western eyes big grain imports prove that the Soviet farm system is an utter failure. In Soviet eyes, they prove that the government is doing its best to put more meat on everybody's plate. Soviet grain production is not all that bad when it comes to feeding people; in fact there is an annual surplus of grain for human consumption. The trouble with the Soviet agricultural system is that it is incapable of feeding all those animals as well. This is because it costs much more to raise animals for food than to raise plants for food. Expressed in energy terms, it takes nine additional calories to provide one calorie for human consumption when grain is converted into animal flesh. Or in terms of protein, it takes four grams of protein in the grains to produce one gram of protein in the meat. In order for the United States to support its current meat consumption habits, 80 percent of the grain grown on United States farms has to be fed to animals. These figures notwithstanding, the USSR has vowed to catch up with the United States. Starting with Nikita Khrushchev's "we will bury you" speech, the Soviets have devoted increasing quantities of their grain crops, supplemented by huge grain imports from abroad, to overtake the United States in the production of meat and milk. While they have come close to achieving their goal for milk—partly as a result of declining milk consumption in the United States—they are far behind in meat production. In fact, they have yet to catch up with Poland.

Are the Poles merely indulging an arbitrary cultural taste? Is their meat hunger nothing but a symbol of the rejection of the Polish brand of state socialism? Both the state bureaucrats and their opponents recognize that meat is a symbol that has the capacity to stir revolutionary thoughts. But it would be an injustice to the Polish people to view their craving for meat as nothing but a symbolic form of hunger. There are good reasons why the Poles and other Eastern Europeans should be concerned about cutbacks in their meat rations.

My argument is that animal foods and plant foods play fundamentally different biological roles in human foodways. Despite recent findings which link the overconsumption of animal fats and cholesterol to degenerative diseases in affluent societies, animal foods are more critical for sound nutrition than plant foods. I don't mean to say that animal foods are so good to eat that we can dispense with plant foods altogether. We are best off when we consume both kinds. Rather, my contention is that while plant foods can sustain life, access to animal foods bestows health and well-being above and beyond mere survival. In agricultural societies animal foods are especially good to eat nutritionally speaking, but they are also especially hard to produce. Animal foods get their symbolic power from this combination of utility and scarcity. I do not think that it is an arbitrary cultural fact therefore that all over the world, as well as in Poland, people honor and crave animal foods more than plant foods and are willing to lavish a disproportionate share of their energy and wealth on producing them.

No, I have not forgotten hundreds of millions of people who are vegetarians and who supposedly prefer plant foods over animal foods. But the term vegetarian is misleading. While significant numbers of people spurn meat, fish, fowl, and other flesh, only a tiny minority of cultists, monks, and mystics has ever professed a bias against all foods of animal origin—a bias against eggs, milk, cheese, or other dairy products as well. True vegetarians are technically known as vegans. Like the followers of "macrobiotics" leader George Ohsawa, who aim to exist on nothing but brown rice, soy sauce, and herbal teas, they are few and far between. And for good reason. Vegans no more refute the existence of a universal preference for animal foods than the fasts of holy men refute the preference for food over hunger. The lesson to be drawn from sporadic episodes of veganism, as from the occasional appearance of people who deliberately starve themselves to death, is that such practices are not only unpopular but they don't last long.

No major world religion has ever urged its followers to practice veganism, nor entirely banned the consumption of eggs and animal flesh from the diet of ordinary people. Hindu foodways in this regard simply do not conform to popular stereotypes. In India people delight in consuming as much milk, butter, cheese, and yogurt as they can afford, and ghee, or clarified butter, is the preferred cooking fat in traditional Indian cuisine. As for animal flesh, some members of the priestly Brahman caste reject it entirely; but most Brahmans eat either eggs, poultry, or fish in addition to copious quantities of milk and dairy products. Brahmans, at any rate, constitute a small minority of the Hindu population; all the other castes consume various combinations of dairy products, eggs, poultry, mutton, fish, pork, goat, and even beef. True enough, the total quantity of animal flesh consumed by Hindu Indians amounts to less than a gram per day per capita, but that is because all kinds of animal foods are in scarce supply in relation to the huge population. Agricultural expert Narayanan Nair claims that for most Hindus, goat, sheep, and poultry are a "delicious food . . . they would eat more of it if they could afford it."

Buddhism is the other great world religion whose food preferences Westerners frequently confuse with veganism. Again, only a relatively small number of extremely devout Buddhist priests voluntarily deprive themselves of all animal foods. Buddhists cannot slaughter or witness the slaughter of animals; but they can eat animal flesh as long as they are not responsible for the termination of the animal's life. Buddha himself never gave up eating boar meat, and in Tibet, Sri Lanka, Burma, and Thailand Buddhist priests eat meat as well as dairy products. As for ordinary Buddhists, they tend to eat as much meat or fish as they can afford, especially where ecological conditions prevent the raising of dairy cattle. Buddhists in Burma, Thailand, and Cambodia are great aficionados of fish, which they consume fresh, dried, salted, and fermented. In addition to fish, Thai Buddhists consume significant quantities of pork, buffalo meat, beef, chicken, ducks, silkworms, snails, shrimp, and crab. During the rainy season they may eat as much as a pound of frogs a week. Cambodian Buddhists consume fish, crabs, frogs, mussels, and certain highly esteemed species of hairy spiders. Buddhist religious principles are flexible. As in Christianity, practice often falls short of or circumvents exalted ideals: witness Genghis Khan and his Buddhist Mongol hordes, who not only lived and died by the sword but were great lovers of mutton and horsemeat (more about this later). As Buddhists grow older they worry a great deal about complying with the ban on killing animals, but they can always get someone else to do the dirty work. In Thailand and Burma, to be truly virtuous, one should never crack an egg. Shopkeepers routinely evade this restraint by keeping a supply of eggs that have been "accidentally" cracked. Wealthy Buddhists ask their servants to break their eggs; the master escapes blame because he didn't do the killing, and the servant escapes blame because he was ordered to do it.

The explanation of aversions to animal flesh among Brahmans, Buddhists, and members of less influential religious groups such as the Jains and Seventh-Day Adventists would take me far afield. For the moment, all I need to say is that less than 1 percent of the world's population voluntarily spurns every type of flesh food, and less than one-tenth of 1 percent are bona fide vegans. Involuntary rather than voluntary abstinence characterizes the animal food patterns of people in less developed countries. This can be seen from the changing proportions of plant and animal foods in relation to improvements in per capita income. The Japanese experience should be taken as a harbinger of Asian things to come: between 1961 and 1971 Japanese consumption of animal protein rose 37 percent while plant protein consumption fell by 3 percent. On a worldwide basis the consumption of grain by livestock is rising twice as fast as the consumption of grain by people. Within most societies, developed as well as under-

developed, the higher the income bracket, the greater the proportion of animal products in the diet. A classic study of this
relationship showed that in over fifty countries higher-income
groups derive far more of their fats, proteins, and calories from
animal sources than do lower-income groups. Proportionate to
income, calories from animal fats replace calories from vegetable
fats and starchy carbohydrates; and calories from animal protein
replace calories from plant proteins. In Jamaica, for example,
wheat flour is the number one source of protein for the poorest
25 percent of the population, with chicken and beef ranking tenth
and thirteenth. But for the top 25 percent of Jamaicans, beef and
chicken rank first and second while wheat flour rank seventh.
This relationship holds around the world. The elites in Madagascar consume twelve times as much animal protein as the people at the bottom of the social hierarchy. Even in the United
States, people at the top eat 25 percent more meat than those
at the bottom. In India, the highest-income groups consume over
seven times more animal protein that the lowest.

Many different kinds of cultures, from hunter-gatherer bands
to industrial states, exhibit similar preferences for animal food.
Anthropologists living in remote parts of the world regularly report cases of meat hunger which invite comparison with modern-
day efforts to increase meat consumption. The phenomenon is
especially common among the native peoples of South America,
perhaps because they lack any domesticated animals that could
provide them with animal products. Janet Siskind recounts how
the daily life of the Sharanahua, a jungle village people of eastern
Peru, revolves around the problem of meat shortages. Sharanahua
women relentlessly cajole and taunt their menfolk to go hunting
and bring back more meat. If two or three meatless days go by,
the women get together, put on their beads and face paint, and
corner each man in the village one by one. They gently tug at
the man's shirt or belt and sing him a song: "We are sending you
to the forest, bring us back meat." The men pretend not to hear,
but they go hunting the next morning. They know that the women
will not sleep with them if there is no meat in the village. Siskind

comments: "The Sharanahua are continually preoccupied with the topic of meat, and men, women, and children spend an inordinate amount of time talking about meat, planning visits to households that have meat and lying about the meat they have in their own households." Other ethnographers who have lived with South American jungle peoples report remarkably similar attitudes and behavior: Jules Henry on the Kaingang: "meat is the principal article of diet, everything else is garnish"; Robert Carneiro on the Amahuaca: "No Amahuaca meal is really complete without meat"; Allan Holmberg on the Siriono: "Meat is the most desired item of the Siriono"; David Maybury-Lewis on the Shavanté: "Meat far and away transcends other forms of food in the Shavanté esteem and in their conversation."

Reports about band and village peoples from other continents paint a similar picture. In his study of the !Kung of Africa's Kalahari desert, Richard Lee states that both men and women value meat more highly than plant food. "When meat is scarce in the camp, all people express a craving for it, even when vegetable foods are abundant." The native peoples of Australia and the South Pacific islands express similar sentiments. In New Guinea, despite the ready availability of yams, sweet potatoes, sago palm flour, taro, and other vegetable foods, people devote an inordinate amount of time to raising pigs; they relish pork more than any other food, and hold great pig feasts at which they stuff themselves to the point of nausea.

Out of necessity, meat portions are more likely to be small and to be eaten in combination with grains and starchy tubers. But even the presence of a few ounces of animal food can make people feel good. Hunter-gatherers and village horticulturalists commonly complain that they are "meat hungry," a condition which their languages denote by words which are different from the words for ordinary hunger. Among the Canela of the Amazonia, *ii mo plam* means "I am hungry" but *iiyate* means "I am hungry for meat." The Semai, natives of the jungles of Malaysia, do not consider a meal which lacks rice or another starch to be satisfactory; but a man who has not had animal flesh recently will say,

"I haven't eaten for days." The Yanomamo, who also have special ways of expressing their meat hunger, regulate the amount of starchy plantains (a kind of banana) they consume by the amount of meat available. They like to alternate bites of meat with bites of plantains—which are seldom in short supply. This seems to accord well with the nutritional concept of "protein-sparing" diets. If meat is not accompanied by calorie-rich carbohydrate foods, the protein in the meat will be used as a source of energy and will not be available for other physiological functions.

Virtually every band or village society studied by anthropologists expresses a special esteem for animal flesh by using meat to reinforce the social ties that bind campmates and kinfolk together. Far more often than plant foods, animal products must be shared reciprocally between producers and consumers. Meat eating is the quintessential social occasion in all of the groups I have mentioned so far. Yanomamo hunters, for example, believe that if they do not share their catch, they will lose their hunting skills. Individuals and families rarely share their plantains and other crops, but they never consume a hunter's catch without cutting it up into portions and distributing it to all the important men in the village, who in turn make further distributions to the women and children. Lorna Marshall depicts meat distribution among the !Kung as progressing in waves from the hunter to his helpers to primary relatives on to more distant relatives and in-laws until everybody in the camp gets some, even if it is only a single mouthful. The !Kung cannot imagine one family eating meat and others not. "Lions do that," they say, "not men." By sharing meat, Marshall writes, "the fear of hunger is mitigated; the person with whom one shares will share in turn when he gets some meat; people are sustained by a web of mutual obligation." While the !Kung also share other foods, nothing else occasions the care and concentration that accompanies meat being passed from one hearth to another.

The preoccupation with meat has another side to it. Meat hunger can be a powerfully disruptive as well as harmonious force. In band and village societies, especially those which do not possess significant domesticated sources of animal flesh, eggs, or milk, lack of success in the hunt may lead to quarrels, a split in the community, and the outbreak of warfare between neighboring camps and settlements. There need not be any actual "scarcity" of meat or animal or plant protein from a nutritional point of view in order for meat distributions to take a quarrelsome turn. As among the Poles, groups such as the Yanomamo are generally well nourished, average as much as seventy-five grams of animal protein per capita per day, and show few signs of protein deficiency disease. But when the population of a village gets bigger, its hunters deplete the nearby game. There are more meatless days, complaints about meat hunger increase, and some men find it increasingly difficult to fulfill their obligation to reciprocate the gifts of meat they have received. The "web of mutual obligation" turns into a web of mutual suspicion. Portions must be cut smaller and smaller, and some villagers may have to be left out altogether. Resentments build and soon hunters begin to slight each other deliberately. As their communal supply of meat dwindles and tensions mount, groups like the Yanomamo split up into hostile factions which move off to establish new villages in areas that have more game. Or they may step up their attacks on enemy villages as a means of gaining access to additional hunting grounds. Recent studies show that the problem of dwindling animal resources lies behind much of the endemic warfare found in native Amazonia and other tropical forest habitats.

A preoccupation with animal flesh also dominates the foodways of more complex societies. It is no accident that chiefs and heroes the world over celebrate their victories by hosting feasts and bestowing large portions of meat on followers and guests. Nor is it an accident that priestly castes such as those described in the Hebrews' Book of Leviticus or the Hindus' Rig Veda made ritual slaughter and consumption of domestic animals a principal focus of their sacraments. The very idea of sacrifice, fundamental to the formative doctrines of Christianity, Hinduism, Judaism, and Islam, arose from the sharing of meat in the camps and villages of prehistoric times. With the domestication of herds and flocks, meat, blood, and milk had to be shared with the ancestors and gods, just as hunters had to share the day's catch with each other, to create a web of mutual obligations, to prevent jealousies and strife, and to preserve communities that embraced both the invisible rulers of the world and their earthly creations. In hallowing animal butchery as sacrifice, and in feeding the gods on animal flesh, ancient peoples expressed their own craving for meat and other animal products. Or taking a slightly different point of view, animal flesh was so good to eat that humans would consume it only if they took precautions to make sure that the gods were willing to share it with them.

All these cultural convergences and recurrences support my theory that animal foods play a special role in the nutritional physiology of our species. In addition we seem to have descended from a long line of meat-hungry animals. Not so long ago anthropologists believed that monkeys and apes were strict vegetarians. Now, after closer and more meticulous observation in the wild, most primates turn out to be omnivorous just like us. And many species of monkeys and apes are not only omnivorous, but they further resemble humans by making a big fuss when they dine on meat.

Being rather small creatures, monkeys prey mostly on insects rather than game. But they expend much more time on capturing and eating insects than anyone previously believed. This has cleared up a long-standing puzzle about the way monkeys feed in the wild. As they make their way through the forest canopy, many species of monkeys send down a constant rain of half-chewed pieces of leaves and fruit. Further study of the morsels they consume versus the morsels they discard indicates that they are not being sloppy but finicky. Monkeys do a lot of sniffing, feeling, exploratory nibbling, and spitting out before they pick the fruit they want. But they are not looking for the perfect, ripe, unblemished Garden of Eden apple; they are trying to find the ones with the worms inside. In fact, some Amazonian species are more interested in the insect larva than in the fruit. They open a weevil-infested fig, eat the weevil, and discard the fig. Some eat both fruit and larva, spitting out the portion that hasn't been spoiled. Some simply ignore fruits that show no signs of insect-induced decomposition. In seeking out insect-containing fruits, monkeys foreshadow human foodways that combine calorie-rich carbohydrates and meat for their "protein-sparing" effect. Where humans alternate bites of meat with bites of plantains, monkeys achieve the same effect simply by selecting plantains that have lots of insects in them.

We now also know that several species of monkeys not only consume insects but actively pursue small game. Baboons are especially keen hunters. During a single year of observation in Kenya, Robert Harding saw baboons kill and eat forty-seven small vertebrates including infant gazelles and antelopes. Baboons normally spend most of their time in the wild eating plant foods. But as among many involuntary "vegetarian" human populations, the reason baboons consume only small quantities of meat may be more a matter of necessity than choice: they have difficulty finding and capturing suitable prey. Whenever there is a choice, claims William Hamilton, the baboons he has observed in Namibia and Botswana prefer to feed on animal matter first; roots, grass seeds, fruits, and flowers second; and leafy materials and grass third. During seasons when insects were abundant, Hamilton found that baboons spent as much as 72 percent of the time eating them.

The most startling discovery about nonhuman primate meat eating is that chimpanzees, our closest relatives in the animal kingdom, are devoted and fairly effective hunters. (So much for the ever-popular theory that humans are unique "killer apes.") On the basis of a decade of observation in Gombe National Park in Tanzania, Geza Teleki estimates that chimpanzees use about 10 percent of their time to hunt small mammals—mostly young baboons, other kinds of monkeys, and "bushpigs." Also at Gombe, R. W. Wrangham observed chimpanzees capturing and eating colobus monkeys, bushpig, bushbuck, redtail monkeys, blue monkeys, and baboons in descending order of frequency. Teleki estimates that the adult males eat noninsect meat about once every two weeks. Chimpanzee hunters frequently cooperate with each other. As many as nine chimpanzees, mostly males, position and reposition and coordinate their movements, sometimes for an hour or more, to surround their quarry and effectively prevent its escape. After capturing their prey, chimpanzees typically spend several hours tearing the carcass apart and eating it. Many individuals get a share. Some "beg" for morsels by holding the palms of their hands upward under the chin of a dominant male; some snatch pieces from one another, and dart in and out to recover dropped fragments—behavior that seldom occurs when they dine on plant foods. Through one means or another, as many as fifteen different individuals—mostly males—share in eating a single prey animal.

I do not see how it can be either arbitrary or coincidental that animal foods evoke special behavior among so many human groups as well as among our primate cousins. But this does not mean that I believe humans are compelled by genetic programming to seek out and consume such foods, the way lions or eagles and other true carnivores are driven to eat meat. There is too much variation in the ratios of plants to animals in the foodways of different cultures to support the idea that we instinctively recognize animal foods as something we *must* eat. A more plausible explanation is that our species-given physiology and digestive processes predispose us to learn to prefer animal foods. We and our primate cousins pay special attention to foods of animal origin because such foods have special characteristics which make them exceptionally nutritious.

What's so nutritious about them? First of all, per cooked portion they are a better source of protein than most plant foods. As compared with most foods of plant origin, a higher percentage by weight of cooked meat, poultry, or fish consists of protein. And with one or two exceptions, the quality of proteins in foods of animal origin is higher than the quality of the proteins in plant foods.

The nutritional importance of protein is that the body uses it to promote and regulate tissue growth. Muscles, organs, cells, hormones, and enzymes all consist of different kinds of proteins formed by particular combinations of amino acids linked into long, complex chains. Between 15 percent and 40 percent by weight of cooked meat, fish, fowl, and milk solids consists of proteins. In contrast, the protein content of cooked cereals ranges from about 2.5 percent to 10 percent. Cooked legumes—beans, peanuts, lentils, peas—fall in the same range (they have higher percentages by dry weight, but they cannot be digested uncooked). Starchy root crops such as potatoes, yams, and manioc, along with fruits and green, leafy vegetables, rarely contain more than 3 percent protein by weight. Nuts, peanuts, and soybeans are the only plant foods that are as proteinaceous as meat, fish, fowl, and milk solids. But with the exception of soybeans, the quality of the proteins in plant foods—including nuts and legumes—is significantly lower than the quality of proteins in foods of animal origin. This point needs to be clarified.

As I said, proteins consist of amino acids. It takes about twenty-two amino acids to build all of the body's thousands of different proteins. Out of molecules obtained through eating other kinds of nutrients such as starches, sugar, vegetable fats, and water, the body itself can synthesize twelve of these amino acids. But there are ten amino acids which it cannot synthesize. These ten are called the "essential" amino acids. We can only get essential animo acids by eating a plant or animal that has the ability to synthesize them or that has eaten them for us. When we eat a food containing proteins, the proteins get broken down into their constituent amino acids, and the amino acids are then distributed throughout the body to form a "pool," which is drawn upon as needed by the cells in various organs and tissues. When we stop eating foods containing the essential amino acids, the assembly of amino acids into proteins needed for maintenance, repair, and growth continues until the essential amino acid which is in shortest supply gets used up. As soon as this single "limiting" essential amino acid gets used up, the assembly of amino acids into proteins ceases, regardless of how much of each of the other essential amino acids still remains in the pool. (If amino acids are not used for protein assembly, they are quickly converted into energy and either burned up or deposited as fat).

Many plant foods as well as animal foods contain all ten of the essential amino acids. But the problem is that the ratios in which they occur one to another limit their ability to be converted into proteins. The ratios of essential amino acids in plant foods are very different from the ratios in which they occur in the human body. They therefore cease to be useful for protein assembly more quickly than animal foods since the the least abundant essential amino acids in plants are precisely the ones most needed by the human body. For example, humans need twice as much of the essential amino acid methionine as of threonine, but beans have four times as much threonine as methionine.

Strictly speaking, human flesh itself contains the highest-quality protein that one can eat. To avoid cannibalistic innuendos, nutritionists conventionally settle for the protein composition of chicken eggs as their reference standard. Taking into account their relative digestibility once they get into the human gut, the quality of most animal proteins can be said to be about 25 percent to 50 percent higher than the best proteinaceous plant foods such as legumes, wheat, and corn (soybeans being again a conspicuous exception).

As every nutrition buff knows, there are strategies which can raise the protein quality of diets based on plant foods. If one eats cereals along with legumes, the essential amino acid balance can be considerably improved. For example, a relative lack of the essential amino acid lysine limits the protein utilization efficiency of wheat flour to about 42 percent of eggs. Beans have about the same low protein efficiency because of limits imposed by the deficit of methionine. Eating wheat and beans together at the same meal improves their utilization rate to about 90 percent. But does this happy outcome alter the relative nutritional value of plants and animals as sources of protein? Not at all. Both quantitatively and qualitatively animal foods remain a better source of proteins than plant foods.

Perhaps I also need to clairfy how the controversy over calories versus proteins as a solution to world hunger and malnutrition affects my argument. Some nutritionists claim that Western scientists were foolish in trying to raise protein consumption as a means of combating malnutrition in the Third World. They charge that a more realistic approach to alleviating malnutrition would be simply to increase the supply of grains or even root crops, and that by adding legumes, a safe daily allowance of proteins can be achieved without using any animal products at all. In this view, the world food problem is not that plant foods are an inferior source of amino acids but that a deficit of calories in the diet prevents the amino acids in plants from being "spared" and used as protein rather than as energy. Raise the energy component of the diet, and the problem of protein malnutrition will disappear, they say. Instead of seeing a "protein crisis" and an urgent need to close a supposed "protein gap," these scientists see a "protein myth" or even a "protein fiasco."

During the 1970s this view resulted in a downward revision of recommended daily protein allowances. But at the meeting of the United Nations World Health/Food and Agricultural Organization committee on nutrition in 1981, this allowance was revised sharply upward from .57 to .75 grams of protein per kilogram of body weight per day, an increase of 30 percent over 1973 standards. The pro-protein nutritionists had long been arguing that the 1973 standard was too low since it was based on what was safe for a fully grown, healthy, normal adult and did not take into account what happened when a person was neither an adult, healthy, nor normal. For example, people who are trying to recover from an infection-related disease were not safe under the old standards. As explained by Nevin Scrimshaw of the Department of Food Science and Nutrition at M.I.T., infections result in an increased need for amino acids. Under stress, the body mobilizes all the amino acids it can draw on from muscles and other tissues and converts them into glucose for extra energy. But at the same time the body needs to step up the production of antigens that provide immunological defense. "The net result of the multiple effects of infections is the need for a margin above normal protein requirements to allow for rapid repletions before the next acute episode worsens the degree of depletion." Young people especially stand to benefit from a margin above the normal safe level. After coming down with a childhood disease such as measles or diphtheria, children can experience growth spurts five times higher than normal—provided they can get enough protein in their diet.

Women who are pregnant or lactating also can benefically consume far more than the ordinary recommended level for adults. (Why they often seem to get less rather than more is a puzzle we'll come to much later on.) And anyone who has intestinal or blood parasites, wounds, or burns falls into a similar category. If people in any of these risky situations are already deriving most of their proteins from plant foods, they are unlikely to benefit from additional amounts of plant foods. Their diet would already be so bulky that to derive additional proteins from grains or a combination of grains and legumes they would have to eat nonstop meals and stuff themselves beyond the point of satiety. Meat, fish, fowl, and dairy products make it possible to obtain extra "catch-up" proteins without bulky meals that people are unlikely to be able to eat, especially if they are recovering from stressful traumas and infections. This is one of the reasons why "man cannot live by bread alone." Wheat contains all of the essential amino acids, but to get enough of the ones that are in scarce supply a man weighing 176 pounds (80 kilos) would have to stuff himself with 3.3 pounds (1.5 kilos) of whole wheat bread a day. To reach the same safe level of protein, he would need only .75 pounds (340 grams) of meat.

But the higher quality and greater concentration of protein is only one, and not necessarily the most important, nutritional reason why humans find animal foods so attractive. Meat, fish, fowl, and dairy products are also a concentrated source of vitamins such as vitamin A and the entire B complex, as well as vitamin E. And they are the only source of vitamin B_{12}, a deficiency of which leads to pernicious anemia, neural disorders, and psychotic behavior. If vegans do not regularly develop B_{12} deficiencies, it is only because the plant foods in their diet are contaminated by insect residues or by certain cobalt-digesting bacteria. This explains why when Hindu vegans migrate from India to England they suffer an increase in the incidence of pernicious anemia. In England the use of pesticides and vigorous washing of fruits and vegetables wipes out their B_{12} supply. Vegans are also at risk for rickets, a bone-crippling disease caused by vitamin D deficiency. Normally we can get enough vitamin D from the action of sunlight falling on our skin. But in the higher latitudes where winters are long and there are many misty, cloudy days, dietary vitamin D often becomes critical, and animal foods, especially eggs, fish, and liver, are the best sources. Animal foods even contain enough vitamin C to satisfy daily recommended allowances. By eating copious amounts of animal flesh and bone marrow, the Eskimo maintained themselves in excellent health on an all-meat diet without the slightest trace of scurvy or other vitamin C–deficiency disease. (Recently, through contact with outsiders, Eskimo health and diet have deteriorated as a result of the consumption of sweets and starches.)

Animal foods are also concentrated sources of essential minerals. Iron, needed for oxygen transport in the blood, occurs in animal foods—except milk—in greater abundance and in a more usable form than in spinach and other leafy plant foods. Milk and dairy products are the best sources of calcium, essential for bone growth. Animal foods are good-to-excellent sources of zinc, essential for male fertility, as well as copper, iodine, and almost every other element needed in trace amounts.

To say that animal foods are especially good to eat is not to say that we can dispense entirely with plant foods or that we can eat all kinds of animal foods in unlimited quantities without harming ourselves. A glaring deficiency in the animal foods package is fiber, which paradoxically is not a nutrient. Fiber adds bulk and roughage to the content of the large intestine, stimulates peristalsis, and is excreted without being digested. The evidence which links diets that are deficient in fiber to cancer of the colon must be taken seriously. One theory is that in the absence of fiber, the transit time of digested matter is delayed and carcinogenic substances accumulate in the bowels. Another theory stresses that phytic acid, one of the components of cereal fiber, binds to potential carcinogens and aids in their excretion. While fiber deficiency has become a serious problem in affluent industrial societies, throughout history and prehistory the problem has been too much rather than too little fiber. Until the twentieth century, fiber was always the easiest and cheapest food element to acquire, and its absence from animal foods was a positive rather than a negative aspect of the animal food package. Everybody used to get more fiber than they needed simply by consuming imperfectly milled cereals. Additional fiber from vegetables and fruit was not only useless but posed several dangers. Fiber, having no nutritive value, does not even provide "empty" calories; it simply fills people up.

In fact, one of the most distinctive features of human physiology is that our digestive tract can only cope with small amounts of fiber. In order to derive essential nutrients and energy from a high-fiber diet an animal needs to have a long and voluminous gut, or special fermentation "vats" such as cattle and sheep possess. (More about these "vats" later on.) To live on fibrous plants, an animal must spend most of the day eating. Some of the great apes display many of the characteristics of animals that are adapted to a high-fiber, nutritionally unconcentrated diet of leaves and woody plants. Gorillas eat continuously, digest slowly, and process cellulose fiber by fermentation in their voluminous colons ("big intestines"). Experiments indicate that about thirty-five hours elapse between the time a gorilla or chimpanzee eats something and its first appearance as fecal matter. Humans, like gorillas and chimpanzees, have a lengthy small intestine, but our colon is conspicuously smaller. Although some absorption of nutrients takes place in the human colon, its main function (besides elimination) is to resorb body fluids. Transit time in the human gut is quite fast. It takes human subjects who swallow small plastic markers with their meals only about twenty-five hours to pass them in their stools. What this evidence indicates is that our gut is not well adapted for high-fiber diets; rather, we seem to be adapted to "high quality dietary items that are volumetrically concentrated and rapidly digested." Animal foods are exactly what this formula calls for.

Alarming reports about diets deficient in fiber long antedate the discovery of a possible linkage with cancer. This was due to the discovery that the fibrous outer covering of wheat, rice, and other cereals is a major source of vitamin B_1. As a result of a preference for finely milled grains and flours from which the outer covering had been removed, the vitamin B_1–deficiency disease known as beriberi became widespread throughout the Orient. Today the preference for finely milled flour as exemplified in the industrial masterpiece called white bread is often cited as one of the prime examples of a food preference which is not only arbitrary but harmful. But when the rise of this preference is placed in proper historical context within systems of preindustrial food production, a very different picture emerges. Recent studies have shown that populations which cannot afford finely milled flour are at risk for deficiency anemias caused by the binding of phytic acids to iron and zinc. It is a toss-up as to which is worse— beriberi or these anemias. In any event, the addition of small amounts of animal food to the diet compensates totally for the thiamine lost as a result of too *much* milling as well as for the zinc or iron lost as a result of too *little* milling. A population whose diet contains significant amounts of meat, fish, or poultry need not shrink from enjoying the products made possible by the technology for mass-producing fine flour. These products include not only much-criticized industrial loaves of white bread but the entire European repertory of pastries and cakes, whose consumption in former times was the exclusive privilege of royalty.

While the absence of fiber does not substantially detract from the package of nutrients in animal food, the presence of other substances—especially fat and cholesterol—seems to render them considerably less good to eat than my argument requires. For example, much evidence links the overconsumption of cholesterol and saturated animal fats with coronary heart disease. Dietary cholesterol only occurs in animal foods, especially in eggs. We get our supply of it both by synthesis in the liver and by consuming it in our diets. In general, societies which consume large quantities of cholesterol and animal fats have higher mortality rates from heart attacks. Also, as shown by several studies, lowering cholesterol levels lowers the risk of coronary heart disease. In the Lipid Research Clinics Coronary Primary Prevention Trial—the best-designed of these studies—middle-aged men were divided into two groups. One was given the cholesterol-lowering drug cholestryamine, the other a placebo. After seven years the group that was not treated had experienced 19 percent more "coronary events" such as heart attacks.

Despite this evidence, the nature of the causal links between high animal fat and cholesterol consumption, cholesterol and fat in the diet, and coronary heart disease remains obscure. There are many unexplained facts. For example, in the Prevention Trial, the effectiveness of cholestryamine therapy varied from one participating clinic to another. At five out of the twelve clinics involved, the placebo groups had the same number of coronary incidents as the treated group; and in one of them, the group taking the placebo actually fared better than the one taking the drug. Moreover, the death rate of the two groups from all causes including coronary incidents was the same.

Fifty percent to 60 percent of patients with heart disease do not have elevated cholesterol counts. And many groups with extremely high animal fat and cholesterol diets such as the Eskimo and the Lapps have lower than expected rates of cardiovascular disease. Also, while diet and anticholesterol drugs may reduce pathologically high cholesterol levels in humans, no studies have yet shown that diet alone can lead to pathologically high levels of cholesterol in otherwise healthy people. In the Prevention Trial, all the men selected for the study had pathologically high levels of cholesterol to begin with. This presents a problem that is analogous to interpreting the occurrence of high levels of blood sugar in diabetics: diet can lower the sugar level, but diet alone may not cause the disease.

All of this indicates that much more than cholesterol and animal fats are probably involved in the high incidence of coronary heart disease found in countries that consume large amounts of cholesterol and animal fats. Other known dietary risks for heart disease include overconsumption of calories, too much salt, and too much alcohol. (Too much calcium is the latest entry in this bad-for-your-heart contest.) And beyond what we eat, many other factors put people at risk for heart attacks: high blood pressure, smoking cigarettes, air pollution, lack of exercise, and chronic repressed anger—just to mention a few. No one knows what proportion of the risk associated with high cholesterol and animal fat intake reflects the combined effect of the other dietary and nondietary risk factors as they interact with cholesterol and animal fat among people who have modern life-styles.

The state of understanding of the linkage between animal foods and cancer is no less fragmentary. Dietary fat—not cholesterol—is a risk factor in cancer of the breast and colon. But no one knows if the problem arises from too much fat of all types or too much saturated animal fat in particular. Saturated fats are denser, harder, and have a higher melting point than unsaturated fats. There is even some evidence that the least-saturated fats—the polyunsaturated vegetable fats—which are supposedly better from the standpoint of preventing cardiovascular disease are worse from the standpoint of preventing cancer. Cancer of the colon has increased severalfold since World War II, precisely the period during which margarine and other polyunsaturated vegetable fats and oils substantially replaced butter and lard in the United States diet.

Despite the contradictory and fragmentary nature of the evidence, the rational thing for affluent industrial societies to do—or, as the Senate's Select Committee on Nutrition and Human Needs put it, the "prudent thing" to do—is to cut back on cholesterol and animal fat consumption. But we must maintain a distinction between prudently cutting back on some of the possibly hazardous components of animal foods and imprudently giving up the entire animal food package.

In our haste to reverse the harmful effects of overnutrition in affluent societies, we must not lose sight of the fact that no one knows what will happen if we drastically reduce the amount of dietary cholesterol for the entire population starting in childhood. Also, there may be hidden dangers in reducing fat intake. Fat, after all, is necessary for a healthy diet if for no other reason than it is needed for the absorption, transport, and storage of vitamins A, D, E, and K—the "fat-soluble" vitamins—which respectively enhance vision, bone strength, fertility, and blood coagulation. Diets severely limited in fat content, for example, hamper the body's ability to absorb the precursor of vitamin A, which can lead to a form of blindness known as xerophthalmia, a disease about which I shall have more to say much later on.

The increasing unpopularity of animal foods as a source of dietary fats must also be placed in a historical context. Just as animal foods formerly were more rather than less desirable because they contained little fiber, so until recently they were more rather than less desirable if they contained a lot of fat. Much of the nearly worldwide hunger for meat is really a craving for fatty meat. The reason for this is that lean meat needs to be supplemented by calorie-rich substances in order to prevent the meat's amino acids from being converted into energy rather than into body-building proteins. Although calorie for calorie carbohydrates are about 13 percent more efficient than fats in sparing proteins, fats provide 100 percent more calories than carbohydrates (such as sugar or starch) per gram. This means that far fewer grams of fat than carbohydrates are needed to achieve a given protein-sparing effect. Fatty meat in other words does away with the need to alternate bites of manioc or fruit with bites of meat.

Prior to the development of industrial methods of stuffing cattle, pigs, and chickens with grains, fish meal, growth hormones, and antibiotics, the problem with most meats was that they were too lean to achieve a protein-sparing effect. Modern high-fat carcasses are 30 percent or more fat. In contrast, a survey of fifteen different species of free-living African herbivores revealed an average carcass fat content of only 3.9 percent. This explains a practice often observed among people who depend on hunting for their protein supply and which appears to be utterly irrational and arbitrary. During the height of their "hungry season" when all sources of nourishment are scarce, hunter-gatherers frequently refuse to eat certain cuts of meat or even whole animals which they have hunted and killed. The Pitjandjara of Australia, for example, have been observed to walk up to a slain kangaroo, inspect its tail for signs of body fat, and then walk away, leaving the animal to rot, if the signs were negative. Archaeologists have also long puzzled over ancient bison kill sites in the American Great Plains from which only a few parts of the slain animals were removed and presumably eaten, while the rest of the carcass was left unbutchered and uneaten exactly where the animal fell. The explanation for these seemingly irrational and arbitrary practices is that hunters run the risk of starving to death if they rely too much on lean meat. Vilhjalmur Stefansson, who learned from years of living among the Eskimo how to remain in excellent health by eating nothing but uncooked meat, warned that such a diet would work only if the meat were fatty. He left a vivid description of a phenomenon which Eskimos, Indians, and many earlier explorers of the Far West recognized as a symptom of eating too many lean rabbits and which they called "rabbit starvation":

> If you are transferred suddenly from a diet normal in fat to one consisting wholly of rabbit you eat bigger and bigger meals for the first few days until at the end of about a week you are eating in pounds three or four times as much as you were at the beginning of the week. By that time you are showing both signs of starvation and of protein poisoning. You eat numerous meals; you feel hungry at the end of each; you are in discomfort through distention of the stomach with much food and you begin to feel a vague restlessness. Diarrhoea will start in from a week to 10 days and will not be relieved unless you secure fat. Death will result after several weeks.

Incidentally, serious dieters will recognize in this prescription the moneymaking, effective, but highly dangerous diet of Irwin Maxwell Stillman, M.D., which lets people eat as much as they want of lean meats, poultry, and fish and nothing else. (The first diet club that corners the market on lean rabbits will make even more money.)

Not only is there less fat in wild animals but its composition is different. Wild game contains over five times more polyunsaturated fats per gram than is found in domestic livestock. Equally important for placing the present panic over meat consumption in proper perspective is that wild animal carcasses contain a polyunsaturated fat (called eicosapent-aenoic acid) which is currently under study as an antiatherosclerotic factor. Domesticated beef does not contain this fat, except in negligible amounts.

Despite the newly arisen threat to health associated with eating too much cholesterol and fat of animal origin, there is no strictly nutritional justification for lowering the consumption of meat, fish, poultry, and dairy products from the levels they have reached in the United States and other affluent countries. Why not? Because high levels of consumption of animal foods and high levels of consumption of cholesterol and unsaturated fats need not go together, as the phenomenon of "rabbit starvation" demonstrates.

Various government committees recommend that saturated animal fat be reduced to 10 percent of energy intake and that the consumption of cholesterol be no more than three hundred milligrams a day. This reduction can easily be achieved without reducing current levels of consumption of animal foods by selecting meats, fish, and dairy products that are low in cholesterol and saturated fat—lean cuts of beef and pork, more fish and poultry, more skim milk and skim milk products. (There is even a place for eggs since the cholesterol is in the yolk, not in the white.) Here are the numbers: lean meats, fish, and poultry contain less than thirty milligrams of cholesterol and less than sixty calories per ounce. One could therefore eat as much as 283 grams (10 ounces) of lean red meat, fish, or poultry a day without exceeding either the recommended fat or cholesterol percentages. That adds up to 228 pounds a year, about the amount of meat, poultry, and fish that Americans currently consume.

Before we decide to blame cancer and heart disease indiscriminately on eating too much animal flesh, we had better take a look at what our hunter-gatherer ancestors were doing during the hundred thousand or so years prior to the domestication of plants and animals. By piecing together evidence from archaeology, paleontology, and the study of contemporary hunter-gatherers, an estimate can be made of how much animal flesh our Paleolithic forbears consumed. S. Boyd Eaton and Melvin Konner of Emory University, Atlanta, conservatively suggest in an article published in the *New England Journal of Medicine* that temperate climate preagricultural peoples regularly derived 35 percent of their calories from meat. This means that for the major portion of our species' history, our bodies were adapted to the consumption of about 788 grams of red meat a day, which is four times the average per capita consumption of the amount of beef, pork, sheep, and goats Americans now consume. Our ancestors also probably consumed twice the amount of cholesterol, but one-third less fat. This is the pattern "for which human beings are in essence genetically programmed." Incidentally, cereal grains could have contributed only an insignificant part of the calories or proteins in the Paleolithic diet. It was only after the adoption of agricultural modes of production a mere ten thousand years ago that grains became the staple foods of humankind. Anyone who contends there is something inherently more "natural" about a diet rich in wheat or rice than one rich in meat knows little about either culture or nature. Of course if it's the chemical adulterants, preservatives, and polyunsaturated fat that one has in mind, what we are eating by way of meat is clearly not what our ancestors ate. (But then again, neither did they eat our chemically nourished grains.)

Before we decide to blame cancer and heart disease indiscriminately on diets rich in animal foods, we had also better pay closer attention to the fact that these maladies result from long-term degenerative processes. The basic reasons why heart disease and cancer have become the number one and number two causes of death in the United States and other affluent societies is that people are living longer. This is not to say that heart disease and cancer are caused by old age or are in some sense inevitable, but that the effects of all the risk factors—dietary and nondietary— take a long time to express themselves. Generally, one has to live a long time before these diseases break through the body's defenses. What has made it possible for us to live long enough for this to occur? In the rush to reduce the toll of heart disease and cancer, some of us may be in danger of forgetting that increased consumption of animal foods and decreased consumption of grains are strongly associated with increased longevity. Between 1909 and 1976 United States life expectancy at birth rose by 40 percent. During the same period per capita consumption of red meat, fish, and poultry rose by 35 percent (milk product consumption fell by 52 percent). Nor is this experience unique to the United States. All countries whose citizens have the highest life expectancies have undergone similar dietary changes.

A simple correlation of course is not evidence of causality, but knowing that animal foods contain essential proteins, minerals, and vitamins in concentrated form, would it not be imprudent to conclude that improved longevity is due entirely to other factors? Since the beneficial effects of high levels of animal food consumption have been achieved in spite of the putatively deleterious effects of the fats and cholesterol they contain, we simply ought to remove these offending substances and thereby further improve the nutritive value of the animal food package. And of course this is exactly what is happening as evidenced by the rapid rise in the United States consumption of lean cuts of meat and of fish and fowl since 1980.

In Third World countries where undernutrition rather than overnutrition is the prime danger, from a nutritional point of view, meat, fish, fowl, and dairy products retain a clear-cut nutritional advantage over plant foods, even without reducing their fat and cholesterol level. The continuing world hunger for more meat, fish, fowl, and/or milk therefore represents a thoroughly rational preference that arises from the interaction of human biology and the nutritive composition of alternative foods. It will never be in the best interest of any country to eat less animal food (as distinct from less animal fat and cholesterol) as a health measure. To return to Poland, no one can blame a nation that does not rush to embrace such a fate. Perhaps someone should tell the Poles that they would be better off eating leaner meats, more fish, more poultry, fewer eggs, more skim milk, and less butter and lard. But woe to the would-be savior of socialism who decides to appease Poland's meat hunger by telling people to go home and eat more bread and beans.

CHAPTER THREE

THE RIDDLE OF
THE SACRED COW

SINCE ANIMAL FLESH is so nutritious one would expect every society to stock its larder with the meat of every available animal species. Yet exactly the opposite seems to prevail. All over the world people in dire need of the very proteins, calories, vitamins, and minerals that meat provides in such concentrated form refuse to consume certain kinds of flesh. If meat is so nutritious, why are so many animals bad to eat? Take India, for example, and the most famous of all irrational foodways, the ban on the slaughter of cattle and the consumption of beef.

There is a section of India's federal constitution called the Directive Principles of State Policy which sets forth guidelines for laws to be enacted by state legislatures. Article 48 calls for prohibiting "the slaughter of cows and calves and other milk and draft animals." All but two Indian states—Kerala and West Bengal—have passed some form of "cow protection" law with "cow" meaning both male and female members of *Bos indicus*, India's native species of cattle. But Hindu holy men and numerous cow-protection societies continue to agitate for a total ban on cattle slaughter. In 1966, rioting by 125,000 nude cow-protectionists threatened to shut down the Indian parliament in New Delhi, and in 1978, a Hindu leader, Acharaya Bhave, provoked a national crisis by threatening to fast until Kerala and West Bengal enacted antislaughter legislation.

India has the largest number of cattle in the world—about 180 million *Bos indicus* (plus 50 million buffalo), a situation which might reasonably be attributed to the fact that no one seems to want to kill or eat them. India also has the distinction of possessing the largest number of sick, dry, barren, old, and decrepit cattle in the world. According to some estimates one-quarter to one-half of the total are "useless" creatures that roam over the country's fields and highways and city streets—a situation which, if true, one might again reasonably attribute to the ban on slaughter and the aversion to beef. India also has 700 million people. Since no one denies that much of this huge human population is sorely in need of more proteins and calories, the refusal to kill and eat cattle seems to be "plainly contrary to economic interest." Has not the very phrase *sacred cow* passed into common usage as an idiom denoting stubborn adherence to customs and practices that have no rational justification?

On one level of explanation, cow protection, beef avoidance, and the large number of useless cattle can all be safely attributed to religious zeal. Hinduism is the dominant religion of India, and cattle worship and cattle protection lie at the very heart of Hinduism. Few Westerners realize, for example, that one of the reasons for the saintly reputation and mass appeal of Mohandas Gandhi is that he was an ardent believer in the Hindu doctrine of cow protection. In Gandhi's words: "the central fact of Hinduism is cow protection. . . . Cow protection is the gift of Hinduism to the world . . . Hinduism will live as long as there are Hindus to protect the cow."

Hindus venerate their cows (and bulls) as deities, keep them around the house, give them names, talk to them, deck them with flowers and tassels, let them have the right of way on busy thoroughfares, and try to place them in animal shelters when they become sick or old and can no longer be cared for at home. Shiva, the avenger god, rides the heavens on Nandi, the bull, whose likeness appears at the entrance to every temple dedicated to Shiva. Krishna, god of mercy and childhood, perhaps the most popular deity in India today, describes himself in Hindu sacred literature as a cowherd, protector of cows, who are his wealth. Hindus believe that everything that comes out of a cow (or a bull) is sacred. The priests make a holy "nectar" composed of milk, curds, butter, urine, and dung which they sprinkle or daub on statues and worshippers. They light the temples with lamps that burn ghee, clarified cow's butter. And they bathe temple statues daily with fresh cow's milk. (In contrast, buffalo milk, butter, curds, urine, and dung have no ritual value.)

At festivals commemorating Krishna's role as protector of cattle, priests mold the god's likeness out of cattle dung, pour milk over the navel, and crawl around it on the temple floor. When in due course the image must be removed, Krishna does not tolerate human hands to break it up. A calf must trample on it first, for Krishna does not mind his image being walked on by his favorite creature. At other festivals, people kneel in the dust raised by passing cattle and daub their foreheads with the fresh droppings. Housewives use dried cattle dung and cattle dung ashes to clean and ritually purify their floors and hearths. Village doctors even collect the dust in the hoofprints of cattle and use it for medicinal purposes. Just to look at a cow gives many Hindus a sense of pleasure. The priests say that to take care of a cow is in itself a form of worship, and that no household should deny itself the spiritual enjoyment which comes from raising one.

Cow protection and cow worship also symbolize the protection and adoration of human motherhood. I have a collection of colorful Indian pinup calendars depicting jewel-bedecked cows with swollen udders and the faces of beautiful human madonnas. Hindu cow worshippers say: "The cow is our mother. She gives us milk and butter. Her male calves till the land and give us food." To critics who oppose the custom of feeding cows that are too old to have calves and give milk, Hindus reply: "Will you then send your mother to a slaughter house when she gets old?"

The sacredness of the cow is linked in Hindu theology to the doctrine of transmigration. Hinduism portrays all creatures as souls which have risen or fallen from various stages of progress toward Nirvana. It takes eighty-six transmigrations to rise from a devil to a cow. One more transmigration and the soul acquires human form. But the soul can always slip back. The soul of a person who kills a cow can expect to return to the lowest rung and start all over again. Gods live inside of cows. Hindu theologians put the number of gods and goddesses in a cow's body at 330 million. "Serving and praying to the cow will lead to Nirvana for 21 generations to come." To assist a departed loved one's soul in its journey to salvation, relatives donate money for feeding herds of cows kept by Hindu temples. They believe that the dead must cross a fiery stream and that these donations buy the departed the right to hold onto a cow's tail while swimming across. For the same reason, orthodox Hindus request that they be given a cow's tail to cling to during their dying moments.

The cow is a political as well as a religious symbol. For centuries, Hindus and Moslems have been whipping up communal strife with stereotypes of Moslems as cow-killers and Hindus as tyrants bent on forcing everyone to accept their peculiar foodways. The fact that the raj from England was an even more prodigal cow-killer and beef eater than the Moslems served as the focus for waves of civil disobedience which led to India's independence after World War II. In the earliest days of the new state the dominant Congress party preempted the picture of a cow and a calf as its national logo, immediately giving its candidates an advantage among illiterate voters who vote by making an X over the picture of their choice. The opposition parties soon struck back by spreading the rumor that a cross placed over the Congress party's logo was a vote for slaughtering one more cow and calf.

As anyone can see, all this is a matter of religion. Were Americans to believe that Nandi is Shiva's vehicle, that Krishna is a cowherd, that there are eighty-six reincarnations from devil to cow, and that each cow contains 330 million gods and goddesses, they wouldn't go around asking, "Where's the beef?" But the rejection of beef because of Hindu beliefs is the puzzle, not the answer. Why is cow protection "the central fact of Hinduism"? Most major religions regard cattle as good to eat. Why is Hinduism different?

Both politics and religion obviously play a role in reinforcing and perpetuating the beef and slaughter taboos, but neither politics nor religion explains why cattle slaughter and beef eating have achieved symbolic prominence. Why the cow and not the pig, horse, or camel? I do not doubt the symbolic power of the sacred cow. What I doubt is that the investment of symbolic power in one particular kind of animal and one particular kind of meat results from an arbitrary and capricious mental choice rather than from a definite set of practical constraints. Religion has affected Indian's foodways, but India's foodways have affected India's religion even more. My justification for saying this lies in the history of Hinduism.

The central fact of that history is that cow protection was not always the central fact of Hinduism. The earliest sacred texts of Hinduism—the Rig Veda—celebrate the gods and customs of the Vedas, a cattle and farming people who dominated northern India from 1800 B.C. to 800 B.C. Vedic society and religion already recognized the four main castes of modern Hinduism including the priestly Brahmans, the ruling warrior chiefs or Kshatriyas, the merchants or Vaisyas, and the Sudras or menials. The Vedas neither spurned beef nor protected the cow. In fact in Vedic times the Brahman caste's religious duties centered not on protecting cows but on slaughtering them. As I mentioned in the chapter before this, the Vedas were one of the early warrior-pastoral peoples of Europe and southwestern Asia among whom ritual slaughter of animals and sumptuous feasting on meat went together. On ceremonial occasions, Vedic warriors and priests, like the Celts and Israelites, generously distributed meat to their followers as a material reward for loyalty and as a symbol of wealth and power. Whole villages and districts participated in these meat-eating feasts.

While the Vedas permitted animal slaughter only as a religious rite carried out under the supervision of Brahman priests, this restriction did not limit the amount of meat available for human consumption. The gods conveniently ate the spiritual portion of the animal, while the worshippers dined heartily on the corporeal residue. And since no culture is ever at a loss for ceremonies, confining the consumption of meat to ceremonial occasions probably did little to inhibit the rate of animal slaughter. Battlefield victories, marriages, funerals, and visits from allies all called for animal sacrifice and lavish meat eating. The compulsive attention paid by the Brahman priests to the size, shape, and color of cattle suitable for particular ritual occasions bears a close resemblance to the detailed instructions found in the Book of Leviticus pertaining to similar ancient Israelite sacrificial feasting. The animals specified by the sacred Hindu texts included: a drooping horned bull with a white blaze on the forehead; a polled ox; a white ox; a five-year-old humpless dwarf bull; a thick-legged cow; a barren cow; a cow that has recently miscarried; a three-year-old humpless dwarf heifer; a black cow; a two-colored cow; and a red cow. All this suggests that the Vedas sacrificed cattle more often than other animals and that beef was the commonest flesh consumed in northern India during most of the first millennium B.C.

The period of lavish cattle slaughter and general beef eating came to an end when the Vedic chieftains could no longer keep large herds of cattle as a reserve of wealth. Population grew, forests shrank, grazing lands were put to the plow, and the old semipastoralist way of life gave way to intensive farming and dairying. Simple energy relationships underwrote the transition: more people can be fed by limiting meat eating and by concentrating on dairying, growing wheat, millet, lentils, peas, and other plant foods. As I mentioned in the last chapter, if grains are consumed by animals and then the animals are consumed by people, nine out of every ten calories and four out of five grams of protein are lost for human consumption. Dairying can cut these losses by a significant amount. Modern dairy cattle convert feed into calories five times more efficiently than modern beef cattle convert feed into edible meat calories; and they convert feed into edible protein six times more efficiently than modern beef cattle.

These figures include the calories and proteins in the edible portion of the cow's carcass at the end of its life, but as I'll show in a moment, the beef-eating taboo probably never prevented the cow from making a terminal contribution in the form of meat. As long as population density remained low, cattle could be grazed on uncultivated land and per capita beef production could be maintained at a high level. With denser human populations, cattle came to compete with humans for food, and their meat soon became too costly to be shared with the traditional openhanded generosity of the Vedic chieftains at public beef-feasting sacrifices.

Gradually the ratio of cattle to humans declined and with it the consumption of beef, especially among the lower castes. But there was a Catch-22 in the process: cattle could not simply be eliminated to make way for more people. Farmers needed oxen to pull plows, which were needed in turn to penetrate the hard-packed soils found throughout much of northern India. In fact, it was the use of ox-drawn plows to break the plains bordering the Ganges River that started the whole cycle of population increase and the shift away from meat eating in general and of beef eating in particular. Naturally, all ranks of society did not give up their beef-eating habits at the same time. The privileged Brahmans and Kshatriyas continued to slaughter cattle and gorge themselves on beef long after it was impossible to invite ordinary people to share in their good fortune.

By about 600 B.C. peasant living standards were in decline, and wars, droughts, and famines inflicted great suffering. The old Vedic gods seemed to be failing, and new religious leaders found ordinary people increasingly hostile to animal sacrifices both as a symbol and as a material manifestation of the inequalities of the caste system.

Out of this stressful social and economic situation arose Buddhism, the world's first nonkilling religion. Gautama, later known as the Buddha, lived between 563 B.C. and 483 B.C. His principal teachings reflect the suffering of ordinary people and were directly opposed to the Hindu beliefs and practices of his times.

As set forth in the Buddhist Eightfold Way—the equivalent of Judaism's Ten Commandments—Buddha condemned the taking of life in animal or human form, banned animal sacrifice, condemned butchers, and substituted meditation, vows of poverty, and good deeds for ritual and prayers as the means of gaining salvation. Buddha did not single out beef eating as a special evil, but since cattle were the principal objects of ritual slaughter, his condemnation of animal sacrifice implies that beef eaters were among the worst offenders.

I feel confident that the rise of Buddhism was related to mass suffering and environmental depletions because several similar nonkilling religions equally opposed to animal sacrifice arose in India at the same time. Jainism, the best known of these lesser antikilling sects, has survived into the present and has numerous temples serving about two million devotees in India. Jains take heroic measures to avoid killing or eating any form of animal life; their priests cannot walk down a path or a street without having broom-wielding assistants go ahead to sweep away small insects or spiders that might accidentlly get stepped on. They also wear gauze masks over their nose and mouth to prevent the accidental inhalation and destruction of mosquitos or flies. Jains to this day maintain numerous animal shelters where they take care of stray or injured cats, dogs, rats, birds, and cattle. The most remarkable Jain shelters are rooms set aside for insects. In Ahmadabad, the capital of Gujarat, devout Jains from all over the city bring to such a room carefully preserved dirt and sweepings containing insects in need of protection. Attendants place the dirt and sweepings together with a small amount of grain inside, and when the room is full, they seal it tightly. After ten or fifteen years the inhabitants are presumed to have died a natural death, and the attendants open the room, shovel out its contents, and sell the remains for fertilizer.

The Buddhist ban on the consumption of beef implicit in the opposition to cattle sacrifice must have resonated with the aspirations of the poorer farmers. At a time when ordinary people were starving and in need of oxen to plow their fields, the Brahmans went on killing cattle and getting fat from eating them. I cannot say precisely how the Brahmans and Kshatriyas continued to obtain cattle for their gluttonous feasts, but taxation, confiscation, or other coercive measures would have been necessary once the peasants were unable or unwilling to donate surplus animals to the temples. Traces of a "let-them-eat-cake" type of arrogance show up in some early Brahmanic texts. Against the argument that beef should not be eaten because the gods had given cattle cosmic power, a Brahman sage replied: "That may very well be, but I shall eat of it nevertheless if the flesh be tender." Recognizing that the nonkilling religions had great mass appeal, the rulers of India's earliest Ganges River empires let them flourish and even encouraged their spread. Buddhism was especially favored when in 257 B.C. Asoka, grandson of the founder of the Maurya Dynasty and the first emperor of all India, became a follower of Gautama. Although Asoka did not prevent cattle from being slaughtered and eaten, he did attempt to stamp out the practice of animal sacrifice. (As I mentioned, Buddhists can eat meat as long as they are not responsible for killing the animal from which it comes.)

Over the course of nine centuries, Buddhism and Hinduism struggled for possession of the stomachs and minds of the Indian people. Hinduism eventually won, but not before the Brahmans overcame the Rig Veda's obsession with animal sacrifice, adopted the principle of nonkilling—known today as *ahimsa*—and set themselves up as the protectors rather than the destroyers of cattle. The gods, they argued, did not eat meat, so the sacrifices described in the Rig Veda were merely metaphorical and symbolic acts. Milk, not meat, now became the principal ritual food of Hinduism as well as the main source of animal protein for members of the Brahman caste. The Brahmans were able to gain an advantage over the Buddhists because they could give free rein to the popular tendency to worship cattle and to identify Krishna and other gods with domestic animals. Buddhists never attempted a similar apotheosis of cattle nor worship of Krishna or comparable deities, being directed by Gautama's example to

seek salvation through meditation rather than by prayers. Buddhism's popular base began to erode, and by the end of the eighth
century A.D. Gautama's religion disappeared entirely from the
land of its birth.

The account I have just given of the struggle between Hin-
duism and Brahmanism was first pieced together by Rajandra
Mitra, a great Sanskrit scholar of the late nineteenth century.
This is what he wrote in 1872:

> When the Brahmans had to contend against Buddhism which
> emphatically and so successfully denounced all sacrifices,
> they found the doctrine of respect for animal life too strong
> and too popular to be overcome, and therefore gradually and
> inperceptibly adopted it in such a manner as to make it
> appear as part of their [teachings].

What I would add to Mitra's brilliant insight is that by becoming
cow protectors and by abstaining from beef, the Brahmans were
able to co-opt a more productive system of agriculture as well as
a more popular religious doctrine. It is no accident that India is
the home of hardy humpbacked zebu breeds which are world-
renowned for their ability to render service as plow animals amid
heat, drought, and other adverse conditions while consuming
very small amounts of feed and fodder. Contrary to popular stereotypes, the presence of large numbers of these animals in the
Indian countryside under the protection of the antislaughter and
beef-eating taboos is indicative neither of waste nor folly. They
seldom compete with humans for resources since they seldom
graze on planted pasture nor on any lands which can be used for
growing human food crops. The density of the human population
long ago became too great for any such luxuries. Instead these
animals are kept in a semistarved condition until they are needed
for work. In between stints of plowing they eat stalks, chaff,
leaves, and household garbage. At plowing time they get extra
rations of oilcakes pressed from humanly inedible residues of
cottonseed, soybeans, and coconut. They are resistant to disease,
have great stamina, and literally work until they drop dead, which

usually does not happen until they have rendered a dozen or more years of grueling service. Farmers value their oxen not only for traction power but also for the fertilizer and fuel they produce. Cattle manure is still India's main source of fertilizer. In addition, lack of wood, coal, and fuel oils obliges millions of Indian housewives to depend upon dried cattle dung for cooking. When employed for this purpose, the dung produces a clean, steady, odorless flame that requires little attention and is well suited for simmering vegetarian dishes.

But nowadays isn't it terribly inefficient to use oxen instead of tractors to pull plows? Not at all. Virtually every study that has ever been carried out to determine the relative efficiency of tractors versus oxen shows that the animals are more cost-efficient per unit of crop produced under the conditions which prevail throughout most of India. While a thirty-five-horsepower tractor can plow a field almost ten times faster than a pair of oxen, the initial investment in the tractor is over twenty times greater than the investment in the animals. Unless the tractor is used for more than nine hundred hours per year, the hourly cost of operating the tractor exceeds the hourly cost of a pair of oxen. This means that tractors are more efficient than oxen only on very large farms. The majority of Indian farms are very small, and the use of tractors can only be rationalized if elaborate provisions are made to lease or rent the machines. But similar provisions also easily lower the cost of using animal traction. Despite a significant increase in the number of tractors in India since 1968, there has been no reduction in the number of draft animals, even in the regions where tractors have become most common. The explanation for that is that repair services and spare parts remain too precarious to risk operations without standby animal power. Some evidence also exists which indicates that after a period of initial enthusiasm, many tractor owners are now trading in their machines and replacing them with new breeds of fast oxen.

In order to have oxen, one must have cows, and in the traditional regimen, the prime function of cows is to give birth to cheap, hardy oxen. Milk and dung are valuable by-products which help pay for the cow's upkeep. Even more than oxen, cows play the role of village scavengers, subsisting on straw, chaff, garbage, leaves, patches of roadside grass and other substances that humans cannot digest.

Does the beef-eating, cattle-slaughter ban significantly and arbitrarily reduce the amount of animal foods available for human consumption? I doubt it. As part of a preindustrial agricultural system burdened with supporting a dense population in reasonably good health, the Hindu ban on cattle slaughter and beef consumption remains an asset rather than a liability. One of the principal problems confronting this system has always been the tendency to slaughter animals which are energetically and nutritionally more useful alive than dead in order to satisfy a craving for meat. The religious proscription against beef eating contributes to the solution of this problem, not only by preventing ritual slaughter itself, but by counteracting the temptation to eat temporarily barren or emaciated animals during periods of stress caused by prolonged dry seasons and droughts. Without preserving the life of their temporarily useless cows or oxen, farmers could not resume the agricultural cycle when conditions improved. To the extent that the beef taboo strengthens their resolve to preserve their breeding stock as long as possible, it enhances rather than diminishes the long-term effectiveness of the agricultural system and reduces caste-based inequalities in the consumption of essential nutrients.

Although sacrificial cults based on slaughter and beef consumption are a thing of the past, modern Indian and foreign entrepreneurs itch to get their hands on India's "surplus" cattle for slaughter and sale overseas, especially to the oil-rich, meat-hungry nations of the Middle East. To the extent that the Hindu aversion to beef helps to prevent the development of large-scale domestic or international markets for Indian beef, it continues to protect the typical smallholder from bankruptcy and landlessness. Unfettered development of large-scale beef markets would inevitably push up the price of Indian cattle to the levels of international beef prices; cattle feeds and supplement would be devoted to raising beef; and small farmers would find it increasingly difficult to raise, rent, or buy animals for plowing. A few traders and wealthy farmers would reap the benefits while the rest of the farming population would sink to a lower level of production and consumption, as the acreage diverted to feeding animals rather than people increased.

Another problem with the scheme for slaughtering India's "surplus" and "useless" cattle is that the animals which Western agronomists regard as surplus or useless are not surplus or useless in the eyes of their owners. Despite the ban on slaughter, Hindu farmers systematically rid themselves of most of the animals for which they have no use. This is shown by the finely tuned adjustments they make in the ratio of oxen to cows according to their needs and circumstances. Depending on the average size of a farm, the pattern of rainfall, the crops grown, and the proximity to cities where milk can be marketed, different regions have remarkably different cattle sex ratios. In northern India, for example, where wheat is the major crop and farm holdings are large, farmers concentrate on raising cattle for plowing, and there are almost twice as many oxen as cows. But in parts of southern India where rice is the principal crop, and the typical half-acre "postage-stamp" farms are too small to support plow animals, farmers raise three times as many cows as oxen. Since the total numbers of cattle in the two regions are widely discrepant, there is no chance that this inversion of cattle sex ratios has been brought about by breeding oxen to the north and cows to the south. Interregional trade does not exist on the requisite scale. Research conducted by the Center for Development Studies in Trivandrum, Kerala, shows rather that male and female calves have drastically different mortality rates in differing regions depending on whether the local farmers want to end up with more cows or more oxen. When I asked farmers to explain this discrepancy, they insisted that no one in their village would deliberately shorten the life of any of their beloved calves. But they did admit that they took better care of the locally more useful sex, allowing whichever they needed most to suckle longer at the mother's teats. Now starvation may seem an inefficient form of getting rid of unwanted animals, but the calf's slow demise has a definite payoff for its owner. Since most of India's cattle are not milk breeds, Indian cows will not "let down" and give milk unless they are stimulated by the presence of their calves. What the farmer is doing in keeping an unwanted calf alive in a semistarved condition therefore is minimizing the cost and maximizing yields of its mother's milk.

In modern India, Hindu farmers have recourse to an additional method for ridding themselves of unwanted animals. They sell them to Moslem traders, who remove the animals from the village and resell them at local fairs. Many of these animals eventually end up being butchered legally or otherwise by other Moslems whose religion does not inhibit them from such activities and who as a result enjoy a lucrative monopoly over the slaughter business. Moslems, Christians, and lower-caste Hindus purchase a considerable amount of cattle flesh either knowingly as beef or somewhat unwittingly as "mutton," a catch-all label which helps keep the peace between Moslems and their Hindu customers and neighbors. But even before the arrival of the Moslems in the eighth century A.D., similar beef-eating segments of the population must have existed. A royal edict issued by King Chandragupta II in A.D. 465 equated the crime of killing a cow with the crime of killing a Brahman priest. This implies that there were people who rejected both the ban on beef and the reverence for Brahmans. Perhaps it was the followers of the Tantric branches of Buddhism and Hinduism who were the targets of Chandragupta's edict. Tantrism presents a persistent countercurrent to the ascetic, contemplative, and monastic mainstream of Indian religion and philosophy. Tantrics seek oneness with the universe through eating meat, drinking alcohol, taking drugs, dancing, and ritual sexual intercourse.

To the beef-eating Tantrics, Moslems, Christians, and other non-Hindus, we must add the members of various untouchable castes who consume beef in the form of carrion. Millions of Indian cattle die each year from a combination of neglect and natural causes. The corpses become the property of carrion eaters, who are called in by higher castes and who skin and then consume the edible parts. Boiling the meat eliminates most of the danger. Of course, the amount of beef they get per animal is only a fraction of what they could obtain from a fat, healthy steer. But untouchables cannot afford to eat meat from fat, healthy steers, and even small amounts of meat help to improve their meager diet.

Just how many "useless" and "surplus" animals does all this culling, beef eating, and carrion eating leave us with? One economist calculated that India's 72.5 million draft oxen would require for maintenance only 24 million productive well-fed breeding cows rather than the actual 54 million cows which now exist. This led him to conclude that largely as a result of the slaughter and beef-eating taboo, 30 million cows are surplus and could be killed off or shipped overseas to everyone's benefit. The flaw in this argument is that most of the less productive cows—cows that are neither breeding regularly nor giving much milk—are owned by the poorest farmers. While the calving rate and milk yield of these cows are ridiculously low, they nonetheless represent a cost-efficient and vital asset for the economically weakest segment of the peasant population. Why is it the poorest peasants who keep the bulk of the most unproductive cows? Because owning little land, it is they who are forced to feed their animals on marginal rations derived from village waste, roadside grass, water hyacinths, and the leaves of trees. It is the fact that cattle scavenge for a good deal of their subsistence that creates the impression that useless stray cattle are wandering all over the landscape, blocking traffic, and begging and stealing from food stands in the cities. But almost all of these strays have owners who know and encourage what their animals are doing. Although "strays" may sometimes invade cultivated fields and destroy someone else's crops, the loss—if it can be called that from an impoverished animal owner's viewpoint—must be weighed against the advantages of the more socially responsible forms of scavenging.

Despite the semistarved condition of most of the females, the hardiness of their zebu ancestry shows through, and many "barren" cows sooner or later calve and give milk. Even if a cow only produces a calf every three or four years and gives only two or three liters of milk a day, the combined value of the calves and milk, plus dung, yields a profit boosting the household income of the poor by a third or more. The birth of a male calf which they may rear as a down payment on a replacement for their oxen or as a means of acquiring oxen for the first time adds to the cow's contribution. Of course, from the point of view of modern animal husbandry, it would be far more efficient to feed a smaller number of cows properly and to get rid of the underfed specimens. But there is another point of view: getting rid of surplus and useless cows is tantamount to getting rid of surplus and useless peasants. To be able to own even one cow, however emaciated, gives poor farmers an extra toehold on their land, possibly saving them from the clutches of the moneylenders and from being forced to join the exodus of landless families who have no place to go but the streets of Calcutta.

But what about those famous old-age homes for cattle? Don't they prove that vast numbers of "surplus" and "useless" cattle are kept alive in India for no reason other than religious senti- ment? About three thousand Indian facilities for housing animals represent themselves as being concerned with animal protection. They house a total of 580,000 cattle. Some of the shelters are indeed primarily religious and charitable institutions which main- tain their cattle at a net loss. Others are essentially for-profit dairy businesses which maintain a small number of useless cattle as tokens of piety and as "pets" (more about "pets" in a later chapter). Jains rather than Hindus run most of the shelters which contain genuinely useless animals and which depend on charitable do- nations of feed and money to balance their books. Piety is scarcely the only motivation for making contributions. Jain animal shelters keep strays off the streets and out of people's farms and gar- dens. In this regard they resemble animal shelters in the West: the ASPCA, for example, must also balance its books by means of charitable donations. And in both instances, unless someone claims a shelter animal, its life expectancy is not very great. Indian shelters substitute starvation for lethal injections, but they share with the ASPCA the necessity to terminate guests in order to discharge their annual animal-catching duties.

Deryck Lodrick, the principal authority on these matters, estimates that about a third, or 174,000, of the cattle in the Jain and Hindu shelters combined are useless. I suspect that most of them belong to the Jains, but let us accept the combined total. It amounts to less than 0.1 percent of the 180 million bovines in India. Even if we also accept the unlikely proposition that the people who run the cattle shelters make an equal effort to feed the useless and useful animals in their care, the costs of these charitable enterprises does not loom large in national perspective. Animal shelters are part of a whole system of values, ideas, and rituals whose historic payoff—the prevention of wasteful beef eating by elites—rationally justifies the expenditures incurred by a handful of pious cow-shelter enthusiasts. No system is perfect. Even corporate America hasn't quite figured out how to eliminate "wasteful" rituals such as support for public broadcasting programs and Little League baseball teams.

As I see it then (and many of my colleagues in India now agree), the "irrationality" of the Hindu taboo on the slaughter of cattle and the consumption of beef is a figment of the imagination of Westerners who are accustomed to raising cattle for beef or for milk and who can use tractors for plowing. On balance, the aversion to beef makes it possible for India's huge population to consume more rather than less animal food.

Let me pause here to make sure that what I have just said does not get distorted into something with which I strongly disagree, namely that the traditional system is flawless, cannot be improved, and is as efficient today as it was in the past. There is a vicious circle operating which makes any such conclusions quite absurd. Human population growth, the reduction in the size of holdings, overgrazing, erosion, and desertification have contributed to a rise in the cost of cattle feeds and fodders relative to other production costs. This in turn has increased the demand for smaller and cheaper cattle breeds, which in turn has led to a gradual deterioration in the quality of traction animals available to the poorer households. In the words of the geographer, A. K. Chakravarti:

> Because of the increasing pressure of human population on land and less and nutritionally unbalanced feed available for cattle, the quality of cattle has deteriorated with declining milk yield and draft efficiency . . . the effort has been to compensate the declining efficiency by increasing the number of cattle. . . . the increase in the number of cattle in turn has resulted in further shortages of feed and fodder.

There is now (and always has been) much room for improving existing breeds both from the point of view of traction power and milk production. As part of a comprehensive scheme to improve traction power and milk yields, it might be advantageous to slaughter cattle more freely than is possible today. (It would help to be able to get rid of stray animals and nondescript temple herds.) But by no stretch of the imagination can the declining efficiency of the traditional system be blamed on the aversion to beef. Blame population growth, colonialism, the caste systems, or land tenure, but don't blame the use of cattle for milk rather than meat! Bad as India's food situation may have become, there is no evidence that the removal of the ban on the slaughter of cattle by itself would ever have led to a broadly based improvement in the Indian diet.

During the past two decades India has actually made considerable progress in raising per capita cereal and dairy production. Thus far the diversions of grains to the production of animal foods is slight compared with what is happening in beef-eating nations like Mexico and Brazil, where beef cattle are now eating better than from one-third to one-half of the people at the bottom of the social pyramid. While the ban on cattle slaughter may eventually place a ceiling on the further improvement of traction and dairy breeds, the most pressing problem remains how to provide feed and fodder for these animals without diminishing the supply of food grains for people. The advantages involved in preventing the diversion of grain to meat production therefore probably outweigh the losses which the ban on slaughter imposes on programs aimed at raising milk and traction production through improved breeding.

To return to Mohandas Gandhi. For all of his sentimental and mystical devotion to cattle, Gandhi was well aware of the practical significance of cow love to his followers. Like them, he never lost sight of the bottom line: "Why the cow was selected for apotheosis is obvious to me," he said. "The cow was in India the best companion. She was the giver of plenty. Not only did she give milk but she made agriculture possible." This perception takes us a long way toward answering the principal remaining question: why did cattle and not some other animal become the quintessential symbol of Hinduism? The answer is that no other animal (or entity) could perform so many vital services for human beings. No other creature had the versatility, stamina, and efficiency of India's zebu cattle. To enter the contest for animal mother of India, a domestic species had to be at least big and strong enough to pull the plow. This immediately eliminates goats, sheep, and pigs, not to mention dogs and cats. We are left with camels, donkeys, horses, and water buffalo. Why not apotheosize the camel? Many farmers do actually employ camels for pulling plows in the arid northwestern regions of India. But the specifications for the ideal Indian plow animal call for a creature that also thrives during wet weather. Camels quickly become a sodden mass during the monsoon rains that fall on most of India. A camel mired in the mud is a sorry sight. It can easily break a leg if it tries to free itself. Donkeys and horses? They also pull plows, but for reasons that will become clear in a later chapter, they need to consume much more grass and straw per pound of body weight than cattle, and they lack the ability of cattle to subsist on various kinds of emergency rations such as leaves and rinds. Now we are down to water buffalo, the principal source of modern India's milk supply. Water buffalo milk is creamier than cow's milk, and in deep mud the males can pull better than oxen. But buffalo lack the stamina and resiliency of zebu cattle.

They are costlier to raise and maintain, and they have far less resistance to drought than cattle. They cannot even survive northern India's normal dry periods without having their skins watered down each day. While the males are good in mud, they are far inferior to zebu oxen when it comes to plowing the typical Indian farmer's hard-packed, sun-baked, and dusty patch of earth. Finally, the use of buffalo for milk production is a modern innovation associated with the growth of urban markets and the development of specialized milk breeds. Clearly, this limited kind of creature could not attract the adoration of India's masses as the all-enduring mother of life.

I would only make some slight additions to Gandhi's explanation of the apotheosis of the cow: not only did she give milk but she was the mother of the cheapest and most efficient traction animal for India's soils and climate. In return for Hindu safeguards against the reemergence of energetically costly and socially divisive beef-eating foodways, she made it possible for the land to teem with human life.

CHAPTER FOUR

THE ABOMINABLE PIG

AN AVERSION to pork seems at the outset even more irrational than an aversion to beef. Of all domesticated mammals, pigs possess the greatest potential for swiftly and efficiently changing plants into flesh. Over its lifetime a pig can convert 35 percent of the energy in its feed to meat compared with 13 percent for sheep and a mere 6.5 percent for cattle. A piglet can gain a pound for every three to five pounds it eats while a calf needs to eat ten pounds to gain one. A cow needs nine months to drop a single calf, and under modern conditions the calf needs another four months to reach four hundred pounds. But less than four months after insemination, a single sow can give birth to eight or more piglets, each of which after another six months can weigh over four hundred pounds. Clearly, the whole essence of pig is the production of meat for human nourishment and delectation. Why then did the Lord of the ancient Israelites forbid his people to savor pork or even to touch a pig alive or dead?

> Of their flesh you shall not eat, and their carcasses you shall not touch; they are unclean to you [Lev. 11:1] . . . everyone who touches them shall be unclean [Lev. 11:24].

Unlike the Old Testament, which is a treasure trove of forbidden flesh, the Koran is virtually free of meat taboos. Why is it the pig alone who suffers Allah's disapproval?

These things only has He forbidden you: carrion, blood, and
the flesh of swine [Holy Koran 2, 168].

For many observant Jews, the Old Testament's characterization
of swine as "unclean" renders the explanation of the taboo self-
evident: "Anyone who has seen the filthy habits of the swine will
not ask why it is prohibited," says a modern rabbinical authority.
The grounding of the fear and loathing of pigs in self-evident
piggishness goes back at least to the time of Rabbi Moses Maimonides, court physician to the Islamic emperor Saladin during
the twelfth century in Egypt. Maimonides shared with his Islamic
hosts a lively disgust for pigs and pig eaters, especially Christian
pigs and pig eaters: "The principal reason why the law forbids
swine-flesh is to be found in the circumstance that its habits and
food are very filthy and loathsome." If the law allowed Egyptians
and Jews to raise pigs, Cairo's streets and houses would become
as filthy as those of Europe, for "the mouth of a swine is as dirty
as dung itself." Maimonides could only tell one side of the story.
He had never seen a clean pig. The pig's penchant for excrement
is not a defect of its nature but of the husbandry of its human
masters. Pigs prefer and thrive best on roots, nuts, and grains;
they eat excrement only when nothing better presents itself. In
fact, let them get hungry enough, and they'll even eat each other,
a trait which they share with other omnivores, but most notably
with their own masters. Nor is wallowing in filth a natural characteristic of swine. Pigs wallow to keep themselves cool; and they
much prefer a fresh, clean mudhole to one that has been soiled
by urine and feces.

In condemning the pig as the dirtiest of animals, Jews and
Moslems left unexplained their more tolerant attitude toward
other dung-eating domesticated species. Chickens and goats, for
example, given motivation and opportunity, also readily dine on
dung. The dog is another domesticated creature which easily de-
velops an appetite for human feces. And this was especially true
in the Middle East, where dung-eating dogs filled the scavenging
niche left vacant by the ban on pigs. Jahweh prohibited their

flesh, yet dogs were not abominated, bad to touch, or even bad to look at, as were pigs.

Maimonides could not be entirely consistent in his efforts to attribute the abstention from pork to the pig's penchant for feces. The Book of Leviticus prohibits the flesh of many other creatures, such as cats and camels, which are not notably inclined to eat excrement. And with the exception of the pig, had not Allah said all the others were good to eat? The fact that Maimonides's Moslem emperor could eat every kind of meat except pork would have made it impolitic if not dangerous to identify the biblical sense of cleanliness exclusively with freedom from the taint of feces. So instead of adopting a cleaner-than-thou attitude, Maimonides offered a proper court physician's theory of the entire set of biblical aversions: the prohibited items were not good to eat because not only was one of them—the pig—filthy from eating excrement but all of them were not good for you. "I maintain," he said, "that food forbidden by the Law is unwholesome." But in what ways were the forbidden foods unwholesome? The great rabbi was quite specific in the case of pork: it "contained more moisture than necessary and too much superfluous matter." As for the other forbidden foods, their "injurious character" was too self-evident to merit further discussion.

Maimonides's public health theory of pork avoidance had to wait seven hundred years before it acquired what seemed to be a scientific justification. In 1859 the first clinical association between trichinosis and undercooked pork was established, and from then on it became the most popular explanation of the Jewish and Islamic pork taboo. Just as Maimonides said, pork was unwholesome. Eager to reconcile the Bible with the findings of medical science, theologians began to embroider a whole series of additional public health explanations for the other biblical food taboos: wild animals and beasts of burden were prohibited because the flesh gets too tough to be digested properly; shellfish were to be avoided because they serve as vectors of typhoid fever; blood is not good to eat because the bloodstream is a perfect medium for microbes. In the case of pork this line of rationalization had a paradoxical outcome. Reformist Jews began to argue that since they now understood the scientific and medical basis of the taboos, pork avoidance was no longer necessary; all they had to do was to see to it that the meat was thoroughly cooked. Predictably, this provoked a reaction among Orthodox Jews, who were appalled at the idea that the book of God's law was being relegated to the "class of a minor medical text." They insisted that God's purpose in Leviticus could never be fully comprehended; nonetheless the dietary laws had to be obeyed as a sign of submission to divine will.

Eventually the trichinosis theory of pork avoidance fell out of favor largely on the grounds that a medical discovery made in the nineteenth century could not have been known thousands of years ago. But that is not the part of the theory that bothers me. People do not have to possess a scientific understanding of the ill effects of certain foods in order to put such foods on their bad-to-eat list. If the consequences of eating pork had been exceptionally bad for their health, it would not have been necessary for the Israelites to know about trichinosis in order to ban its consumption. Does one have to understand the molecular chemistry of toxins in order to know that some mushrooms are dangerous? It is essential for my own explanation of the pig taboo that the trichinosis theory be laid to rest on entirely different grounds. My contention is that there is absolutely nothing exceptional about pork as a source of human disease. All domestic animals are potentially hazardous to human health. Undercooked beef, for example, is a prolific source of tapeworms, which can grow to a length of sixteen to twenty feet inside the human gut, induce a severe case of anemia, and lower the body's resistance to other diseases. Cattle, goat, and sheep transmit the bacterial disease known as brucellosis, whose symptoms include fever, aches, pains, and lassitude. The most dangerous disease transmitted by cattle, sheep, and goats is anthrax, a fairly common disease of both animals and humans in Europe and Asia until the introduction of Louis Pasteur's anthrax vaccine in 1881. Unlike trichinosis, which does not produce symptoms in the majority of infected individuals and rarely has a fatal outcome, anthrax runs a swift course that begins with an outbreak of boils and ends in death.

If the taboo on pork was a divinely inspired health ordinance, it is the oldest recorded case of medical malpractice. The way to safeguard against trichinosis was not to taboo pork but to taboo undercooked pork. A simple advisory against undercooking pork would have sufficed: "Flesh of swine thou shalt not eat until the pink has been cooked from it." And come to think of it, the same advisory should have been issued for cattle, sheep, and goats. But the charge of medical malpractice against Jahweh will not stick.

The Old Testament contains a rather precise formula for distinguishing good-to-eat flesh from forbidden flesh. This formula says nothing about dirty habits or unhealthy meat. Instead it directs attention to certain anatomical and physiological features of animals that are good to eat. Here is what Leviticus 11:1 says:

Whatever parts the hoof and is cloven footed and chews the cud among animals, you may eat.

Any serious attempt to explain why the pig was not good to eat must begin with this formula and not with excrement or wholesomeness, about which not a word is said. Leviticus goes on to state explicitly of the pig that it only satisfies one part of the formula. "It divideth the hoof." But the pig does not satisfy the other part of the formula: "It cheweth not the cud."

To their credit, champions of the good-to-eat school have stressed the importance of the cud-chewing, split-hoof formula as the key to understanding Jahweh's abomination of the pig. But they do not view the formula as an outcome of the way the Israelites used domestic animals. Instead they view the way the Israelites used domestic animals as an outcome of the formula. According to anthropologist Mary Douglas, for example, the cud-chewing, split-hoof formula makes the split-hoof but non–cud-chewing pig a thing that's "out of place." Things that are "out of place" are dirty, she argues, for the essence of dirt is "matter out of place." The pig, however, is more than out of place; it is neither here nor there. Such things are both dirty and dangerous. Therefore the pig is abominated as well as not good to eat. But doesn't the force of this argument lie entirely in its circularity? To observe that the pig is out of place taxonomically is merely to observe that Leviticus classifies good-to-eat animals in such a way as to make the pig bad to eat. This avoids the question of why the taxonomy is what it is.

Let me attend first to the reason why Jahweh wanted edible animals to be cud-chewers. Among animals raised by the ancient Israelites, there were three cud-chewers: cattle, sheep, and goats. These three animals were the most important food-producing species in the ancient Middle East not because the ancients happened capriciously to think that cud-chewing animals were good to eat (and good to milk) but because cattle, sheep, and goats are ruminants, the kind of herbivores which thrive best on diets consisting of plants that have a high cellulose content. Of all domesticated animals, those which are ruminants possess the most efficient system for digesting tough fibrous materials such as grasses and straw. Their stomachs have four compartments which are like big fermentation "vats" in which bacteria break down and soften these materials. While cropping their food, ruminants do little chewing. The food passes directly to the rumen, the first of the compartments, where it soon begins to ferment. From time to time the contents of the rumen are regurgitated into the mouth as a softened bolus—the "cud"—which is then chewed thoroughly and sent on to the other "vats" to undergo further fermentation.

The ruminant's extraordinary ability to digest cellulose was crucial to the relationship between humans and domesticated animals in the Middle East. By raising animals that could "chew the cud," the Israelites and their neighbors were able to obtain meat and milk without having to share with their livestock the crops destined for human consumption. Cattle, sheep, and goats thrive on items like grass, straw, hay, stubble, bushes, and leaves—feeds whose high cellulose content renders them unfit for human consumption even after vigorous boiling. Rather than compete with humans for food, the ruminants further enhanced agricultural productivity by providing dung for fertilizer and traction for pulling plows. And they were also a source of fiber and felt for clothing, and of leather for shoes and harnesses.

I began this puzzle by saying that pigs are the most efficient mammalian converters of plant foods into animal flesh, but I neglected to say what kinds of plant foods. Feed them on wheat, maize, potatoes, soybeans, or anything low in cellulose, and pigs will perform veritable miracles of transubstantiation; feed them on grass, stubble, leaves, or anything high in cellulose, and they will lose weight.

Pigs are omnivores, but they are not ruminants. In fact, in digestive apparatus and nutrient requirements pigs resemble humans in more ways than any mammal except monkeys and apes, which is why pigs are much in demand for medical research concerned with atherosclerosis, calorie-protein malnutrition, nutrient absorption, and metabolism. But there was more to the ban on pork than the pig's inability to thrive on grass and other high-cellulose plants. Pigs carry the additional onus of not being well adapted to the climate and ecology of the Middle East. Unlike the ancestors of cattle, sheep, or goats, which lived in hot, semiarid, sunny grasslands, the pig's ancestors were denizens of well-watered, shady forest glens and riverbanks. Everything about the pig's body heat-regulating system is ill suited for life in the hot, sun-parched habitats which were the homelands of the children of Abraham. Tropical breeds of cattle, sheep, and goats can go for long periods without water, and can either rid their bodies of excess heat through perspiration or are protected from the sun's rays by light-colored, short fleecy coats (heat-trapping heavy wool is a characteristic of cold-climate breeds). Although a perspiring human is said to "sweat like a pig," the expression lacks an anatomical basis. Pigs can't sweat—they have no functional sweat glands. (Humans are actually the sweatiest of all animals.) And the pig's sparse coat offers little protection against the sun's rays. Just how does the pig keep cool? It does a lot of panting, but mostly it depends on wetting itself down with moisture derived from external sources. Here, then, is the explanation for the pig's love of wallowing in mud. By wallowing, it dissipates heat both by evaporation from its skin and by conduction through the cool ground. Experiments show that the cooling effect of mud is superior to that of water. Pigs whose flanks are thoroughly smeared with mud continue to show peak heat-dissipating evaporation for more than twice as long as pigs whose flanks are merely soaked with water, and here also is the explanation for some of the pig's dirty habits. As temperatures rise above thirty degrees celsius (eighty-six degreees Fahrenheit), a pig deprived of clean mudholes will become desperate and begin to wallow in its own feces and urine in order to avoid heat stroke. Incidentally, the larger a pig gets, the more intolerant it becomes of high ambient temperatures.

Raising pigs in the Middle East therefore was and still is a lot costlier than raising ruminants, because pigs must be provided with artificial shade, extra water for wallowing, and their diet must be supplemented with grains and other plant foods that humans themselves can eat.

To offset all these liabilities pigs have less to offer by way of benefits than ruminants. They can't pull plows, their hair is unsuited for fiber and cloth, and they are not suited for milking (I'll explain why in a later chapter). Uniquely among large domesticated animals, meat is their most important produce (guinea pigs and rabbits are smaller equivalents; but fowl produce eggs as well as meat).

For a pastoral nomadic people like the Israelites during their years of wandering in search of lands suitable for agriculture, swineherding was out of the question. No arid-land pastoralists herd pigs for the simple reason that it is hard to protect them from exposure to heat, sun, and lack of water while moving from camp to camp over long distances. During their formative years as a nation, therefore, the ancient Israelites could not have consumed significant quantities of pork even had they desired it. This historical experience undoubtedly contributed to the development of a traditional aversion to pig meat as an unknown and alien food. But why was this tradition preserved and strengthened by being written down as God's law long after the Israelites had become settled farmers? The answer as I see it is not that the tradition born of pastoralism continued to prevail by mere inertia and ingrown habit, but that it was preserved because pig raising remained too costly.

Critics have opposed the theory that the ancient Israelite pork taboo was essentially a cost/benefit choice by pointing to evidence of pigs being raised quite successfully in many parts of the Middle East including the Israelites' promised land. The facts are not in dispute. Pigs have indeed been raised for ten thousand years in various parts of the Middle East—as long as sheep and goats, and even longer than cattle. Some of the oldest Neolithic villages excavated by archaeologists—Jericho in Jordan, Jarmo in Iraq and Argissa-Magulla in Greece—contain pig bones with features indicative of the transition from wild to domesticated varieties. Several Middle Eastern pre–Bronze Age villages (4000 B.C. to 2000 B.C.) contain concentrated masses of pig remains in association with what archaeologists interpret as altars and cultic centers, suggestive of ritual pig slaughter and pig feasting. We know that some pigs were still being raised in the lands of the Bible at the beginning of the Christian era. The New Testament (Luke) tells us that in the country of the Gadarenes near Lake Galilee Jesus cast out devils from a man named Legion into a herd of swine feeding on the mountain. The swine rushed down into the lake and drowned themselves, and Legion was cured. Even modern-day Israelis continue to raise thousands of swine in parts of northern Galilee. But from the very beginning, fewer pigs were raised than cattle, sheep, or goats. And more importantly, as time went on, pig husbandry declined throughout the region.

Carlton Coon, an anthropologist with many years of experience in North America and the Levant, was the first scholar to offer a cogent explanation of why this general decline in pig husbandry had occurred. Coon attributed the fall of the Middle Eastern pig to deforestation and human population increase. At the beginning of the Neolithic period, pigs were able to root in oak and beech forests which provided ample shade and wallows as well as acorns, beechnuts, truffles, and other forest floor products. With an increase in human population density, farm acreage increased and the oak and beech forests were destroyed to make room for planted crops, especially for olive trees, thereby eliminating the pig's ecological niche.

To update Coon's ecological scenario, I would add that as forests were being destroyed, so were marginal farmlands and grazing lands, the general succession being from forest to cropland to grazing land to desert, with each step along the way yielding a greater premium for raising ruminants and a greater penalty for raising swine. Robert Orr Whyte, former director general of the United Nations Food and Agriculture Organization, estimated that in Anatolia the forests shrank from 70 percent to 13 percent of the total land area between 5000 B.C. and the recent past. Only a fourth of the Caspian shorefront forest survived the process of population increase and agricultural intensification; half of the Caspian mountainous humid forest; a fifth to a sixth of the oak and juniper forests of the Zagros Mountains; and only a twentieth of the juniper forests of the Elburz and Khorassan ranges.

If I am right about the subversion of the practical basis of pig production through ecological succession, one does not need to invoke Mary Douglas's "taxonomic anomaly" to understand the peculiarly low status of the pig in the Middle East. The danger it posed to husbandry was very tangible and accounts quite well for its low status. The pig had been domesticated for one purpose only, namely to supply meat. As ecological conditions became unfavorable for pig raising, there was no alternative function which could redeem its existence. The creature became not only useless, but worse than useless—harmful, a curse to touch or merely to see—a pariah animal. This transformation contrasts understandably with that of cattle in India. Subject to a similar series of ecological depletions—deforestation, erosion, and desertification—cattle also became bad to eat. But in other respects, especially for traction power and milk, they became more useful than ever—a blessing to look at or to touch—animal godheads.

In this perspective, the fact that pig raising remained possible for the Israelites at low cost in certain remnant hillside forests or swampy habitats, or at extra expense where shade and water were scarce, does not contradict the ecological basis of the taboo. If there had not been some minimum possibility of raising pigs, there would have been no reason to taboo the practice. As the history of Hindu cow protection shows, religions gain strength when they help people make decisions which are in accord with preexisting useful practices, but which are not so completely self-evident as to preclude doubts and temptations. To judge from the Eight-fold Way or the Ten Commandments, God does not usually waste time prohibiting the impossible or condemning the unthinkable.

Leviticus consistently bans all vertebrate land animals that do not chew the cud. It bans, for example, in addition to swine, equines, felines, canines, rodents, and reptiles, none of which are cud-chewers. But Leviticus contains a maddening complication. It prohibits the consumption of three land-dwelling vertebrates which it specifically identifies as cud-chewers: the camel, the hare, and a third creature whose name in Hebrew is *shāphān*. The reason given for why these three alleged cud-chewers are not good to eat is that they do not "part the hoof":

> Nevertheless, these shall ye not eat of them that chew the cud . . . the camel because he . . . divideth not the hoof. And the *shāfān* because he . . . divideth not the hoof. . . . And the hare, because he . . . divideth not the hoof. [Lev. 11:4–6]

Although strictly speaking camels are not ruminants, because their cellulose-digesting chambers are anatomically distinct from those of the ruminants, they do ferment, regurgitate, and chew the cud much like cattle, sheep, and goats. But the classification of the hare as a cud-chewer immediately casts a pall over the zoological expertise of the Levite priests. Hares can digest grass but only by eating their own feces—which is a very uncudlike solution to the problem of how to send undigested cellulose through the gut for repeated processing (the technical term for this practice is coprophagy). Now as to the identity of the *"shāphān"*. As the following stack of Bibles shows, *shāphān* is either the "rock badger," "cherogrillus," or "cony":

BIBLES TRANSLATING SHĀPHĀN AS "ROCK BADGER"
 The Holy Bible. Berkeley: University of California Press.
 The Bible. Chicago: University of Chicago Press, 1931.
 The New Schofield Reference Library Holy Bible. (Authorized King James Version). New York: Oxford University Press, 1967.
 The Holy Bible. London: Catholic Truth Society, 1966.
 The Holy Bible. (Revised Standard Version). New York: Thomas Nelson and Sons, 1952.
 The American Standard Bible. (Reference Edition). La Habra, CA: Collins World, 1973.
 The New World Translation of the Holy Scriptures. Brooklyn, NY: Watchtower Bible and Tract Society of Pennsylvania, 1961.
BIBLES TRANSLATING SHĀPHĀN AS "CONY"
 The Pentateuch: The Five Books of Moses. Edited by William Tyndale. Carbondale: Southern Illinois University Press, 1967.
 The Interpreter's Bible: The Holy Scriptures. 12 vols. New York: Abingdon Press, 1953.
 The Holy Bible: King James Version (Revised Standard Version). Nashville: Thomas Nelson and Sons, 1971.
 Holy Bible: authorized version. New York: Harpers.
 Holy Bible: Revised. New York: American Bible Society, 1873.
 Modern Readers Bible. Edited by Richard Moulton. New York: Macmillan, 1935.
BIBLES TRANSLATING SHĀPHĀN AS "CHEROGRILLUS"
 Holy Bible. (Duay, translated from Vulgate). Boston: John Murphy and Co., 1914.
 The Holy Bible (translated from the Vulgate by John Wycliffe and his followers). Edited by Rev. Josiah Forshall and Sir Frederick Madden. Oxford: Oxford University Press, 1850.

All three terms refer to a similar kind of small, furtive, hoofed herbivore about the size of a squirrel that lives in colonies on rocky cliffs or among boulders on hilltops. It has two other popular aliases: "dassie" and "damon." It could have been any of these closely related species: *Hyrax capensia, Hyrax syriacus,* or *Procavia capensis.* Whichever it was, it had no rumen and it did not chew the cud.

This leaves the camel as the only bona fide cud-chewer that the Israelites couldn't eat. Every vertebrate land animal that is not a ruminant was forbidden flesh. And only one vertebrate land animal that is a ruminant, the camel, was forbidden. Let me see if I can explain this exception as well as the peculiar mixup about hares and *shāphān.*

My point of departure is that the food laws in Leviticus were mostly codifications of preexisting traditional food prejudices and avoidances. (The Book of Leviticus was not written until 450 B.C.—very late in Israelite history.) I envision the Levite authorities as undertaking the task of finding some simple feature which good-to-eat vertebrate land species shared in common. Had the Levites possessed a better knowledge of zoology, they could have used the criterion of cud-chewing alone and simply added the proviso, "except for the camel." For, as I have just said, with the exception of the camel, all land animals implicitly or explicitly forbidden in Leviticus—all the equines, felines, canines, rodents, rabbits, reptiles, and so forth—are nonruminants. But given their shaky knowledge of zoology, the codifiers could not be sure that the camel was the only undesirable species which was a cud-chewer. So they added the criterion of split hooves—a feature which camels lacked but which the other familiar cud-chewers possessed (the camel has two large flexible toes on each foot instead of hooves).

But why was the camel not a desirable species? Why spurn camel meat? I think the separation of the camel from the other cud-chewers reflects its highly specialized adaptation to desert habitats. With their remarkable capacity to store water, withstand heat, and carry heavy burdens over great distances, and with their long eyelashes and nostrils that shut tight for protection

against sandstorms, camels were the most important possession
of the Middle Eastern desert nomads. (The camel's hump con-
centrates fat—not water. It acts as an energy reserve. By concentrating the fat in the hump, the rest of the skin needs only a
thin layer of fat, and this facilitates removal of body heat.) But
as village farmers, the Israelites had little use for camels. Except
under desert conditions, sheep and goats and cattle are more
efficient converters of cellulose into meat and milk. In addition,
camels reproduce very slowly. The females are not ready to bear
offspring and the males are not ready to copulate until six years
of age. To slow things down further, the males have a once-a-
year rutting season (during which they emit an offensive odor),
and gestation takes twelve months. Neither camel meat nor camel
milk could ever have constituted a significant portion of the ancient Isarelites' food supply. Those few Israelites such as Abraham
and Joseph who owned camels would have used them strictly as
a means of transport for crossing the desert.

This interpretation gains strength from the Moslem acceptance
of camel meat. In the Koran, pork is specifically prohibited while
camel flesh is specifically allowed. The whole way of life of Mohammed's desert-dwelling, pastoral Bedouin followers was based
on the camel. The camel was their main source of transport and
their main source of animal food, primarily in the form of camel
milk. While camel meat was not daily fare, the Bedouin were
often forced to slaughter pack animals during their desert journeys as emergency rations when their regular supplies of food
were depleted. An Islam that banned camel flesh would never
have become a great world religion. It would have been unable
to conquer the Arabian heartlands, to launch its attack against
the Byzantine and Persian empires, and to cross the Sahara to
the Sahel and West Africa.

If the Levite priests were trying to rationalize and codify dietary
laws, most of which had a basis in preexisting popular belief and
practice, they needed a taxonomic principle which connected the
existing patterns of preference and avoidance into a comprehensive cognitive and theological system. The preexisting ban on

camel meat made it impossible to use cud-chewing as the sole taxonomic principle for identifying land vertebrates that were good to eat. They needed another criterion to exclude camels. And this was how "split hooves" got into the picture. Camels have conspicuously different feet from cattle, sheep, or goats. They have split toes instead of split hooves. So the priests of Leviticus added "parts the hoof" to "chews the cud" to make camels bad to eat. The misclassification of the hare and *shāphān* suggests that these animals were not well known to the codifiers. The authors of Leviticus were right about the feet—hares have paws and *Hyrax* (and *Procavia*) have tiny hooves, three on the front leg and five on the rear leg. But they were wrong about the cud-chewing—perhaps because hares and *shāphān* have their mouths in constant motion.

Once the principle of using feet to distinguish between edible and inedible flesh was established, the pig could not be banned simply by pointing to its nonruminant nature. Both its cud-chewing status and the anatomy of its feet had to be considered, even though the pig's failure to chew the cud was its decisive defect.

This, then, is my theory of why the formula for forbidden vertebrate land animals was elaborated beyond the mere absence of cud-chewing. It is a difficult theory to prove because no one knows who the authors of Leviticus were or what was really going on inside their heads. But regardless of whether or not the good-to-eat formula originated in the way I have described, the fact remains that the application of the expanded formula to hare and *shāphān* (as well as to pig and camel) did not result in any dietary restrictions that adversely affected the balance of nutritional or ecological costs and benefits. Hare and *shāphān* are wild species; it would have been a waste of time to hunt them instead of concentrating on raising far more productive ruminants.

To recall momentarily the case of the Brahman protectors of the cow, I do not doubt the ability of a literate priesthood to codify, build onto, and reshape popular foodways. But I doubt whether such "top-down" codifications generally result in adverse nutritional or ecological consequences or are made with blithe disregard of such consequences. More important than all the zoological errors and flights of taxonomic fancy is that Leviticus correctly identifies the classic domesticated ruminants as the most efficient source of milk and meats for the ancient Israelites. To the extent that abstract theological principles result in flamboyant lists of interdicted species, the results are trivial if not beneficial from a nutritional and ecological viewpoint. Among birds, for example, Leviticus bans the flesh of the eagle, ossifrage, osprey, ostrich, kite, falcon, raven, nighthawk, sea gull, hawk, cormorant, ibis, waterhen, pelican, vulture, stork, hoopoe, and bat (not a bird of course). I suspect but again cannot prove that this list was primarily the result of a priestly attempt to enlarge on a smaller set of prohibited flying creatures. Many of these "birds," especially the sea birds like pelicans and cormorants, would rarely be seen inland. Also, the list seems to be based on a taxonomic principle that has been somewhat overextended: most of the creatures on it are carnivores and "birds of prey." Perhaps the list was generated from this principle applied first to common local "birds" and then extended to the exotic sea birds as a validation of the codifiers' claim to special knowledge of the natural and supernatural worlds. But in any event, the list renders no disservice. Unless they were close to starvation and nothing else was available, the Israelites were well advised not to waste their time trying to catch eagles, ospreys, sea gulls, and the like, supposing they were inclined to dine on creatures that consist of little more than skin, feathers, and well-nigh indestructible gizzards in the first place. Similar remarks are appropriate vis-à-vis the prohibition of such unlikely sources of food for the inland-dwelling Israelites as clams and oysters. And if Jonah is an example of what happened when they took to the sea, the Israelites were well advised not to try to satisfy their meat hunger by hunting whales.

But let me return to the pig. If the Israelites had been alone in their interdictions of pork, I would find it more difficult to choose among alternative explanations of the pig taboo. The recurrence of pig aversions in several different Middle Eastern cultures strongly supports the view that the Israelite ban was a response to recurrent practical conditions rather than to a set of beliefs peculiar to one religion's notions about clean and unclean animals. At least three other important Middle Eastern civilizations—the Phoenicians, Egyptians, and Babylonians—were as disturbed by pigs as were the Israelites. Incidentally, this disposes of the notion that the Israelites banned the pig to "set themselves off from their neighbors," especially their unfriendly neighbors. (Of course, after the Jews dispersed throughout pork-eating Christendom, their abomination of the pig became an ethnic "marker." There was no compelling reason for them to give up their ancient contempt for pork. Prevented from owning land, the basis for their livelihood in Europe had to be crafts and commerce rather than agriculture. Hence there were no ecological or economic penalties associated with their rejection of pork while there were plenty of other sources of animal foods.)

In each of the additional cases, pork had been freely consumed during an earlier epoch. In Egypt, for example, tomb paintings and inscriptions indicate that pigs were the object of increasingly severe opprobrium and religious interdiction during the New Kingdom (1567–1085 B.C.). Toward the end of late dynastic times (1088–332 B.C.) Herodotus visited Egypt and reported that "the pig is regarded among them as an unclean animal so much so that if a man in passing accidentally touches a pig, he instantly hurries to the river and plunges in with all his clothes on." As in Roman Palestine when Jesus drove the Gadarene swine into Lake Galilee, some Egyptians continued to raise pigs. Herodotus described these swineherds as an in-marrying pariah caste who were forbidden to set foot in any of the temples.

One interpretation of the Egyptian pig taboo is that it reflects the conquest of the northern pork-eating followers of the god Seth by the southern pork-abstaining followers of the god Osiris and the imposition of southern Egyptian food preferences on the northerners. The trouble with this explanation is that if such a conquest occurred at all, it took place at the very beginning of the dynastic era and therefore does not account for the evidence that the pig taboo got stronger in late dynastic times.

My own interpretation of the Egyptian pig taboo is that it

reflected a basic conflict between the dense human population crowded into the treeless Nile Valley and the demands made by the pig for the plant foods that humans could consume. A text from the Old Kingdom clearly shows how during hard times humans and swine competed for subsistence: ". . . food is robbed from the mouth of the swine, without it being said, as before 'this is better for thee than for me,' for men are so hungry." What kinds of foods were robbed from the swine's mouth? Another text from the Second Intermediate period, boasting of a king's power over the lands, suggests it was grains fit for human consumption: "The finest of their fields are ploughed for us, our oxen are in the Delta, wheat is sent for our swine." And the Roman historian, Pliny, mentions the use of dates as a food used to fatten Egyptian pigs. The kind of preferential treatment needed to raise pigs in Egypt must have engendered strong feelings of antagonism between poor peasants who could not afford pork and the swineherds who catered to the tastes of rich and powerful nobles.

In Mesopotamia, as in Egypt, the pig fell from grace after a long period of popularity. Archaeologists have found clay models of domesticated pigs in the earliest settlements along the lower Tigris and Euphrates rivers. About 30 percent of the animal bones excavated from Tell Asmar (2800–2700 B.C.) came from pigs. Pork was eaten at Ur in predynastic times, and in the earliest Sumerian dynasties there were swineherds and butchers who specialized in pig slaughter. The pig seems to have fallen from favor when the Sumerians' irrigated fields became contaminated with salt, and barley, a salt-tolerant but relatively low-yielding plant, had to be substituted for wheat. These agricultural problems are implicated in the collapse of the Sumerian Empire and the shift after 2000 B.C. of the center of power upstream to Babylon. While pigs continued to be raised during Hammurabi's reign (about 1900 B.C.), they virtually disappear from Mesopotamia's archaeological and historical record thereafter.

The most important recurrence of the pig taboo is that of Islam. To repeat, pork is Allah's only explicitly forbidden flesh. Mohammed's Bedouin followers shared an aversion to pig found everywhere among arid-land nomadic pastoralists. As Islam spread westward from the Arabian Peninsula to the Atlantic, it found its greatest strength among North African peoples for whom pig raising was also a minor or entirely absent component of agriculture and for whom the Koranic ban on pork did not represent a significant dietary or economic deprivation. To the east, Islam again found its greatest strength in the belt of the semiarid lands that stretch from the Mediterranean Sea through Iran, Afghanistan, and Pakistan to India. I don't mean to say that none of the people who adopted Islam had previously relished pork. But for the great mass of early converts, becoming a Moslem did not involve any great upending of dietary or subsistence practices because from Morocco to India people had come to depend primarily on cattle, sheep, and goats for their animal products long before the Koran was written. Where local ecological conditions here and there strongly favored pig raising within the Islamic heartland, pork continued to be produced. Carlton Coon described one such pork-tolerant enclave—a village of Berbers in the oak forests of the Atlas Mountains in Morocco. Although nominally Moslems, the villagers kept pigs which they let loose in the forest during the day and brought home at night. The villagers denied that they raised pigs, never took them to market, and hid them from visitors. These and other examples of pig-tolerant Moslems suggest that one should not overestimate the ability of Islam to stamp out pig eating by religious precept alone if conditions are favorable for pig husbandry.

Wherever Islam has penetrated to regions in which pig raising was a mainstay of the traditional farming systems, it has failed to win over substantial portions of the population. Regions such as Malaysia, Indonesia, the Philippines, and Africa south of the Sahara, parts of which are ecologically well suited for pig raising, constitute the outer limits of the active spread of Islam. All along this frontier the resistance of pig-eating "pagans," pig-eating Moslem heretics, and pig-eating Christians has prevented Islam from becoming the dominant religion. In China, one of the world centers of pig production, Islam has made small inroads and is confined largely to the arid and semiarid western provinces. Islam, in other words, to this very day has a geographical limit which coincides with the ecological zones of transition between forested regions well suited for pig husbandry and regions where too much sun and dry heat make pig husbandry a risky and expensive practice.

While I contend that ecological factors underlie religious definitions of clean and unclean foods, I also hold that the effects do not all flow in a single direction. Religiously sanctioned foodways that have become established as the mark of conversion and, as a measure of piety, can also exert a force of their own back upon the ecological and economic conditions which gave rise to them. In the case of the Islamic pork taboos, the feedback between religious belief and the practical exigencies of animal husbandry has led to a kind of undeclared ecological war between Christians and Moslems in several parts of the Mediterranean shores of southern Europe. In rejecting the pig, Moslem farmers automatically downgrade the importance of preserving woodlands suitable for pig production. Their secret weapon is the goat, a great devourer of forests, which readily climbs trees to get at a meal of leaves and twigs. By giving the goat free reign, Islam to some degree spread the conditions of its own success. It enlarged the ecological zones ill suited to pig husbandry and removed one of the chief obstacles to the acceptance of the words of the Prophet. Deforestation is particularly noticeable in the Islamic regions of the Mediterranean. Albania, for example, is divided between distinct Christian pig-keeping and Moslem pig-abominating zones, and as one passes from the Moslem to the Christian sectors, the amount of woodland immediately increases.

It would be wrong to conclude that the Islamic taboo on the pig caused the deforestation wrought by the goat. After all, a preference for cattle, sheep, and goats and the rejection of pigs in the Middle East long antedated the birth of Islam. This preference was based on the cost/benefit advantages of ruminants over other domestic animals as sources of milk, meat, traction, and other services and products in hot, arid climates. It represents an unassailably "correct" ecological and economic decision embodying thousands of years of collective wisdom and practical experience. But as I have already pointed out in relation to the sacred cow, no system is perfect. Just as the combination of population growth and political exploitation led to a deterioration of agriculture in India, so too population growth and political exploitation took their toll in Islamic lands. If the response to demographic and political pressures had been to raise more pigs rather than more goats, the adverse effects on living standards would have been even more severe and would have occurred at a much lower level of population density.

All of this is not to say that a proseletyzing religion such as Islam is incapable of getting people to change their foodways purely out of obedience to divine commandments. Priests, monks, and saints do often refuse delectable and nutritious foods out of piety rather than practical necessity. But I have yet to encounter a flourishing religion whose food taboos make it more difficult for ordinary people to be well nourished. On the contrary, in solving the riddle of the sacred cow and abominable pig, I have already shown that the most important food aversions and preferences of four major religions—Hinduism, Buddhism, Judaism, and Islam—are on balance favorable to the nutritional and ecological welfare of their followers.

What about Christianity? There is only one animal whose consumption mainstream Christianity has ever explicitly banned. And that animal is the subject of the next riddle.

CHAPTER FIVE

HIPPOPHAGY

WHY DON'T Americans eat horsemeat? Horsemeat is redder than beef, but Americans like red meat. Horsemeat is sweeter than beef, but would that bother people who dump sweetened ketchup and steak sauce on their T-bones and sirloins? As for texture, horsemeat has a peculiar advantage. Even though horses have never been bred for the quality of their meat, they are tender not only as colts, but in their old age. Only horses whose muscles have recently been under strain tend to be tough. Horsemeat is also lean and unmarbled. In these diet-conscious times, what could be more appealing than tender red meat minus a lot of calories and cholesterol?

The horsemeat puzzle deepens as we look about us to other cultures. People eat horsemeat throughout most of continental Europe. The French, Belgians, Dutch, Germans, Italians, Poles, and Russians all think horsemeat is good to eat and consume significant quantities during the course of a year. In France where about one out of three people eats horsemeat, average per capita consumption is 4 pounds (1.8 kilos) per year, which is more than the average amount of veal, lamb, and mutton consumed per person in the United States. Despite a decline in sales since World War II, there are still about three thousand butcher shops in France that specialize in horsemeat. Many Europeans believe

that horsemeat is not only tastier but healthier than other meats.
In Japan, horsemeat eating is on the rise. A popular ingredient
in sukiyaki dishes and in chopped meat products, horsemeat
accounts for 3 percent of meat protein in the Japanese diet. Prime
hindquarter steaks sell for the price of the most expensive cuts
of beef in supermarkets and fancy Tokyo restaurants. Incidentally,
the Japanese like to eat their horsemeat raw, a gustatory preference which is obviously predicated on the tenderness of the
meat.

Horsemeat eating has gone through a strange series of ups and
downs. Back in the Stone Age, Old World hunters gorged themselves on the flesh of wild horses. The Asiatic pastoralists who
first tamed and domesticated the horse continued to relish horsemeat as did the pre-Christian peoples of northern Europe. Taboos
against horseflesh first appear with the rise of ancient Middle
Eastern empires. The Romans also refused to eat horses, and
during early medieval times, the horse seemed on the verge of
becoming a kind of European sacred cow when it was banned as
flesh to all Christians by papal decree. About the time of the
French Revolution, horsemeat began to return to favor in Europe. By the late nineteenth century, Europeans—except for the
British—were once more consuming it in a big way. Parisians ate
thirteen thousand tons of it per year just before World War I.
But since World War II, as I already mentioned, the trend has
reversed yet another time. Today the once commonplace French
and Belgian horsemeat restaurants are slowly fading away. Why
the strange on-again, off-again pattern in Europe? And why did
horsemeat never catch on in England and the United States?

Let's go back to the Stone Age. At the bottom of a cliff near
Solutré-Pouilly in Burgundy, France, lies a pile of fossilized horse
bones that covers two-and-a-half acres three feet deep. This famous equine graveyard was formed when Paleolithic hunters
repeatedly stampeded herds of wild horses over the cliff's edge
and then descended to cut off favorite parts, leaving the rest of
the carcass where it had fallen (like the bison hunters of the Great
Plains). The caves in which these hunters lived are also full of

horse bones, cracked and split, mementos of many a bygone
marrow-sucking, finger-licking feast. Stone Age peoples not only
ate more horses per capita per year than anyone before or since,
but they also painted more pictures of horses on the walls of their
caves than of any other animal (bison were the runner-up, and
third place went to deer and reindeer). Does this mean that they
ate more horses than any other animal? Or does it mean simply
that they just couldn't get enough horsemeat? I don't have the
answer, but I'm sure of one thing: only consummate admirers of
living as well as of dead horses could have created the stunningly
beautiful creatures that gallop across the walls and ceilings of
Europe's cave-art galleries. I mention this in order to disabuse
modern horse lovers of the notion that horses cannot be both
good to see and good to eat at the same time.

The great epoch of horse hunting soon passed away—soon in
geological terms at least. The climate grew warmer. Forests replaced grasslands, and horses could no longer graze in dense
numbers in Western Europe. But in Asia, treeless steppes
stretching from the Ukraine to Mongolia remained covered with
sparse grass, enough to support remnant herds of wild horses.
And so it was in that vast expanse of semiarid grasslands that
human beings first tamed the horse and brought it within the
fold of domesticated species. I cannot tell you precisely where
or when the horse was first domesticated. But one crucial point
is known: it happened very late compared with the domestication
of other animals. Sometime between 4000 B.C. and 3000 B.C., a
people, or several peoples, living on the margins of the Asiatic
steppes and already familiar with oxen and sheep, developed the
first tame breeds. Anthropologists have tried to reconstruct something about the role of horses in these earliest horse cultures.
We have studies of certain central Asiatic pastoral nomads such
as the Yakut, Kirghiz, and Kalmuck, who until recently still followed many of the ways of their ancestors. The whole existence
of these pastoralists depended on the horse, not only because
they used it for food, but because the horse made it possible for
them to raise cattle and sheep on the sparse natural pasture which

the steppes afford. The only way they could make a living in their wind-blown, treeless world was to disperse cattle and sheep over hundreds of square miles and to keep them moving in perpetual search of grass and water. In the West, closer to Europe where the rainfall is heavier and the grass somewhat lusher, the mounted nomads herded more cattle than sheep, while in the East, closer to Mongolia, where semidesert conditions prevail, they herded more sheep than cattle. In either situation, what the horse contributed was mobility, enabling its owners to care for widely dispersed herds, and to move rapidly to ward off threats from hostile neighbors who were more interested in stealing other people's animals than in raising their own.

The horse was the Asiatic pastoralists' most crucial instrument of production and their most prized possession. They gave horses grass and water before tending to their own needs or the needs of their other animals. During the summer months when the ewes and cows stopped giving milk for lack of nourishment, the nomads concentrated on feeding their horses, especially the mares, whose milk they drank in the form of a fermented and mildly intoxicating concoction known as *kumiss*. They had a reputation for being kind to their mounts; they sang about them in their love songs, and never wantonly beat one. But none of this inhibited them from slaughtering fat mares for the feasts of heroes and "big men," nor from serving boiled horsehead and horsemeat sausages to wedding guests. In this regard, the central Asian pastoralists resembled the Bedouin camel pastoralists of the Arabian heartlands who were discussed in the previous chapter. On long journeys, horsemeat was indispensable as an emergency ration. To judge from the behavior of the later Mongol armies, the freedom to consume horseflesh was a military necessity for them. On the march they drank horse blood until an animal keeled over, and then they devoured its corpse. But more about this in a moment.

The first taboos on horseflesh probably did not appear until after densely populated agrarian civilizations in Asia and the Middle East began to import horses from their nomad neighbors and to adapt them to their own needs. The early Middle Eastern empires with their dense populations of humans and herds of ruminants were hard-pressed to feed large numbers of horses. Since horses thrive on grass they are less competitive than pigs, but they need a lot more grass than cattle, sheep, or goats. As the Israelites recognized, the horse does not chew the cud. Horses digest fibrous materials in a greatly enlarged section of the gut known as the caecum, located between the large and small intestine. With no cud to chew and its fermentation vat placed at the end of the small intestine rather than at the beginning, the horse is only two-thirds as efficient in digesting grass as cattle or sheep. Horses feeding on natural pasture, in other words, need 33 percent more grass than cattle or sheep just to maintain their own weight. But the actual disadvantage is even greater. Horses are active animals, with higher metabolic rates. They burn up calories much faster than cattle and require correspondingly more food for each pound that they weigh. To put it more strongly, the domestication of the horse presumes the prior domestication of more efficient grass-eating ruminant sources of milk and meat. That is why the horse was domesticated so late. No one would ever have tamed and bred it for meat or milk; it is too wasteful of grass to be used primarily for such purposes. This also explains why not even the surviving central Asiatic nomads with their passion for *kumiss* had ever bothered to select mares for higher milk yields—a lapse which incidentally made the milking of mares among the Kirghiz a highly dangerous activity entrusted solely to experienced male practitioners.

What did the agrarian civilizations want horses for? Soon after the horse was domesticated and the art of harnessing them to carts had been learned, they acquired a use which dominated the objectives of horse breeders down to medieval times. All the ancient agrarian civilizations which grew up on the perimeters of Asia wanted the horse as an engine of war. Early Bronze Age warriors from China to Egypt raced into battle on horse-drawn chariots, shooting bows and arrows and jumping on and off to engage in hand-to-hand combat. The use of horses as mounts for cavalry began about 900 B.C., coincident with the rise of the Assyrian, Scythian, and Median empires. Thereafter, with the invention of saddles and stirrups, soldiers had to learn to wield swords, lances, and bows and arrows while seated astride their mounts. For three thousand years empires were to rise and fall literally on the backs of horses—horses bred for swiftness, stamina, and steadiness in the heat of battle, not for meat or milk. Cavalry assaults by the Huns against China were the reason the Great Wall was built starting in 300 B.C. And the Roman conquest of Britain began with a raid by Caesar's Roman cavalry in 54 B.C.

A wonderful passage in the Book of Job shows why horses were worth so much more for war than for food throughout much of the ancient world:

> Hast thou given the horse strength?
> Hast thou clothed his neck with thunder?
> Canst thou make him as afraid as a grasshopper?
> The glory of his nostrils is terrible.
> He paweth in the valley, and rejoiceth in his strength:
> He goeth on to meet the armed men.
> He mocketh at fear, and is not affrighted;
> Neither turneth he back from the sword.
> The quiver rattleth against him,
> The glittering spear and the shield.
> He swalloweth the ground with fierceness and rage;
> Neither believeth he that it is the sound of the trumpet.
> He saith among the trumpets, Ha, ha;
> And he smelleth the battle afar off.
> The thunder of the captains, and the shouting.

This passage again underscores the difference between an animal that is too costly to be raised for food but that renders valuable services and an animal that is too costly to be raised for food and does not render valuable services. Despite the fact that the horse was not a cud-chewer (nor hoof-splitter) and therefore was not good to eat, it remained for the Israelites, as for all of the people of antiquity, good to look at and good to touch.

The Romans were as little inclined as the Israelites to dine on horseflesh. Roman haute cuisine, otherwise noted for its exotic concoctions, would have none of it. Significantly, dishes made out of the horse's smaller and militarily dispensable relation, the ass, were a favorite banquet item, even though an ass was worth more than a slave. In abstaining from horseflesh the Romans acknowledged in fact that the horse was for them priceless, and events eventually proved this to be all too true. Many theories have been advanced to explain the underlying causes for the collapse of the Roman Empire. But one can say without fear of contradiction that whatever else may have been responsible for Rome's social and political troubles, it was the horse that defeated its armies. Southern Europe, densely populated with people and ruminants, lacked natural pasture and was therefore ill suited to the task of rearing large numbers of horses for war. Furthermore, native-born Romans made excellent foot soldiers, but as horsemen they were at a disadvantage. To defend itself against the equestrian barbarians who threatened the empire from the other side of the Danube, Rome hired its own barbarian horsemen— Scythians, Sarmatians, and Huns—men who learned to sit on a horse before they learned to walk, who grew up with horses, shot arrows from bows at full gallop, ate horseflesh, drank mare's milk, and in emergencies could nourish themselves on blood taken from a vein in their mount's neck. Commenting on the Huns, the Roman historian Marcellinus wrote: "The huns fall at every step—they have no feet to walk; they live, wake, eat, drink, and hold counsel on horseback." Beyond the Danube there were always new tribes with more horses than people pushing against the border. These were the "barbarians" to whom Rome finally succumbed; Goths and Visigoths who defeated the Roman legions at Adrianople in A.D. 378 and who sacked the city of Rome itself in A.D. 410; and Vandals who swept through Roman Gaul and Spain all the way to North Africa in A.D. 429. The Mongol horsemen who much later conquered Eurasia from China to the plains of Hungary were of the same ilk. Genghis Khan's warriors could easily advance a hundred miles a day. I already mentioned that on forced marches they lived by drinking horses' blood. Each warrior traveled with a string of eighteen horses, opening a vein in a different one in turn at ten-day intervals, and eating those which could not keep up the pace.

Europe, the bastion of Christianity, was in fact threatened from the south, north, and west by advancing hordes of mounted pastoral nomads. During the early Middle Ages, after the fall of Rome, Islamic warriors intent on spreading their faith through holy war posed the greatest threat. A scant seventy years after the death of Mohammed in A.D. 632, the Moslems under their general Al-Tarik had reached the rock which henceforth would be known as Jabal-al-Tarik or (say it fast) "Gibraltar," that is, "Tarik's Mountain," poised to invade Spain. In those seventy years they had spread their dominion from Mesapotamia to the Atlantic. Although it was the camel that made possible their initial conquest of Arabia, the horse was their principal military weapon thereafter. The Prophet's warriors used the camel to transport supplies, but not to fight from except in deep desert encounters. The extraordinary pace of their conquests was due almost entirely to their being mounted on a small, swift, hardy breed of horse which, "mare or no, possessed the undisputed staying power and courage that distinguishes the Arabian breeds today." The Arabs had a proverb which said that each grain of oats a man gave a horse was recorded in heaven as a good dead. Although not prohibited by the Koran, they would only consume horseflesh in the direst emergency.

The Islamic forces crossed the Straits of Gibraltar in 711, conquered all of Spain, and had crossed the Pyrenees into France in 720, penetrating as far north as the Loire Valley. They were engaged by an army of Frankish soldiers under Charles Martel near Tours in A.D. 732 in what was one of the most important battles of history. There are two competing versions of how the Christians defeated the Moslems. One has it that Martel had put together a force of heavily armored cavalrymen mounted on big horses which could not be dislodged by the lightly armed Arabs on their small horses. The other version is that the Arab cavalry was unable to penetrate the compact phalanx of stout Frankish foot soldiers. Even if foot soldiers did triumph over cavalry in Tours, it was only by absorbing heavy casualties. Moreover, Martel himself and his nobles survived the battle encased in armour—astride heavy steeds. Everyone agrees that from then on Europe's plan of battle shifted from dependence on large numbers of infantry conscripts to "a numerically much smaller but very well equipped mounted contingent of noble vassals." If Martel did not win the day with cavalry, it was simply because there were not as yet sufficient numbers of armored nobles and heavy horses. All subsequent major battles in Europe were decided by heavily armored cavalry riding horses bred to bear the extra load of armor.

Meanwhile, to the north, there remained many pagan peoples, from Poles to Icelanders, who continued to practice their ancient customs with regard to animal sacrifice and who slaughtered horses and consumed horseflesh. With their survival threatened by Moslem cavalry, the Church fathers could only take a dim view of an appetite for horseflesh, and in A.D. 732 Pope Gregory III wrote a letter to his missionary among the Germans, Boniface, ordering an end to the consumption of horsemeat. It is obvious from the tone of the pope's letter that he was shocked by the thought that anyone would eat a horse:

> Among other things, you also mentioned that some of [the Germans] eat wild horse and even more eat domesticated horse. Under no circumstances holy brother, should you ever permit this to be done. Rather impose on them an appropriate punishment by any means with which, with the help of Christ, you are able to prevent it. For this practice is unclean and detestable.

Was it coincidence that A.D. 732 was also the date of the battle of Tours? I doubt it. To defend the horse was to defend the faith.

The papal taboo on horseflesh was an extraordinary departure from the established principles governing the Church's definition of what was good to eat. Taboos against specific foods were antithetical to the universalist proseletyzing thrust of Christianity. From the time of Saint Paul, the church was opposed to any food taboos that placed obstacles in the path of potential converts. As stated in Acts 5:29, God only asks of Christians that "Ye abstain from meats offered to idols, and from blood and from things strangled." The horse is the one exception (aside from fast days and the unwritten taboo on human flesh).

After Gregory III's edict, horses were seldom slaughtered anywhere in Europe for their meat, unless they were lame, ill, or decrepit or unless they were needed as emergency rations during famine and sieges.The horse remained an extremely expensive animal, the more so as the population density of northern Europe began to approach that of the south, and the forests, wastelands, and remaining natural pastures began to disappear. Increasingly, horses had to be fed on grains—barley in the south, oats in the north—thereby directly competing with humans for food. A census of feudal holdings carried out in three English counties in A.D. 1086 shows that there was only 0.2 horses per peasant farm, compared with 0.8 head of cattle, 0.9 goats, 3.0 pigs, and 11.0 sheep.

During medieval times, to own a horse was the essence of being a knight or a lord. "Chivalry," from *cheval*, the French word for horse, tells the story. It represents the premium placed upon the heavily armed cavalryman—the knight—who was given enough land and labor by a lord to keep him in horse and armor and who owed military services in return. Feudalism was in that perspective essentially a military contract to provide for heavy cavalry. It embodied "the supremacy of cavalry over infantry and the substitution of the castle for the infantry as the base of cavalry operations." But not any horse would do—remember Don Quixote's Rosinante. It took a big one to carry a knight plus 120 pounds of armor and assorted cutlery. As late as the sixteenth century a good war-horse was worth more than a slave. Historian Fernand Braudel relates that even someone as rich as Florence's Cosimo de Medici could go broke trying to maintain a guard of a mere two thousand horsemen. It was a shortage of horses that prevented Spain from consolidating its hold over Portugal; throughout Louis XIV's reign the French had to import twenty thousand

to thirty thousand horses a year to keep their armies in the field;
and it was impossible to buy thoroughbreds in Andalusia or Na-
ples without permission from the king himself. In a sense, the
horse was treated as a rare and endangered species.

None of this means that the poorer classes in Europe abstained
entirely from eating horsemeat. The situation was probably not
unlike that which prevails in India with respect to beef. While
upper castes hold the cow to be sacred and the consumption of
beef akin to cannibalism, millions of aged and unwanted cattle
are eaten by leather-working and carrion-eating castes. Europe's
poorer agricultural classes must also have indulged in a certain
amount of clandestine slaughtering and consumption of unwanted
horses. Perhaps they too ate some horses that died natural deaths.
Authorities on the history of horseflesh consumption agree that
horseflesh eating never completely ceased in Europe, despite
Gregory III's letter and numerous royal and municipal decrees
aimed at stamping it out. Eleventh-century Swiss monks ate "wild
horses"—presumably animals that had escaped from their owners
and that lived in inaccessible valleys. There was a horsemeat feast
in Denmark in 1520, and the Spanish navy ate "red deer," a
euphemism for the flesh of young colts, presumably slaughtered
because of some defect or affliction. Poor people probably ate
horsemeat whenever it was available and especially since much
horseflesh was represented as venison or wild boar or consumed
as sausage meat.

If we allow for the ability of needy peasants to consume occasional small amounts of horseflesh clandestinely, the medieval
laws aimed at discouraging the slaughter of horses for food do
not seem to have created significant hardships or represented
any conspicuous degree of mismanagement of equine resources.
During medieval times, especially after the population had been
cut in half by the great plagues of the fourteenth century, ordinary
people ate quite a lot of meat. In fact, Braudel claims that late
medieval Europe was the world center of carnivory. Who needed
horsemeat when there was such an abundance of pork, mutton,
goat, poultry, and beef, not to mention fish? Almost every family

had its porker, which it raised semiwild on forest floor acorns and put away salted or smoked for winter. If horsemeat was cheaper than other meats, it was only because people obtained it clandestinely from stolen, diseased, or dead animals. They could never have afforded to purchase it at regular markets. As long as the horse population remained small, horsemeat could not have competed with other meats simply because there were not enough unwanted horses available to cull for human consumption (and raising them for meat was out of the question).

But horses were not destined to retain the status of a rare and endangered species for long. Already in medieval times the epoch of the war-horse was giving way to the epoch of the plow horse. All across northern Europe, wealthy farmers were learning how to exploit the heavier, more powerful breeds which had been developed to carry armor-plated knights into battle. Hitched to new, heavy, iron-wheeled plows by means of another great invention, the horse collar, breeds like Drysdales, Belgians, and Shires easily outperformed oxen, especially in the wet soils of the north.

To sustain the growing numbers of horses, farmers had to increase their production of oats. This was done by dividing farms into three fields: one in fallow, one devoted to wheat planted in the fall, and one devoted to oats, planted in the spring. By plowing with horses, and manuring, and rotating fields every year, farmers found that they could feed their horses and still increase the output of cereals and livestock for human consumption. It was a medieval green revolution. But all was not well. Just as with modern-day agricultural revolutions, many farmers grew richer, but more grew poorer. Conversion to horsepower and the three-field system led not only to a rapid increase in agricultural productivity, but to an equally rapid rise in population. To achieve economies of scale, the bigger farmers swallowed up the smaller ones. And thanks in large part to the greater efficiency of the horse, fewer laborers were needed in the agricultural sector. This provoked massive migrations to towns and cities and a worsening of the distribution of income between the wealthier and poorer classes. The remaining forests were cleared to make way for planting more oats, adversely affecting the ordinary family's ability to put meat on the table. The family porker disappeared, hunger and malnutrition increased, and great numbers of people found, not for the first or last time, that technological progress had left them with an essentially vegetarian diet, consisting mostly of rye, oats, and barley, which they consumed in the form of bread and porridges.

And yet in the midst of this miseration and meat hunger, the horse population continued to grow. Braudel estimates that on the eve of the French Revolution there were as many as 14 million horses in Europe, 1,781,000 in France alone. A flurry of royal edicts—1735, 1739, 1762, 1780—simultaneously reinforced the ban on horsemeat and warned that people who ate horseflesh would get sick; evidence, I believe, that meat-hungry people were stepping up their quest for the forbidden flesh. The restraint on the consumption of horsemeat soon became one of the many antagonistic class interests that led to France's revolutionary upheaval. Aristocrats, generals of the army, and rich farmers probably feared that if a legal market for horseflesh were allowed to develop, horses would be reared for meat, the cost of oats would rise, more horses would be stolen for quick disposal at the slaughterhouse, and a great symbol of the rightful ascendancy of men and women of noble birth over the rabble would be befouled. During the Reign of Terror in Paris in 1793 and 1794, the heads of the enemies of the people went into baskets; their horses went into housewives' cooking pots.

French scientists and intellectuals now took the lead in urging the free and open use of horsemeat. One of the most prominent of these advocates was the surgeon-in-chief of Napoleon's armies, Baron Dominique Jean Larrey, inventor of the ambulance. Ordinary soldiers and civilians must have known by then that one could live quite healthfully on horseflesh, provided the animal was not diseased and the meat consumed while still fresh. Baron Larrey apparently was not privy to this information. He was amazed to find that wounded men who ate copious amounts of horsemeat from newly fallen horses after the battle of Eylau in 1807 not only recovered but actually thrived and became immune to scurvy. Thereafter, the officers of the French army no longer hesitated to let their men consume the flesh of horses killed in battle, and the slaughter of horses to relieve hunger during sieges and on long retreats as from Moscow in 1812 became a standard logistic maneuver.

After Napoleon was defeated, conservative French politicians tried to reinstate the ban on horseflesh. But a long line of distinguished nineteenth-century scholars and scientists took up the fight against the lingering resentments and prejudice toward horsemeat and horsemeat eaters expressed by the French aristocracy and many members of the bourgeoisie (probably including people interested in protecting beef, lamb, and pork from a cheaper competitor, but I have no definite information on this). Men like Antoine Parmentier, also known for championing the potato, chief veterinarian of the French army Emile Decroix, and naturalist Isidore Geoffroy Saint-Hilaire argued that the denial of the right to eat horsemeat was a superstitious survival of the *ancien régime* and a threat to the welfare of the French working class. To further the cause, the Parisian pro-horsemeat faction held a series of elegant horsemeat banquets in the 1860s including one at the Grand Hotel and another at the Jockey Club. This was good training for the German siege of Paris in 1871. Pricked by necessity, Parisians ate every horse they could lay their hands on— sixty thousand to seventy thousand of them. (They also ate all the animals in the zoo as well.) By the end of the century horsemeat enthusiasts had succeeded in legalizing the horsemeat industry and in establishing government inspection services to assure consumers that the meat was safe. The municipal council of Paris even exempted horsemeat from the sales tax to which other meats were subject, and to complete the transformation, French doctors suddenly discovered that horsemeat was healthier than beef and prescribed it as a cure for tuberculosis.

Although horsemeat is still regarded as good to eat by many Europeans, the amount of horsemeat being consumed today is much less than in the first half of the century. The reason for this decline is not hard to find. The push to create a legitimate market for horsemeat presumed the existence of large numbers of unwanted horses whose meat would otherwise be marketed clandestinely and in deteriorated, if not hazardous, condition. There were about 3 million horses in France in the late nineteenth century. Their numbers peaked in 1910, declined slowly after World War I, and then crashed from about two million in 1950 to about 250,000 in 1983, probably no more than existed in France before the invention of the horse collar. The decline of course was caused by a shift to motorized transportation, the substitution of tractors for draft animals on the farm, and the replacement of horses by motorized vehicles in the armed forces. As the numbers of French horses available for culling decreased, the demand for horsemeat could only be met by importing frozen horsemeat from abroad. Prices rose; demand fell. Already by the late 1930s, hindquarter cuts were more costly than comparable cuts of beef, and the proletariat could afford neither. Yet horsemeat continued to be identified as poor people's food. France's foremost gourmets never did include horsemeat recipes in their cookbooks. Rising standards of living post–World War II gave Frenchmen access to greater quantities of beef, poultry, and pork than ever before. With horsemeat still identified as poor man's food, with lingering suspicions about its wholesomeness, with the price up to three or four dollars a pound, and with other and more prestigious meats underselling it, a continued decline in its popularity seems assured.

Let me sum up why Europe's taste for horseflesh has followed a peculiar on-again, off-again pattern. When horses were a rare and endangered species needed for war, and other sources of meat were abundant, Church and state banned the consumption of horseflesh; the ban was relaxed and horsemeat consumption increased when horses became abundant and other sources of meat became scarce; but now that horses have once more become scarce, and other sources of meat are more abundant, horsemeat consumption is on the way down.

This equation can be applied to England, with interesting results. As the earliest and most urbanized center of the industrial revolution, England ceased to be self-sufficient in food production during the eighteenth century. The English solved the problem of food supply by using their navy and army to create the largest overseas empire in the history of the world and by imposing terms of trade that permitted them to import foods at low prices relative to the value of their manufactured exports. The paradoxical result of this lack of self-sufficiency was that English commoners were never as deprived of beef, pork, and mutton as their counterparts on the Continent. In effect, as the English expanded their empire during the eighteenth and nineteenth centuries, they were able to obtain control over ever more distant pastures and rangelands on which animals destined to supply them with low-cost meat could be raised. The first region to serve this function was Scotland, large areas of which were deforested and converted to pasture in order to supply England with beef and mutton (and wool). It was upon this basis that the Scottish highlands in the early eighteenth century were drawn into the British sphere of influence and thereafter "relegated to a pastoralist and economically backward role."

Ireland's fate was similar. As English landlords gained control over the Irish countryside, the Irish cottagers were forced off the best farmlands to make way for cattle and pigs. These animals were not destined to be consumed locally; instead they were used to provide cheap salted beef and pork for the English proletariat in such booming industrial centers as Manchester, Birmingham, and Liverpool. Even at the height of the great Irish potato famine in 1846, Ireland exported a half a million pigs to England, and to this day Ireland remains one of the world's major exporters of beef. Toward the end of the nineteenth century English banks gained control over the Argentine beef industry, making cheap Argentinian grass-fed beef a staple in the English diet. While some feeble attempts to market horsemeat were made in England during the nineteenth century, the relative abundance of imported ruminant flesh reduced the pressure to use horsemeat as a by-product of the other services horses rendered.

Turning to the other side of the equation, the relative abundance of horses, I cannot offer any firm statistics. But one thing is clear: the expansion of the British Empire was in large degree contingent upon the superiority of the British cavalry with its superbly groomed and trained mounts and its elite brigades. To abstain from horsemeat was to indulge the aristocratic pretensions of these forces and to hone their fighting edge. It was not much of a deprivation for anyone since the cavalry returned the favor by making it possible for the British to outdo everyone but the Americans as beef, mutton, and pork eaters.

Now for the American part of the puzzle. As elsewhere, horses were never bred for meat or milk in the United States because of their inherent inefficiency compared to cattle and pigs. Horses were abundant from Colonial times onward, but alternative sources of meat were even more abundant. So unlike what happened in Europe, large-scale consumer demand for the culling and marketing of unwanted and overage horses never developed in the United States. Lacking a strong pent-up demand for meat, United States horsemeat packers have never been able to overcome the obstacles placed in their way by established beef and pork interests, horse lovers, and their allies in Congress and state legislatures. While Europeans were repealing legal restrictions on the sale of horsemeat, Americans were passing laws prohibiting its sale. And while Europeans were setting up inspection facilities for horsemeat, Americans were setting up inspection facilities for beef and pork, but not for horsemeat. During the nineteenth century municipal food inspectors ignored horsemeat. Not until 1920 did Congress authorize the U.S. Department of Agriculture to inspect and certify horsemeat in the United States. But there has always been a countercurrent. As in Europe, there was no way to prevent the clandestine marketing of horseflesh for consumption by unsuspecting or less affluent members of the population. Prior to the passage of federal pure food and drug legislation, Americans unknowingly consumed substantial quantities of horsemeat in the form of sausages, ground meat, and even as steak. An article in the *Breeder's Gazette* of 1917 advocating the slaughter of horses to overcome high wartime beef prices put it this way:

> Few indeed are the Americans who have not at one time or another consumed a product the principal ingredient of which was the flesh of a horse or mule or an ass, donkey or burro.

The delay in subjecting horsemeat packers and vendors to government inspection reinforced everybody's suspicions of horseflesh, and the public had plenty to fear. In the early decades of this century, muckrakers evoked strong disgust reactions with exposés of filthy meat-packing plants. For example, they accused the packers of making sausages out of chemically revived moldy meats recovered from filthy, spit-soaked floors or out of rats and the poisoned bread that had killed the rats. "At times too, an employee would fall into a boiling vat and would not be missed until all but his bones had gone forth as Pure Leaf Lard." The clandestine nature of the horsemeat trade guaranteed that abuses of this sort would be greater for horseflesh and that the abuses would linger on after the other meat pckers had been forced to clean up their act. "What is this, horsemeat?" Americans of an earlier generation would say when confronted by an extremely tough, spoiled, or strangely colored piece of "beef."

Today there are still about 8 million horses in the United States—more than in any other country. Most of these are kept for recreational purposes, for racing, for "show," and for breeding; many are "pets." It is understandable why the United States never developed a meat-packing industry based on the rearing of horses for slaughter—given the horse's rather inefficient gut compared to cattle or pigs. But why is so little use made of horsemeat as a by-product of the raising of horses for other purposes?

To begin with, there actually is a substantial horsemeat-packing industry in the United States, but its products are consumed overseas. The United States is the world's number one exporter of horsemeat, and with favorable currency conditions, has been known to sell over 100 million pounds of fresh, frozen, and chilled horsemeat a year to foreign customers. So the question really comes down to why this meat is not eaten in the United States. The recent history of attempts to market horsemeat within the United States indicates that horsemeat is acceptable to many Americans if they have the opportunity to buy it at prices lower than those of other meats. But they seldom get this opportunity because of the organized resistance of beef and pork interests and the aggressive tactics of horse lovers, who, in their effort to protect the horse's noble image, play a role analogous to that of Europe's horse-owning aristocracy. In this regard, the sentiments and interests of people who own horses as "pets" remain quite distinct from the sentiments and interests of ordinary consumers, and it is probably no more correct to say that Americans in general now have a strong aversion to eating horses than it would have been to represent all Frenchmen prior to the French Revolution as being opposed to the consumption of horseflesh.

An irony of horse lover opposition to the consumption of horse- flesh by humans is that for many years after World War II, horse- meat was cheap enough to be used as one of the prime ingredients in dog food. Apparently no one objected if one pet ate another, but what the horse protectors did not realize was that substantial numbers of impoverished Americans found out that dog food was a bargain and were buying it for their own consumption. Today, horsemeat is too expensive to be used as pet food, and the pet food industry has been obliged to make use of the trimmings and organs of cattle, hogs, chickens, and fish. Paradoxically, the in- crease in the high-priced human demand for horseflesh has re- sulted in improved treatment of unwanted horses since horse traders are more inclined to take care of an animal that is worth five hundred dollars at the slaughterhouse than one that is worth only twenty-five.

Consumer surveys carried out in the Northeast indicate that 80 percent of college students are willing to taste samples of horsemeat products, and of this 80 percent, over 50 percent liked what they tasted moderately or better. The fact is that Americans turn out in droves whenever beef prices become excessive and inexpensive U.S.D.A.–inspected horsemeat is offered for sale. That was what happened, for example, in 1973 when the Arab oil shock produced a surge in beef prices and a national boycott of beef by irate United States housewives. Prime horse steaks could temporarily be offered at about one-half the price of comparable cuts of beef. Customers flocked to the horsemeat stores which opened in Connecticut, New Jersey, and Hawaii, and emptied the shelves faster than they could be filled. It did not take long for protestors to appear on horseback, decrying the slaughter of animals whose owners had "petted and brushed them," nor for Senator Paul S. Schweiker of Pennsylvania to try to introduce a bill in the senate banning the sale of horsemeat for human consumption. These protests proved unnecessary because the price of horsemeat soon rose above the price of beef, removing the primary incentive for buying horsemeat. Even with horses reared at the expense of owners interested in them for racing and recreation, there is no way that large-scale trading in horses for meat can result in prime horse steaks that are cheaper than prime beefsteak.

A similar fate overtook an attempt in the early 1980s to create a market for inexpensive flaked and formed horsemeat products. Recognizing the futility of trying to get Americans to buy choice cuts of horse at prices above comparable cuts of beef, the M and R Packing Company of Hartford, Connecticut, tried to market processed horse "steaks" and "horseburgers" made from front-quarter cuts. In international trade, front-quarter cuts of horsemeat are destined for consumption as sausage or ground meat and at much lower prices than comparable front-quarter beef products. After trials in various New England stores, M and R succeeded in 1982 in placing its Chevalean brand U.S.D.A.–inspected "horse steaks" and "horsemeat patties" in three New England naval commisaries—huge supermarkets offering cut-rate prices to naval personnel—located in New Brunswick, Maine; New London, Connecticut; and Newport, Rhode Island. At about the same time, M and R stationed promotional vending carts on busy streetcorners in Boston, Hartford, New Haven, and New

York, featuring "Horsemeat Special Pattie Burgers" and "Super-horsemeat Steak Sandwiches." Business was brisk at the commissaries with the low-priced horsemeat products outselling comparable beef products by a wide margin. At Lexington Avenue and Fifty-third Street, customers lined up twelve deep to taste what New Yorkers inevitably began to call "Belmont Steaks." But M and R's experiment was short-lived. Complaints from irate self-identified horse lovers and the American Horse Council, the Humane Society, and the American Horse Protection Association began to catch the ear of the beef lobby. Senators John Melcher of Montana and Lloyd Bentsen of Texas therewith informed Navy Secretary John F. Lehman, Jr., that they were extremely disappointed in the navy. How did they expect to recruit volunteers if they gave the impression the navy feeds its people on horsemeat? Especially since cattle have been selling for less than their cost of production, and due to the recession and adverse publicity about cholesterol, beef consumption is falling. Shortly thereafter, all three commissaries discontinued their sale of horsemeat.

I said at the outset that puzzling food preferences and avoidances ought to be seen in relation to whole systems of food production—systems which have long-and short-term consequences, do not necessarily dish out benefits equally to everybody, and in which "good to sell" may play a role as prominent as "good to eat." This caveat applies to the explanation of the United States' aversion to horseflesh. I have not as yet given proper recognition to the fact that Americans exhibit a hierarchy of avoidances and preferences for various other kinds of meats and that the horse is by no means the only domesticated animal whose flesh is held in low esteem. What remains to be done, therefore, is to supply an explanation for the overall hierarchy of the principal meats available to the American consumer.

And so, onward to the riddle of why beef became king.

CHAPTER SIX

HOLY BEEF, U. S. A.

AMERICANS CONSUME about 150 pounds of "red meat" per capita per year. About 60 percent by weight is beef and veal; 39 percent is pork; 1 percent is lamb and mutton; and the amount of goat meat consumed is almost too small to measure. Over a three-day period 39 percent of Americans will eat beef at least once, 31 percent will eat pork at least once, and neither lamb nor goat is likely to be eaten at all. During a one-week period 91 percent of United States households purchase beef; 80 percent purchase pork, 4 percent purchase lamb; and practically no one purchases goat. Why is beef "king" in America? Why is pork the runner-up? Why are lamb and mutton so little appreciated? And why is goat meat almost as unpopular as horsemeat?

The preference for beef some say was transplanted from Great Britain along with the English language—a nice explanation as long as you ignore the fact that the English traditionally consumed almost as much mutton as beef, and that the majority of Americans do not have British ancestry. Another notion that we can easily dispense with is that the preference for beef is an ancient heritage shared by all Europeans that harks back to the days when cattle were a medium of exchange and therefore symbolized wealth and power. Or as one "good-to-think" scholar would have us believe, beef eating is part of a "sexual code of food which must go back

109

to the Indo-European identification of cattle . . . with virility."
Even if beef is somehow a sexier meat than its rivals, its status
as an item of consumption has proved to be extremely variable
among the Indo-European family of nations which, after all, includes Hindu India, where, as we saw, it is prohibited, not preferred. Another heavy blow to this explanation is that Americans
were not primarily beef eaters during Colonial times nor during
the last century. In fact, as we'll see, beef consumption in the
United States substantially surpassed pork consumption for the
first time only in the 1950s. The challenge which must be met
is not merely why Americans think beef is good to eat but why
there is an order of preference for beef, pork, lamb, mutton, and
goat which has changed considerably from Colonial times to the
present.

In 1623, Plymouth Colony had six goats, fifty pigs, and many
hens. The first cows provided milk, not beef, and did not arrive
until the next year. Pigs, goats, and sheep were a more important
source of meat then cattle at most of the earliest settlements.
William Wood, writing in the year 1633 about Massachusetts Bay
Colony, asked, "Can they be very poor, where for four thousand
souls there are fifteen hundred cattle, four thousands goats, and
swine innumerable?" In 1634 in Jamestown, pork and kid were
the only "red meats" eaten by the "better houses."

Goat was the first "red meat" to be knocked off the Colonial
dinner table. It faded into the gastronomical great beyond as soon
as there were enough dairy cattle to keep the colonies well supplied with milk. Since the colonists used goats primarily as a
source of milk, goat meat was a by-product. In competition with
cattle, goats can win out as a source of milk and meat only in
lands with small farms and scant pasture, the opposite of the
conditions which existed in Colonial America. With plenty of
land and pasture, American farmers quite reasonably preferred
to own one cow rather than four or five goats to get an equal
amount of milk. As soon as dairy cattle began to multiply, goats
virtually disappeared. To this day the majority of Americans have
never tasted goat meat. In fact one can search through a stack of

American cookbooks from the *Joy of Cooking* to the *James Beard Cookbook* without encountering a single recipe for it. The few Americans who consume goat tend to be low-income southerners, especially blacks, with rural sharecropping or slave ancestry, whose parents never owned enough land to keep a cow. Goats are also in favor among the generation of back-to-the-land ex-hippies whose small farms are better served by one or two small animals rather than one large expensive cow. And not surprisingly, Hispanic Americans who live in the arid scrublands of the Southwest and whose ancestors were small-scale farmers and herders also like goat meat. The association between goat meat and impoverished and exploited racial and cultural minorities has been bad for the goat's gustatory image and helps, I think, to explain why goat meat actively repels the average American almost as much as horse or dog meat.

What about sheep? Sheep—especially lamb—ranks considerably higher in terms of gustatory prestige than goat, but far below cattle and pigs. Per capita consumption of mutton and lamb— mostly lamb—in the United States is tiny compared with the amount of mutton and lamb consumed in other countries. Sheep became bad to eat and bad to think for reasons similar to those which brought about the downfall of the goat. Sheep can only be an efficient large-scale producer of animal flesh if lamb and mutton are by-products. This explains the prominence of lamb and mutton in traditional British cookery; they were by-products of the raising of sheep for wool. The British ate sheep culled from the flocks which provided wool for England's woolens industry. In their haste to shear more sheep, big landowners destroyed the forests of northern England and Scotland and forced the peasants to stop farming and take up herding. Intensive grazing prevented the regrowth of trees, and the peasants went hungry for lack of crops. Sheep thereby acquired a central place in British cuisine as well as a reputation for being an animal that metaphorically ate both trees and people (unlike goats, which literally eat trees).

A curious side effect to the reign of the sheep in Scotland was the appearance of a taboo on the consumption of pork. Bereft of trees, the common folk of Scotland and Ireland stopped raising pigs; they turned against pork and came close to abominating the animal itself in the Old Testament manner. Early in the eighteenth century the pig's reputation had sunk so low in Scotland and Ireland that the mere sight of one brought bad luck. Modern-day Scots find this hard to believe because pork once again ranks high among their preferred foods. What happened was that the pig regained its popularity when potatoes were introduced. Pigs became good to think again when they acquired a new ecological niche, rooting for leftovers in the potato fields. But remnants of the pig taboo show up along the Maine coast where descendants of the early Scotch-Irish immigrants still say that the sight of a pig brings bad luck to mariners.

The American aversion to mutton and lamb was likewise linked to the British woolens industry. English mercantile policy dictated that the American colonies, like Scotland, should grow wool but should not manufacture woolens for export. So raising sheep could not be as profitable as raising pork and beef, which, as I pointed out in the previous chapter, the English were eager to import in prodigious amounts. Gradually the taste of lamb and especially mutton became unfamiliar to the majority of Americans except in New England, where independence led to a surge in woolen manufacture and an increase in sheep grazing, centered in Vermont. Southerners, lacking a woolens industry and happy to wear cotton garments, experienced a more thorough extinction of the taste for lamb and mutton than northerners. In fact many southerners to this day do not distinguish between sheep and goat as a source of meat and regard the one with as much displeasure as the other.

Just before the Civil War, mutton and lamb accounted for about 10 percent of all the fresh meat slaughtered in New York. But as dairying replaced sheepherding throughout New England, the center of sheep production moved further west, and the cost of transportation made lamb and mutton less competitive. Finally, with the twentieth century and the development of synthetic fabrics, wool lost much of its market. Sheepherding became confined to the most remote western rangelands, and despite the twentieth-century boom in meat eating, the consumption of lamb and mutton continues to dwindle.

The other side of America's diminishing interest in raising and eating goats and sheep (and abiding rejection of horsemeat) is the ready availability of pork, beef, and veal as substitutes for goats, mutton, and lamb. Under the ecological and demographic conditions which prevailed during Colonial times, the colonists found pigs and cattle to be more efficient sources of meat than goats or sheep, and this explains why pigs and cattle have until recently been the main contenders for America's most preferred meat (I will get to chickens later on).

The dense American forests provided an especially favorable habitat for raising pigs. All the colonists had to do was rid the woods of Indians and wolves, and thereafter the acorns, beechnuts, hazelnuts, and the hardy breeds known as "wood pigs" did the rest themselves. In the northern colonies pigs rooted for their living during the spring, summer, and fall, but were put in pens for the winter. From Virginia south, farmers left them on their own throughout the year except for brief farrowing roundups when the sows were enticed into pens with bribes of corn. Before long, many farmers discovered that when pigs were fed on corn for a month or so before slaughter, their flesh firmed and they gained weight rapidly. By 1700 "finishing" hogs on corn had become an established commercial practice.

The wedding of pigs and corn was made in heaven. Pigs can convert corn to meat about five times more efficiently than cattle. Pigs, therefore, could be raised for most of their lives on free "pasture"—the bounty of the forest floor—and then brought to market weight by feeding on surplus corn, far more efficiently than cattle could be raised by similar methods. Although some colonists also let their cattle loose to roam in the woods, ruminants could not match pigs as a source of meat under such conditions. Lacking natural pasture, cattle were better used as a source of milk, butter, cheese, and traction, and much of the beef and veal produced on the eastern seaboard originated as a by-product of the culling of dairy herds and the slaughter of over-age oxen.

As the farming frontier moved across the Alleghenies into the Midwest, the center of pig, cattle, and corn production moved with it. Soils and climate were ideal for corn. Farmers in the Ohio Valley could easily harvest more than they could sell, given the rudimentary nature of the roads and the great expense of transport by wagon. The best way to market the surplus was to feed it to pigs and cattle and then walk them back across the mountains to the cities on the eastern seaboard. (Actually, the best way to market the corn was to convert it to bourbon and ship it in jugs, but the federal government taxed away the profits from the distilleries and made "moonshine" illegal.) Under the noisy cracking whips of the drovers—the original southern "crackers"—the corn harvest walked itself to market, and the very feature which had made pigs abominable to the ancient Israelites—their appetite for grains—made them lovable to the American farmer. Soon canals and railroads provided better means of getting across the mountains, putting an end to the colorful era of the whip-cracking drovers and greatly expanding the potential for marketing corn-fed pigs and cattle.

With better means of transport, Corn Belt farmers dispensed with their wood pigs and switched over to new breeds which were heavier and better larded. These "lard pigs" could be raised profitably without supplementary foraging. They were fed almost exclusively on corn and then sent for slaughter and packing to Cincinnati in such great numbers that the city became known as "Porkopolis." Corn on the hoof now became pigs in a barrel or "condensed corn." Pork reigned supreme. Before the Civil War, Americans consumed more of it than any other foodstuff except wheat. Never in human history had such a prodigious quantity of grain been harvested with the sole intent of converting it into animal flesh.

In the developing Corn Belt, farmers raised beef cattle as well as pigs. The cattle ate prairie grass and hay until they matured, and then they were fattened up on corn and trailed across the

mountains to the eastern cities. Pigs and cattle from the Ohio
Valley were often driven together. The cattle ate stores of corn
sold along the trail; the pigs followed behind, feeding on the
cattle dung which contained much undigested corn residue.

Which meat was preferred, beef or pork? During late Colonial
times and the early nineteenth century as far as salted or barreled
meat was concerned, pork was preferred over beef in most sec-
tions of the country. My main evidence for this is that despite
the fact that far more pork than beef was produced, the price of
salted pork was always higher than the price of salted beef. This
was true even in the Northeast, which was the region most partial
to beef (for reasons I'll explain in a moment). For example, in
Philadelphia in 1792, a barrel of pork was worth $11.17 while a
barrel of beef was worth only $8.00. This disparity continued
until the outbreak of the Civil War. Since the ordinary American
was brought up on salted meat, and salted pork cost more than
salted beef, it would be hard to say that beef was the preferred
type of animal flesh. Henry Adams noted that corn was eaten
three times a day—as salt pork. One foreign visitor noted that
in Europe to ask for food was to ask for bread; but in the United
States, to ask for food was to ask for salt pork. And in James
Fenimore Cooper's novel *The Chainbearer*, the rustic housewife
says: "Give me the children that's raised on good sound pork
afore all the game in the country. Yams is good as a relish and
so's bread; but pork is the staff of life."

Admittedly, there were important sectional differences. In the
South and Midwest, the passion for pork was so great that beef
took second place whether it was fresh or preserved. From the
eighteenth century on "Southerners gloried in their pork." Vir-
ginians regarded their hams as superior in flavor to any in the
world, and no Colonial landlord could do business without serving
ham and other cuts of pork. In fashionable Williamsburg it was
the custom "to have a plate of cold ham upon the table; and there
was scarcely a Virginian lady who breakfasts without it." In Colonial North Carolina it was "pork upon pork and pork upon that."
Early in the nineteenth century in places like Tennessee, meat

meant pork; they were synonymous. Kentucky was the "land of pork and whiskey," and in Georgia a doctor from Columbus, alarmed by the eating of "fat bacon and pork, fat bacon and pork only, and that continually morning, noon and night, for all classes, ages and conditions," advocated naming the United States of America "The Great Hog-Eating Confederacy" or the "Republic of Porkdom." One traveler visiting Illinois in 1819 wrote that during the summer when pork was in short supply, "people would rather live on corn bread for a month than eat an ounce of mutton, veal, rabbit, goose or duck," while in Michigan in 1842, pork was "more cherished than sweetening or whiskey, something one could never have too much of," and pigs were so exalted that "not the sacred cow of Isis was the subject of more reverential attention."

New Yorkers and New Englanders apparently never developed a similar passion for pork. To judge from New Yorkers, when fresh meat was available, northerners preferred beef to either fresh or preserved pork. In New York City between 1854 and 1860 a yearly average of 132 million pounds of cattle was sold fresh at wholesale as compared with only 53 million pounds of pork. Yet it was fresh pork, not beef, that was used to celebrate the Fourth of July, the nation's most important public holiday. A visitor to New York in the 1840's painted this picture of how the republic of porkdom celebrated its independence:

> Broadway being three miles long and booths lining each side of it, in every booth there was a roast pig . . . as the center of attraction. Six miles of roast pig! and that in New York City alone; and roast pig in every other town, hamlet and village in the Union.

One obvious reason for the northerners' relative lack of interest in pork is that on the eve of the Civil War northern-grown pigs had become rarer than sheep. Vermont farms, for example, had an average of 25 sheep but only 1.5 pigs in 1860. On a per capita basis the South and Midwest raised about two pigs per person while the North raised less than one-tenth of a pig per person. Pigs became scarce because the forests had been cut down to supply Yankee shipbuilding and manufacturing industries, and little corn was grown because croplands had been converted into pasture to feed herds of diary cattle. Whatever the precise combination of factors preventing northerners from developing a preference for pork, they were not merely acting out their ancestral British preference for beef. The British, after all, settled the South as much as the North, and pork-eating Colonial Virginia was in no way less British than beef-eating Colonial New York.

As a national phenomenon, the American preference for beef originated not overseas in Great Britain, but across the Mississippi in America's Great Plains. Here at last was a habitat ideal for raising cattle, but not for raising pigs. Hungry pigs will eat anything, and on certain grasses such as alfalfa they can even gain weight. But no one was going to turn pigs loose to roam the plains of Texas and Kansas. Grass was to cattle as forest acorns were to pigs. And what had to be done to make the plains safe for cattle was similar to what had been done two centuries earlier to make the forests safe for pigs: Indians and wolves had to be subdued. Buffalo presented a third problem; not being domesticated animals, they could not be walked to market, and they had little long-term commercial value. No one except the Indians preferred them to cattle. The stockmen, farmers, and the U.S. Army soon realized that the best way to get rid of the Indians was to get rid of the buffalo. Contrary to what the schoolbooks say, the extinction of the American bison did not result from careless and wanton overkill. Rather it resulted from a conscious policy connived at by the railroads, the army, and the cattle ranchers as a means of subduing the Indians and keeping them on their reservations. General Philip Sheridan put it to the Texas legislature straight from the hip: "Let the [hunters] kill, skin, and sell until the buffalo is exterminated, as it is the only way to bring about a lasting peace and allow civilization to advance." Hunters like Buffalo Bill shot, skinned, and butchered buffalo on the spot, loading the choicest parts on wagons for delivery to the railroad work camps and to frontier towns, helping to make the plains safe for cattle.

As the buffalo disappeared, herds of cattle took their place, feasting on the endless sea of grass and multiplying faster than they could be butchered. So cheap was the meat from these animals that the army paid ranchers to supply the Indian reservations with beef, to prevent the Indians from starving. Civilian markets could only be reached by cowboys and cattle over long trails, some extending from Texas to cities as far away as Chicago and New Orleans. But railroads soon put an end to marathon western cattle drives just as they had put an end to long-distance pig drives in the East. Even before the rails crossed the cattle trails at Dodge City, Abilene, and Kansas City, beef entrepreneurs were building stockyards, and filling them with cattle awaiting the arrival of the first train. Off the cattle went to be butchered and packed in Chicago, which after the Civil War had replaced Cincinnati as butcher to the world, or to the cities of the East, where they were slaughtered locally and sold as fresh meat. After two or three days in the crowded, swaying cars, the cattle staggered off bruised and ill, prompting a public outcry for a more humane mode of transport. The beef entrepreneurs saw the problem from a slightly different angle. Anyone who could figure out how to cut western steers into sides shipped fresh from Chicago would not only satisfy the animal protectionists but save the cost of transporting 35 percent to 40 percent of the animals—hides, bones, offal—which could be processed for industrial uses just as profitably in Chicago as in New York or Boston. Laying the meat directly on ice gave it "ice-burn." True refrigerator cars, introduced in 1882 by Gustavus Swift for the run between Chicago and New York, kept the ice in special compartments, chilling the air which circulated around the sides of beef hooked to overhead trolleys. The beef barons and packing-house owners—Armour, Swift, Cudahy, Morris—bought up the railroads, cornered the grain markets, and became as rich as modern-day oil sheiks.

But the sea of grass on which the nineteenth-century beef bonanza was premised proved to be as vulnerable as the Indians and the buffaloes. Overgrazing on the lusher parts of the Great Plains and homesteading by farmers dispersed ranching farther

west to arid regions remote from railroads and midwestern stockyards. More feedlot finishing on corn was needed to bring range
cattle up to the market weight; beef lost its price advantage over
pork; and per capita beef consumption fell from a peak of 67.1
pounds at the turn of the century to 54.9 pounds in 1940. The
rangeland beef boom had greatly narrowed the difference between pork and beef consumption, but it did not last long enough
to close the gap. In 1900, there was still a 4.8-pound-per-person
advantage in favor of pork, and as the twentieth century wore
on, the difference increased until on the eve of World War II
Americans were back to eating 18.6 pounds more pork per person
than beef. It seemed as if the pig's incomparable gut was going
to have the last laugh as long as both beef and pork production
continued to depend primarily on the conversion of grains into
flesh.

But the race was not over; the triumph of beef over pork was
only a few years away. By the 1950s Americans were eating equal
amounts of beef and pork; by the 1960s they were eating 10
pounds more of beef; and by the 1970s this advantage had increased to 25 pounds. Finally, during the all-time peak meat-
eating year of 1977, Americans consumed almost twice as much
beef as pork: 97.7 pounds of beef per person to 53.7 pounds of
pork, a difference of 44 pounds per person per year.

How did beef finally manage to become king? Through a combination of changes in the beef production and marketing systems
which were ideally suited to the emergent life-styles of post–
World War II America. As the twentieth century wore on, rangeland played an ever-decreasing role in United States beef production. Time spent on raising "feeders" (calves that will be sent
to feedlots) and the time spent on finishing have grown shorter
and shorter. With improved breeds, planted pasture, and scientific management, feeders can now be brought to four hundred
pounds in four months. Farmers then sell them for shipment to
feedlots where they are induced to eat a mixture of protein-rich
soybeans, fish meal, calorie-rich corn, sorghum, and vitamins,
hormones, and antibiotics all roasted to optimum temperature

and delivered night and day by cement-mixer–type trucks. The cattle eat all day and, under the glare of lights that turns night into day, they eat all night. No matter how much they eat, their trough runneth over, and in four more months they have put on another four hundred pounds and are ready for slaughter.

Just as important as the changes in the way beef was produced, were the changes in the way beef was consumed. First came the growth of suburban homeownership and the use of outdoor living space for cooking and entertaining. To the suburban refugees from the central cities, charcoal broiling represented the fulfillment of pent-up recreational and gustatory aspirations. Aside from its novelty—it was the one mode of preparation that apartment-dwellers had to forego—the backyard charcoal grill offered the convenience of no mess, no pans, and rapid, cooked meals often presided over by husbands who played the role of the great-giver-of-feasts-and-provider-of-meat like the chiefs of old. These backyard redistributors filled their grills with beef. If they submitted pork to smoke and flame, it was as frankfurters, themselves forty or more percent ground beef. Charcoal-broiled steaks were the favorites, made all the more delectable no doubt because they had once been unaffordable. But the charcoal-broiling of prodigious numbers of hamburgers shows that there was more to the beef-grilling mania than mere snob appeal. Technical aspects of backyard cookery, for example, made it difficult to employ pork in ground form. Pork patties cannot be cooked on open grills without falling through, and to prepare them on skillets would defeat the purpose of the flight from kitchen drudgery.

More important perhaps was that pork had to be cooked longer than beef because of the danger of trichinosis. Incredible as it may seem, the U.S. Department of Agriculture does not inspect pork for trichinosis. The only way to detect trichinella in pork is to look for them under the microscope, a time-consuming, costly, and not entirely effective procedure. As a result, about 4 percent of Americans have trichinella worms in their muscles and mistake their trichinosis flare-ups for mild cases of the flu. In lieu of inspection, the U.S.D.A., the surgeon general's office, and the

American Medical Association launched an intensive educational program during the 1930s to get Americans to cook pork until it turns from pink to grey through and through. These warnings ruled out the grilling of pork chops, which upon turning grey through and through also turn tough and dry through and through. Barbecue and pork spareribs present a technically feasible solution because they are well-larded and remain tender and juicy when thoroughly cooked, but they offer much less meat compared with hamburger or steak, are messy to eat, and cannot be put on a bun, placing them at a disadvantage with hamburgers as a convenience food.

The move to suburbia was shortly followed by other social changes that contributed to the beefing of America: the entrance of women into the work force, the formation of families in which both parents work, the rising tide of feminism, and the growing resentment of women against pots, pans, sinks, and stoves. These changes set the stage for an orgy of beef eating outside the home and for the rise of America's most distinctive culinary contribution to world cusine, the fast-food hamburger. For the new postwar, two-wage-earner families, the fast-food hamburger restaurant provides an opportunity to eat out, to be free of the drudgery of the kitchen—even without homeownership and backyard barbecues—at a cost that is comparable to a medium-budget home-cooked meal, especially if you put a price on the housewife's labor, as wage-earning women are increasingly prone to do.

Americans began to dine out on beef patties a long time ago. Some historians date the hamburger's inception to an obscure restaurant owner who ran out of pork sausages and substituted ground beef at an Ohio county fair in 1892. Others claim that the first hamburgers appeared at the St. Louis Fair of 1904. Less confusion surrounds the origin of the ironically unbeeflike name. "Hamburger" undoubtedly originated either with German immigrants who booked passage on the Hamburg-America Line and were served a mixture of chopped beef and onions, or with a chopped beef dish popular in the city of Hamburg itself. Whatever their precise origins, restaurant hamburgers were a novelty

confined to fairs, amusement parks, and beach resorts for most
of the first half of this century. A hint of their potential as mass-
produced restaurant fare came with the founding of the White
Castle hamburger chain in Kansas City in 1921. The chain spread
slowly, taking almost a decade to reach New York. But White
Castle was not a fast-food restaurant, nor were the times ripe for
a fast-food restaurant. It was a cheap central-city eatery catering
to local pedestrian traffic. Its hamburgers were made while customers sat at the counter and lingered over coffee, impeding the
flow of new orders. The first real fast-food chains were spin-offs
of the auto age. They catered to motorized families who preferred
to take their meals inside chromium and glass, high-finned living
rooms on wheels, rather than around the kitchen table. Mc-
Donald's, pioneered in 1955 by Ray Kroc, did not add stools and
tables for sit-down customers until 1966. From then on the formula for success included take-out windows for autos, plenty of
parking space, separate ordering and eating areas, limited menus,
standardized portions, and a clean "family atmosphere." Today
franchise holders own and operate most of the branch restaurants.
In return for the name and national advertising, they buy much
of their food, equipment, and supplies from the parent company
and must abide by uniform standards regulating preparation,
serving, and maintenance. At a McDonald's the hamburgers
themselves arrive from central distributors as frozen patties. Em-
ployees fry them, place them between buns along with relish or
a slice of cheese, and pack them in styrofoam containers at a rate
sufficient to keep a stock on hand so that every customer's order
can be filled without delay. Theoretically, at Burger King, hamburgers must be served within ten minutes after they are cooked.

In the early 1980s, Americans were eating fifty pounds of ground
beef per head, mostly in the form of hamburgers. Every second,
the fast-food restaurants alone were selling an order of one or
two patties on a bun to two-hundred customers to the tune of
6.7 billion per year worth $10 billion. Fourteen million Americans
a day eat in McDonald's alone.

* * *

In my opinion, the rise of the fast-food restaurant was an event that was at least as socially significant as putting a man on the moon. I have in mind Edward Bellamy's prediction in his influential utopian novel, *Looking Backward*, that one of the great achievements of socialism would be to put an end to the capitalist way of eating. Bellamy's hero falls asleep in 1887 and dreams that he does not waken until the year 2000. Among the wonders he encounters, none impresses him more than that Americans no longer separately shop for, prepare, or serve dinner. Instead they eat meals cooked at neighborhood kitchens by ordering from menus published in the newspaper and served at elegant clubs. McDonald's, Wendy's, or Burger King scarcely provide the haute cuisine and luxurious salons Bellamy envisioned, but they go farther toward fulfilling the dreams of affordable dining out than anything the world has ever seen before. Nurtured in the bosom of capitalism, McDonald's, Wendy's, and Burger King are nothing if not centralized, efficient, and communal—the food is cheap, nourishing, and instantly available in unlimited quantities; no one waits on anyone else or washes dishes since plates and utensils simply get thrown away; and the patrons themselves carry the food to the table and clean up when they are done. (Of course there remains lots of drudgery, pressure to speed up, and low wages, but who believes in utopia anyway?)

Beef consumption and the fast-food industry took off together, leaving pork on the launching pad. It was not until the 1980s that pork began to appear on fast-food menus and then only as a component in breakfast specials. (McDonald's gave its McRib, a pork sandwich that oozed barbecue sauce, a field trial involving thirty-five hundred restaurants, but quickly dropped it when customers complained it was too messy and didn't taste good.)

The obvious solution to the problem of finding a way for pork to participate in the fast-food restaurant boom was to sell hamburgers that were a mixture of pork and beef. After all, frankfurters are a mixed pork-and-beef product, and have long been one of the mainstays of the pork industry. But no fast-food company has ever tried to market such a product. All hamburgers sold in the U.S., unlike frankfurters, contain only beef and nothing but beef. There is a simple reason for this, although most Americans don't know it. Legally, there is no such thing as a hamburger which is not an all-beef hamburger. The statutes of the U.S. Department of Agriculture define hamburger as a ground meat patty which contains no meat or fat other than beef or beef fat. If a ground meat patty contains even a smidgin of pork or pork fat, it can be called a "patty," a "burger," or a "sausage," but it cannot be called a "hamburger." In other words, by government decree, the beef industry holds a kind of patent or trademark on America's most popular convenience food. Here is what the operative code of regulations (Code of Federal Regulations 1946, 319.15 subpart B) states:

> *Hamburger.* "Hamburger" shall consist of chopped fresh and/or frozen beef with or without the addition of beef fat as such and/or seasoning, shall not contain more than 30 percent fat, and shall not contain added water, phosphates, binders, or extenders. Beef cheek meat (trimmed beef cheeks) may be used in the preparation of hamburgers only in the accordance with the conditions prescribed in paragraph (a) of this section.

Ground pork can be eaten; ground beef can be eaten; yet to mix the two together and call it a hamburger is an abomination. It all sounds suspiciously like a rerun of Leviticus. Yet as in the original pork taboo, what appears as mumbo jumbo on one level has a hard core of practical sense on another. A key provision is that while hamburgers must be an all-beef product, they can contain up to 30 percent added beef fat, unlike ground beef, whose fat composition is determined solely by the fat present before grinding. Hamburgers, in other words, can be constructed by mixing beef and beef fat from entirely different animals. I have italicized the operative clause in the code governing ground beef:

> *Chopped beef, ground beef.* "chopped beef" or "ground beef" shall consist of chopped fresh and/or frozen beef with

or without seasoning and *without the addition of beef fat* as
such, shall not contain more than 30 percent fat, and shall
not contain added water, phosphates, binders, or extenders.
[italics added]

What all these arcane definitions and mysterious abominations
add up to is federal endorsement of the hamburger as a mixture
of two ingredients—a type of beef and a type of beef fat—neither
of which is marketable as food without the other. The cheapest
beef available, now as always, comes from lean, unfinished range-
fed steers. But if you grind this meat up and try to make hamburgers out of it, the patties will fall apart in cooking. In other
words, to make a hamburger out of range-fed beef, you need fat,
the universal food binder. Any fat, animal or vegetable, would
do, but since you want to make a hamburger, not a patty or a
sausage, it must be fat from a beef animal. The focus now shifts
to the feedlots and to cattle that have been spending twenty-four
hours a day for four or five months eating corn, soybeans, fish
meal, vitamins, hormones, and antibiotics. On their bellies they
carry a paunch which must be trimmed off after they are slaughtered. It is the cheapest beef fat available. The union of feedlot
fat with range-fed lean beef takes place in the industrial grinders
from whence they emerge transubstantiated into the nation's
supply of hamburger meat. Let hamburgers be made of pork with
beef fat, or beef with pork fat, or prevent hamburgers from being
made of beef fat from one animal plus beef from another, and
the entire beef industry would collapse overnight. The fast-food
companies need feedlot waste fat to make cheap hamburgers,
and the feedlots need hamburgers to hold down the cost of feedlot
meat. Since the relationship is symbiotic, when you eat a steak
you are making it possible for someone else to eat a hamburger;
or if you prefer, when you eat a hamburger at McDonald's, you
are subsidizing someone else's steak at the Ritz.
    Despite inquiries addressed to the Department of Agriculture,
I have been unable to learn the history of how the Federal Code's
definition of hamburger was negotiated. When placed alongside

the federal government's failure to develop adequate safeguards against trichinosis, the exclusion of pork and pork fat from hamburgers suggest that beef producers had more influence in government circles than pork producers. If true, this would be the natural outcome of a basic difference in the organization of the two industries which has persisted since the late nineteenth century. Beef production has long been dominated by a relatively small number of very large ranches and feedlot companies, while pig production has been carried out by a relatively large number of small-to-medium farm units. As the more concentrated of the two, the beef industry is probably better able to influence the Department of Agriculture's regulations.

A touchy issue remains. The cheapest sources of lean hamburger meat lie overseas in countries like Australia and New Zealand which have low population densities and plenty of rangeland. If the fast-food chains had their way, they would buy most of their lean beef from abroad. To prevent this from happening the federal government has set up quotas restricting beef imports. Even with these quotas almost 20 percent of all the ground beef that Americans consume is foreign beef. No one knows exactly how foreign beef gets into the consumer's stomach. Once it clears customs no agency records where it goes or what the processors do with it. Some of the fast-food restaurant chains make a point of claiming that their hamburgers are both 100 percent beef and 100 percent American. Others remain silent, adding one more mystery to America's meat-eating ways.

To sum up, beef achieved its recent ascendancy over pork through the direct and indirect influence of all-beef fast-food hamburgers. By combining unfinished range-fed beef with surplus fat from beef feedlots, fast-food chains were able to overcome the pig's natural superiority as a converter of grains to flesh. The U.S.D.A.'s abomination of pork hamburgers as a taxonomic anomaly therefore bears more than a metaphorical resemblance to the taboos of Leviticus. In mediating the age-old struggle between pigs—consummate eaters of grain—and cattle—consummate eaters of grass—the U.S.D.A. had followed ancient precedents. By endowing hamburgers with an all-beef identity, it placed an encumbrance of spirit on the choice of flesh and made beef holier than pork.

The story of America's changing tastes in meat does not end with the triumph of beef over pork. Both of these red meats are being threatened by the rise of fast-food, frozen, and fresh forms of chicken. Americans are now eating 54 pounds of chicken meat per year. While adverse medical findings and rising retail prices have led United States consumers to eat 15 pounds less of beef per capita since 1976, consumption of chicken has zoomed by 11.2 pounds. If these trends continue, Americans will be eating more chicken than beef by the end of the century.

The chicken revolution was long overdue. By nature and breeding, chickens are about as efficient as pigs in converting grain to meat and five times more efficient than cattle. Some of the newest breeds are designed to exceed the efficiency of pigs and convert 1.92 pounds of high-protein feed to one pound of meat, mostly concentrated on the breast. Various technical problems—the susceptibility of chicken flocks to communicable disease, the chickens' tendency to peck each other to death in establishing "pecking orders" within crowded coops, and the difficulty of determining the sex of chicks for flock management—prevented their mass production potential from being realized. These obstacles have been overcome by dosing them with antibiotics, debeaking them with a cauterizing iron, and breeding male chicks to have longer wings than female chicks. Chickens are now "manufactured" in batches of thirty thousand per chicken house, each bird getting less than a square foot of cage to live in. Temperature regulation, ventilation, and waste removal are all automatic. Lights burn twenty-two hours a day to keep them awake so that they can eat nonstop. In forty-seven days after hatching, they weigh over four pounds and are ready to be marketed, half as many days as it took in 1950. In a major brand-name factory, the birds are killed, plucked, eviscerated, cooled, and boxed by automated machines at the rate of 1.5 birds per second. As a result of these innovations, chicken prices have barely risen over the past decade, and chicken products now constitute the fastest-growing component in the entire fast-food industry. "Where's the beef?" may soon apply to its originator. Wendy's abruptly withdrew the slogan that was on everyone's lips during the 1984 presidential campaign because it was interfering with the chain's plan for a newly introduced chicken sandwich.

When food experts tell us that food habits are the parts of culture that change most slowly—so slowly that America's preference for beef harks back to Vedic times—they have obviously not paid much attention to the history of meat consumption in the United States. (Incidentally, chickens were domesticated in the jungles of Southeast Asia and were never part of the basic Indo-European, pastoral-farming complex. They probably first reached Europe only in Greek and Roman times.) The dead hand of tradition has not noticeably slowed the vast gustatory tides that have swept over the United States from Colonial times to the present. In America as never before in history, good to eat is what is good to sell. Yet no less emphatically than in other cases I have been examining, the ups and downs of American tastes in meat are not mere random fashions that aggressive agribusinesses have been able to exploit at will. No less than in Hindu India, the interplay between nature and culture, no matter how ingenious the technology that mediates them, places definite limits on profitability, whether measured in terms of energy, proteins, resources, or dollars and cents. And we must never forget that there are many chickens that have yet to come home to roost. Although I have been emphasizing short-run improvements in the efficiency of converting plant foods to meat, one must not lose sight of the fact that fast-food meats are an energetically inefficient way to feed people. The engineering truimph embodied in the latest superchicken is predicated entirely on the availability of chicken feed which contains not only corn, soybeans, sorghum, and other proteinaceous plant foods, but animal products as well—principally fish meal. This concoction belies its name. It is nutritionally, and energetically too valuable to be called "chicken feed." Nutritionally speaking, all that high protein

plant and fish food means that the average American chicken eats
better than three fifths of the people in the world. And energetically speaking, each calorie of chicken breast costs at least six
calories of fossil fuel. This means that the sumptuous diet of
America's chickens (and pigs and cattle) rests entirely on the
continuing drawdown of still relatively cheap nonrenewable sources
of fossil energy. As I said at the outset, the orgy of carnivory in
America may yet prove to be as transitory as it was in Vedic India.
In the meantime, I hope that I have demonstrated that the principal features of America's meat preference hierarchy—from
horsemeat to beef and chicken—have rapidly adapted to novel
combinations of nutritional, ecological, economic, and political
conditions rather than remaining fixed and unresponsive as an
arbitrary heritage passed on from the remote past.

I am not disputing the fact that some foodways are extremely
tenacious. In addition to preferences and avoidances which last
only decades, there are others which last for millennia. But as
the next riddle shows, the dead hand of tradition is no more
convincing as an explanation for food-ways which persist for thousands of years than it is for those which persist for only decades.

CHAPTER SEVEN

LACTOPHILES
AND LACTOPHOBES

MY INNOCENCE about milk lasted until I encountered the writings of Robert Lowie, a famous anthropologist who was fond of collecting examples of the "capricious irrationality" of human food habits. Lowie found it to be an "astonishing fact that eastern Asiatics, such as the Chinese, Japanese, Koreans, and Indo-Chinese have an inveterate aversion to the use of milk." I shared Lowie's sense of wonder. As an admirer and frequent consumer of Chinese cuisine, I should have realized that there were no milk dishes on Chinese menus—no creamy sauces to go with fish or meat, no cheese toppings or soufflés, and no butter to go with vegetables, noodles, rice, or dumplings. But every Chinese menu I had ever seen offered ice cream for dessert. It never occurred to me that this lone dairy dish was a condescension aimed at pleasing the American palate, and that whole populations of fellow human beings could spurn the "perfect food" of my childhood and youth.

Lowie had put the matter rather mildly. The Chinese and other eastern and Southeast Asian peoples do not merely have an aversion to the use of milk, they loathe it intensely, reacting to the prospect of gulping down a nice, cold glass of the stuff much as Westerners might react to the prospect of a nice, cold glass of cow saliva. Like most of my generation I grew up believing that milk is an elixir, a beautiful white liquid manna endowed with the capacity to put hair on manly chests and peaches and cream on women's faces. What a shock to find others regarding it as an ugly-looking, foul-smelling glandular secretion that no self-respecting adult would want to swallow.

During my youth, the dairy industry, the U.S. Department of Agriculture, and the American Medical Association fervently endorsed the popular stereotype of milk as the "perfect food." Drink a quart of it a day; put it in every school lunchroom; drink it before meals, during meals, between meals, and for midnight snacks. Buy it by the gallon in plastic containers equipped with spigots. Drink some every time you open the refrigerator. Drink it to settle the stomach, treat ulcers, cure diarrhea (boiled), calm the nerves, and relieve insomnia (warmed). Milk could do no wrong.

When the United States was called upon to help feed the underdeveloped countries in the aftermath of World War II, U.S. Agency for International Development officials naturally picked milk as a weapon in the war against hunger. Between 1955 and 1975 various government agencies shipped millions of tons of it (mostly in powdered form) to needy countries around the world. Regardless of the fact that the milk was surplus and that Americans themselves did not like to use it in powdered form, farmers, politicians, and the international aid technicians felt good about shipping their manna to malnourished souls all over the globe. But soon after the first shipments reached their destinations in Africa, Latin America, Oceania, and other needy places, rumors began to be heard about people getting sick from drinking milk— American milk.

I was in Brazil in 1962 when 88 million pounds of powdered milk began to arrive under the Kennedy administration's Food for Peace program. Soon the Brazilians were complaining that the milk made them feel bloated and gave them cramps and diarrhea. United States embassy officials were at first incredulous and then resentful of the way this token of American generosity was being spurned and maligned. "What they're doing," one official told me, "is eating the powder raw by the fistful, throwing it into their mouths without mixing it in water. Naturally that's going to give them one hell of a stomachache." "The problem," said another official, "is that they're mixing the powder with polluted water. There's nothing wrong with the milk. It's just that they don't know enough to boil the water before they mix it." "No," answered my Brazilian friends, "we mix it and we use boiled water, but it still gives us a big stomachache." I should point out that the people who were getting sick were accustomed to using milk only rarely, if at all, and then in small amounts with a morning cup of coffee. They had never before drunk milk by the glassful. Unlike the Chinese and other Asians, Brazilians did not have any strong prejudice against milk prior to their experience with the United States handouts. With their cultural traditions primarily European in origin, they were not repelled by the idea of drinking it. But Brazilians, especially the poorer classes of Brazilians who were the recipients of the handouts, are genetically mixed descendants of Africans and American Indians, as well as of immigrants from Europe. It is important to bear in mind that many Africans lack any tradition of drinking milk, while American Indian peoples without exception were entirely unfamiliar with the practice prior to the arrival of Europeans and their domesticated animals.

As the United States government shipped massive amounts of powdered milk abroad under its foreign aid programs, it was simultaneously distributing surplus whole milk to needy Americans under various antipoverty programs. By the mid-1960s, United States doctors in contact with native Americans and ghetto populations had become aware that blacks and American Indians were getting unpleasant gastrointestinal symptoms after downing as little as a single glass of milk. In 1965, a team of research physicians at the Johns Hopkins Medical School discovered the cause: a large percentage of the people who reported milk-related bowel problems were unable to digest the sugar that is found in milk. This sugar is called lactose and is chemically known as a polysaccharide or complex sugar. All mammalian milk contains lactose, with the exception of the milk of pinnipeds—seals, sea lions, and walruses—an exception whose significance will become apparent later on. Lactose molecules are too complex to pass through the walls of the small intestines. They have to be broken down into monosaccharides or simple sugars, specifically glucose and galactose, before they can be absorbed into the bloodstream and used as a source of energy. The transformation of lactose into simpler sugars depends on the chemical action of an enzyme known as lactase. What the John Hopkins researchers discovered was that about 75 percent of adult blacks had a deficiency of this enzyme as compared with about 20 percent of American whites. After drinking a glass of milk, lactase-deficient individuals are unable to absorb the lactose portion. If the deficiency is severe, the lactose accumulates in their large intestines, begins to ferment, and emits gas. The gut fills and swells with water, and the lactose is flooded out of the body in a liquid stool. For some lactase-deficient individuals, even the milk added to breakfast cereals can produce severe symptoms. The classical description of the symptoms of lactase insufficiency was published by a Sudanese doctor named Ahmed. Here is what Dr. Ahmed wrote in the prestigious British medical journal, *Lancet*.

I am a 31-year-old doctor from Sudan, . . . married with a two-year-old daughter and have been fortunate to have received a good education in my own country and now here in Britain. However, my life has been profoundly influenced by a long-lasting concern and preoccupation with disturbed bowel action. The first clear indication of this that I recall was at the age of 9 or 10 years when I began to experience occasional attacks of colic with watery diarrhea; I became bothered by rumbling sounds in the abdomen, frequent discharge of flatus, and great difficulty in obtaining a satisfactory, if bulky, evacuation. I recall needing to go to the lavatory several times a day and would strain at a stool for hours, only to be rewarded at the end each time by a tiny stringy motion that was shaped like toothpaste squeezed out of a near-empty tube.

The psychological impact became very great, and especially so when I had to leave home for school and live in a boarding house with other students. I soon became famous for blocking access to the toilet for hours. I found it impossible to retain gas for long in my bowel, so I had to dress my plight with a garment of humour based on the ability to pass flatus hugely and freely. Although I joked about my nickname, Gurab El Ful, inside I was utterly miserable. . . .

When I came to this country [England] I noticed a marked deterioration in my condition and this I attributed to the stress of working in the background of a strange culture and my preparation for the [medical] examination. Daily work became an ordeal. Although I took only a light breakfast of cornflakes and milk, the ward-rounds became intolerable. I had to suppress volumes of flatus and abdominal rumbling and after the rounds I would rush home to the toilet to have several explosive bowel actions. . . . I decided . . . to treat myself with bran—this being strongly recommended in the unit as a major component in the treatment of the irritable bowel syndrome. I took gradually to increasing doses of bran, with milk, every morning. To my astonishment this made my condition worse. . . . I was beginning to feel desperate and it was quite by chance that I mentioned my disease during an informal chat with the newly appointed consultant to the unit. She raised the possibility that this was caused by the sugar of milk. Reluctantly I agreed to be investigated, but I had little hope that any such pathology would be found.

My lactose-tolerance test was quite an event. The experience was exactly the same as I had at home with my torrential enteritis due to cholera a few years ago. Within half an hour of taking the lactose I started to be aware of excessive rumbling in my abdomen which was later audible to people at the other end of the ward. Two hours later, when teaching students in a round, I had very severe periumbilical colic and rushed away in a most distressed condition . . .

Within a few days of starting a milk-free diet, I found that I had lost the persistent abdominal distension and the need to pass flatus so frequently. My abdominal rumbling dis-

appeared and for almost the first time in my life I had regular
bowel actions. Although I lost no weight, my waistline started
to shrink and this posed another problem on ward-rounds
when I found my trousers were slipping off my waist. I had
to rush away, not to the toilet but to buy a pair of trouser
braces! Now my morale is high, I have thrown away the
bottle of tranquilisers, and am working on my second publication—the incidence of lactase deficiency in Sudanese doctors in Britain.

Medical and nutrition authorities disagree about the frequency
with which the ingestion of milk by lactose-intolerant individuals
is associated with Dr. Ahmed's complaint, Some experts estimate
that drinking an eight-ounce glass of milk will produce discomfort in as many as 50 percent of lactase-intolerant individuals,
while others claim that their studies show less than 10 percent
experience even mild symptoms after downing the same
amount.

The lack of consensus on this issue proved fatal to the Federal
Trade Commission's celebrated attempt to stop the California
Milk Producers Advisory Board from using the theme "milk is
good for every body" in ad campaigns aimed at getting Califor-
nians to drink more milk. The presiding judge denied the request
for a restraining order on the grounds that the best available
double-blind studies showed that "of the 20% to 25% of the
California population which is lactase deficient, probably at most
only 15% would experience symptoms of any kind from 240 ml
of milk [8 ounces] consumed at a sitting. Of those experiencing
symptoms of some kind, the evidence establishes that in only
15% would the symptoms be of sufficient social or psychological
concern or cause sufficient physical discomfort for the symptoms
to be considered significant." The judge concluded that this worked
out to only .7 percent of the California population being afflicted
with significant symptoms. But since almost all the experts agreed
that symptoms increased in proportion to the size of dose, the
court criticized advertisements which sought to encourage the
consumption of several glasses of milk at once. (In one TV spot,

baseball hero Vida Blue announced that he drank two and a half gallons of milk per day.)

It was unfair and misleading for respondents to represent to lactase-deficient persons, who constitute a substantial seg- ment of the population, that the consumption of large or unlimited quantities of milk at a time is beneficial. Ingestion of large or unlimited amounts of milk by such persons may cause symptoms which are troublesome or discomforting, although not health threatening.

Apparently the severity of symptoms among lactose-intolerant individuals can be moderated by some sort of habituation effect. Lactase-deficient subjects who have had no prior experience with milk drinking are more likely to have pronounced symptoms on imbibing small amounts. Most experiments carried out in the United States have used lactase-deficient subjects who have con- tinued to drink milk in obedience to the prevailing customs of their milk-drenched cultural milieu. We know that gastric symp- toms are sensitive to psychological states and that to a certain degree one can learn to ignore or live with flatus, bloating, and mild cramps just as one can learn to ignore or live with mild arthritic discomfort. In addition, the intestinal flora of habituated milk drinkers may differ from those of nonhabituated milk drink- ers, with the result that different rates of symptom-producing fermentation may occur among individuals with the same levels of lactase deficiency.

Factors such as these may explain why lactase-deficient sub- jects in other countries or in American Indian cultures show a higher rate of more dramatic symptoms after drinking a glass of milk than United States subjects. In Mexico City, for example, 20 percent of lactase-deficient subjects had mild symptoms and 16 percent had severe symptoms after downing a single glass of milk. Adult Pima Indians in Arizona have close to 100 percent lactase insufficiency. After drinking a glass of milk, 68 percent of Pima subjects report symptoms.

After discovery of the biological basis of milk intolerance, medical researchers rushed to identify additional populations that were unable to digest lactose. They initially labeled those who were deficient in lactase as "abnormal," but it soon became evident that lactase deficiency in adulthood is the "normal" condition and lactase sufficiency the "abnormal" condition among adult humans just as it is among virtually all mammals. Less than 5 percent of adult Chinese, Japanese, Koreans, and other eastern Asians can absorb lactose; in some Asian and Oceanian groups such as the Thai, New Guineans, and aboriginal Australians, the percentage of adult lactose absorbers is close to zero. Adult lactose absorbers are almost equally hard to find in West and central Africa—the ancestral homelands of most United States and Brazilian blacks. And that gets us back to all those Brazilian stomachaches. Brazilians of mixed African and American Indian ancestries who complained after drinking powdered milk were undoubtedly victims of lactose malabsorption rather than of dirty water or fistfuls of unmixed powder.

We now know that the greatest concentration of "abnormal" lactose absorbers lives in Europe north of the Alps. Over 95 percent of the Dutch, Danes, Swedes, and other Scandinavians have enough lactase enzyme to digest very large quantities of lactose throughout their lives. South of the Alps, high to intermediate levels prevail, falling to intermediate and low levels in Spain, Italy and Greece and among Jews and city-dwelling Arabs in the Middle East. Intermediate to high levels of absorbers occur again in northern India, while high levels of absorbers occur in isolated enclaves such as the Bedouin nomads of Arabia and certain pastoral groups in northern Nigeria and East Africa.

Mammals obviously have to be able to drink milk in infancy, but why do mammals, including most humans, lose their ability to produce lactase enzyme as juveniles and adults? A possible explanation for postinfancy lactase insufficiency is that natural selection usually does not favor chemical and physical features for which an organism has no use. As infant mammals grow up and become bigger and heavier, their mothers can no longer produce enough milk to satisfy their offspring's nutritional needs.

Furthermore, mammalian mothers must prepare for new pregnancies and the care and feeding of additional offspring by ter-
minating lactation and by obliging their older offspring to engage
in the quest for adult foods. The only way people can include
milk in their diets after being weaned from the mother's breast
is to "steal" it from other lactating mammals tame enough to let
human beings milk them. No advantage existed for humans who
could synthesize lactase after infancy until such milkable species
had been domesticated. For this reason, throughout millions of
years prior to the domestication of the ruminants, natural selection did not favor humans who had an ability to synthesize lactase
after infancy. Yet genes for extending the period of lactase sufficiency into adulthood were present in very low frequencies as
a result of recurrent mutations (we can surmise this from the
occurrence of adult lactase sufficiency in certain species of monkeys). It was only after the domestication of ruminants starting
about ten thousand years ago that natural selection began to favor
the spread of the gene for adult lactase sufficiency among certain
groups which possessed milkable animals. Today every human
population which contains a high percentage of lactase-sufficient
juveniles and adults has had a long history of milking one or more
of the domesticated ruminants and of consuming their milk—the
more copious the quantity consumed relative to the consumption
of other foods, the higher the frequency of the genes for lactase
sufficiency among juveniles and adults.

All this seems to add up to a deceptively simple explanation
of why northern Europeans and their descendants have a more
than 90 percent incidence of adult lactase sufficiency. If people
needed to drink copious quantities of milk in order to satisfy their
nutritional needs, natural selection would have favored the reproductive success of those individuals who had the aberrant gene
for lactase sufficiency and disfavored the reproductive success of
those individuals who had the "normal" genes for lactase insufficiency. But why would anybody need to drink copious quantities
of milk? Our species and its ancestors had gotten along for millions
of years before the first domestic animal was tame enough to be

milked. As the existence of healthy, long-lived non–milk drinkers all over the world proves, most people still do not depend on milk to satisfy any basic nutritional needs. Yet the ability of other populations to get along without milk does not preclude the possibility that there were some special circumstances associated with the environment and prehistory of Europe which obliged Europeans to become milk drinkers. The problem then is to specify under what circumstances milk drinking would become critical for people's health, well-being, and reproductive success.

Milk contains no nutrients that cannot be obtained from other plant and animal foods. Yet milk does contain extra-large doses of one ingredient which Europeans, especially northern Europeans, might have needed in exceptionally large amounts. That ingredient is calcium, a mineral the body used to build, maintain, and repair its bones. The solid portion of milk is the most concentrated of all dietary sources of calcium. Adequate supplies of calcium can also be obtained from eating dark green, leafy vegetables, such as beet greens, turnip greens, and spinach. But these sources must be consumed in large quantities and are far less efficient food "packages" (for lactose-tolerant individuals) than milk, whose fats and sugars are an important source of energy as well as of proteins, vitamins, and minerals. Chewing fish bones and gnawing on the heavy ligaments close to animal bones can also marginally satisfy calcium needs. And this is how the Eskimo get their calcium. But not everyone has access to fish, and gnawing on large bones is hazardous to teeth besides being a total loss as far as energy is concerned.

The mere presence of calcium in a food is no guarantee that it will get absorbed by the intestines. Like many other plant foods dark green, leafy vegetables contain acids which bind to calcium and other minerals, prevent their absorption, and lower their biological value. Milk excels as a dietary source of calcium not only because it contains more calcium than most foods, but because it also contains a substance which promotes its absorption by the intestines. The substance is none other than lactose, but more about this in a moment.

First let me point out that the evolution of the use of milk as an unexcelled source of absorbable calcium is one of the most distinctive features of the mammalian class of vertebrates. Newborn mammals have soft immature skeletons which must harden and grow rapidly even though they cannot obtain solid food on their own. The secretion of the mammary glands therefore contain a superb natural formula for promoting the absorption of calcium and maximum rates of bone growth in nursing infants. Juveniles and adults in need of calcium can also benefit from this formula, provided they have milkable animals and are lactase-sufficient.

Let me be a bit more explicit about one of the things that may happen if children and adults do not get enough calcium. They develop the disease known as rickets when it affects youngsters and osteomalacia when it affects older people. In the young, legs become grotesquely bowed and stunted; the chest collapses, and the female pelvis becomes twisted, rendering the birth canal impassable to the fetus. In later years legs, hips, and arms can become brittle and subject to breakage at the slightest fall or impact. Untreated ricketic children and juveniles would be less likely to get married and reproduce than their healthy counterparts. And ricketic mothers would face a high risk of dying with an unborn child stuck in the birth canal. Is there any evidence of a linkage between lactase insufficiency and bone disease? Yes. Studies show that among whites as many as 47 percent of those with osteomalacia have lactase deficiency. In a population which possessed milkable animals, and poor alternative sources of calcium, lactose intolerance could therefore definitely influence reproductive success.

As I mentioned a moment ago, the effectiveness of milk as a source of dietary calcium is assured by the large amount of calcium in milk and by the fact that milk contains a special substance—namely lactose—which promotes the abosrption of calcium by the intestines. If one is not able to digest lactose, milk drinking will not only be an unpleasant way to obtain calcium, but it will be an inefficient way as well. This point has only recently been clarified. While researchers have generally agreed that severe lactose intolerance could lead to the nonabsorption and waste of the calorie-rich sugary part of milk, there was contradictory evidence concerning whether or not lactose intolerance meant that the calcium in milk also would be passed out of the body without being abosrbed. To test for the effects of lactase insufficiency on the ability to absorb calcium, scientists at the Center for the Study of Bone Disease at the University of Geneva gave groups of lactase-deficient and lactase-sufficient volunteers standard doses of calcium in water. In one experiment the subjects took the calcium with a dose of lactose, and in another they took the calcium alone. Every one of the lactase-deficient subjects showed a significant decline, averaging 18 percent, in their total absorption of calcium when they ingested calcium together with lactose. The importance of this decline can only be appreciated by comparison with what happened when lactase-sufficient subjects took calcium and lactose together. All twelve of them experienced a marked jump in the amount of calcium they were able to absorb— a 61 percent average increase over the absorption total when they ingested calcium without ingesting lactose. These findings (which had been anticipated by earlier experiments using animals and smaller samples of humans) suggest that lactose-tolerant individuals may have as much a 79 percent advantage over lactose-intolerant individuals when it comes to utilizing the calcium in milk.

Incidentally, this new evidence directly contradicts one of the principal arguments at the trial of the California Milk Producers Advisory Board. The judge had been convinced by the preponderance of expert testimony that "milk was essential, necessary, and needed by the people of California . . . including the bulk of those with symptomatic lactose intolerance" because "they obtain all the nutrients contained in milk except possibly the calories present in the lactose" and therefore do need milk to obtain the calcium their body requires. The new data indicate that lactase-deficient individuals cannot obtain enough calcium from milk without drinking more milk than lactase-sufficient people need to drink. And of course the more they drink, the more violent their symptoms (remember Dr. Ahmed!). The prudent response to these facts is not to advise lactase-deficient people to drink milk but to consume more green, leafy vegetables or chewable fish bones.

To sum up: if the ancestors of today's lactase-sufficient Europeans were dependent on milk for their calcium, and if they were at risk for rickets and osteomalacia, then individuals who were unable to drink copious quantities of milk or who could only absorb a small portion of the calcium in what they drank would be at greatest risk.

Who were the ancestors of today's lactose-tolerant Europeans and why were they dependent on animal milk for their calcium supply? Archaeological and linguistic evidence strongly indicates that about ten-thousand years ago, central and northern Europe were heavily forested and sparsely inhabited by hunter-gatherer peoples. The geographic center for the domestication of milkable animals was in the Middle East and eastern Mediterranean regions. Starting about nine or eight thousand years ago, Neolithic farmers and stock raisers began to migrate northward using fire to clear the forests, planting cereals in small gardens, and letting their animals graze on the grasslands which grew up after the trees were burnt off. In this mode of subsistence, there was little room for planting calcium-rich but energy-poor dark green, leafy vegetables. In fact, most of the familiar species of dark green, leafy vegetables were not yet part of the world's inventory of domesticated plants, precisely because they are so unrewarding as a source of energy and protein as compared with cereal grains and animal foods. If Europe's Neolithic pioneers were exceptionally at risk for rickets and osteomalacia, it is far more likely that both cultural and natural selection would select for an increased use of milk rather than the domestication and increased use of dark green, leafy vegetables.

The question now becomes, is there any evidence indicating that the Neolithic pioneers were especially at risk for rickets and osteomalacia? Yes, there is, even though it comes from an entirely unexpected quarter and appears to be unrelated to the domain of food behavior. The evidence consists of the exceptionally light complexion of northern Europeans and the way skin color in Europe gradually darkens as one journeys from the British Isles and Scandinavia to the lands surrounding the Mediterranean. In a quantitative sense, extremely fair skin ranging into shades of pink is as "abnormal" as is lactase sufficiency in adulthood. Most of humankind possesses brown or dark skin, and perhaps as recently as ten-thousand years ago no humans anywhere had skin which resembled that of modern-day northern Europeans. The doubly exceptional combination of fair skin and lactase sufficiency is not a coincidence. Fair skin, like lactase sufficiency, increases the absorption of calcium. It does this by permitting certain wavelengths of light to penetrate beneath the outer skin and convert a form of cholesterol found in the epidermis into vitamin D_3. The blood carries vitamin D_3 from the skin to the intestines (technically making it a hormone rather than a vitamin) where it plays a vital role in the absorption of calcium. Vitamin D can also be obtained directly from dietary sources, but these are remarkably limited, consisting mainly of marine fish oils, especially marine fish and sea mammal liver (freshwater fish will not do). An essential fact to be kept in mind is that milk itself (unless enriched) does not contain significant amounts of vitamin D. Why should it? It contains lactose, which by itself is capable of substituting for vitamin D in enhancing the absorption of the calcium which milk provides in abundance. This helps to explain the curious anomaly of the absence of lactose in pinniped milk. As opposed to the milk of other mammals, sea lion, seal, and walrus milk is rich in vitamin D, and therefore there is no need for it to have lactose to enhance the absorption of calcium. What this substitution of vitamin D for lactose points to is the fact that the diet of sea mammals consists almost entirely of vitamin D–rich fish. Assured of a plentiful supply of vitamin D by their fish-eating habits, the pinnipeds, unlike other mammals, were able to dispense with the complex need for mothers to produce lactose in the mammary gland and for infants to produce lactase in the intestine.

The beneficial effect of fair skin on calcium absorption may seem odd in view of what I have just said about brown being the "normal" color of our species. If calcium is such an important nutrient, and if light skin color promotes the synthesis of vitamin D and the absorption of calcium, why is fair skin so "abnormal"? The answer is cancer—cancer of the skin.

Human skin owes its color to the presence of particles known as melanin, the same substance which allows lizards to change their color and which makes octopus ink black. In humans the primary function of melanin is to protect the upper levels of the skin from being damaged by the ultraviolet band of sunlight that penetrates the atmosphere. This radiation poses a critical problem for our species because we lack the dense coat of hair that acts as a sunscreen for most mammals. Hairlessness has its advantages; it allows abundant sweat glands to cool our bodies through evaporation, thereby bestowing on our species a unique ability to pursue and run down swift game animals over long distances during the midday heat. But hairlessness has its price. It exposes us to two kinds of radiation hazards: ordinary sunburn with its blisters, rashes, and risk of infection; and skin cancers, including malignant melanoma, one of the deadliest diseases known. Melanin is the body's first line of defense against these afflictions. The more melanin particles, the darker the skin, and the less risk of sunburn and all forms of skin cancer.

Malignant melanoma is primarily a disease of light-skinned individuals of northern European parentage with a history of exposure to intense solar radiation. One of the highest rates of all forms of skin cancer is found in Australia, where the white population is primarily of northern European descent. Solar radiation is implicated for two reasons: the rate quadrupled in thirty years coincident with an increase in outdoor sports and the wearing of scanty attire; and the rate varies with the amount and intensity of solar radiation from north to south.

In the United States, where one-third of all new cancers per year are skin cancers, the rate of malignant melanoma increased sixfold from 1935 to 1975, again in tandem with the rise in popularity of outdoor sports and the relaxation of dress codes. Predictably, malignant melanoma occurs most frequently among whites who live in cities like Dallas and Fort Worth and least frequently among those who live in Detroit or Minneapolis. Men, more likely to go shirtless than women, get it on the upper torso. Women get it on their legs, less frequently on their backs, and practically never on their seldom-exposed breasts. In contrast, malignant melanoma rarely occurs among heavily pigmented central Africans and their New World descendants. An added twist is that when very dark-skinned individuals get malignant melanoma, they get it on the most depigmented parts of their bodies—the soles of their feet, palms of their hands, and their lips.

In Europe the evidence seems contradictory: Norwegians get malignant melanoma twenty times more frequently than sundrenched Spaniards. But there is an obvious explanation. Not only are Norwegians and Swedes generally fairer than Spaniards, they have taken to nude and seminude sunbathing with fanatic zeal, at home during their short summer and abroad during their winter vacations. The particular color of a human population's skin therefore represents in a large degree a trade-off between the hazards of too much versus too little solar radiation: acute sunburn and skin cancer on one hand, and rickets and osteomalacia on the other. It is this trade-off that largely accounts for the preponderance of brown people in the world and for the general tendency for skin color to be darkest among equatorial populations and lightest among populations dwelling at higher latitudes.

At middle latitudes the skin follows a remarkable strategy of changing colors with the seasons. Around the Meditteranean basin, for example, exposure to the summer sun is high risk for cancer but low risk for rickets; more melanin is produced and people grow darker (i.e., they get suntans). Winter reduces the risk of sunburn and cancer; less melanin is produced and the tan wears off, assuring the synthesis of adequate amounts of vitamin D_3.

Now to begin to put all of this together: as the Neolithic pioneers moved northward, the risks from rickets and osteomalacia outweighed the risks from skin cancer. The winters became longer and colder and the sun more often obscured by mists and clouds. At the same time, they had to reduce the area of skin that they could expose to vitamin D–inducing radiation since they had to bundle up to protect themselves against the cold. Finally, since they were inland farmers and stock raisers, the pioneers could not emulate the Eskimo and substitute fish oil for sunshine as a source of vitamin D_3 (thousands of years were to pass before the technology became available for the exploitation of the Atlantic North Sea and Baltic fisheries). Under these circumstances, fair-skinned, nontanning individuals who could utilize the weakest and briefest doses of sunlight to synthesize vitamin D_3 would have been strongly favored by natural selection. Much of the population lost its ability to tan altogether. And since only a small circle of face could be left to peek out at the winter sun through the heavy clothing, the northerners acquired peculiar translucent patches of pink on their cheeks—veritable windows into the skin to facilitate vitamin D_3 synthesis.

Since Vitamin D_3 will only prevent rickets or osteomalacia if calcium intake is adequate, fair skin and lactose sufficiency may therefore have evolved in tandem, as adaptations to the same set of selection forces. Calculations by the population geneticist Cavalli-Sforza show that the changeover from suntanning, brown skin, lactase-deficient Mediterraneans to fair skin, lactase-sufficient Scandinavians could have been completed in well under five thousand years, assuming that in each generation the individuals who possessed the genes for fair skin color and lactase sufficiency had on the average 2 percent more offspring than those who had genes for darker skin and lactase insufficiency.

There is an alternative scenario which I also ought to mention. Some archaeologists doubt that a south-to-north migration of brown-skinned peoples bearing the milk-and-cereal complex out of the Middle East actually took place. Instead, hunter-gatherer populations already living in Europe may simply have passed the milk-and-cereal complex from one group to another. And parts of the complex—for example, the domestication of milkable cattle—may even have been invented independently by the Europeans themselves. This scenario has the same implications as the previous one for selective pressure in favor of lighter skin color and lactase sufficiency. We know that the predecessors of the milk-and-grain peoples lived primarily along the seacoasts and had ample supplies of vitamin D–rich fish and sea mammals. The more northerly of these groups probably lived under arctic conditions much like modern-day Eskimo (although much farther south). And like modern-day Eskimo, who are also not greatly stressed for vitamin D, these populations could have been considerably browner than their descendants, who gave up hunting and fishing, moved to the less desirable interior zones of Europe, and took up a way of life dependent on milk drinking and cereal eating.

The principal elements for explaining the origins of milk preferences and avoidances are now ready for final assembly. But I must first attend to certain objections raised by scholars who prefer to believe along with my old nemesis, Robert Lowie, that food habits are largely a matter of cultural whim and fancy. I can easily dispose of one long-standing objection based on the apparent ability of some lactase-insufficient individuals to remain symptomless as long as they drink milk in small quantities. The challenge confronting our Neolithic pioneers was not merely to be able to tolerate milk in copious amounts without experiencing "Dr. Ahmed's complaint" but to maximize the absorption of the calcium in what they were drinking. The finding that lactase-sufficient individuals may have as much as a 78 percent advantage over lactase-insufficient individuals in absorbing calcium in the presence of lactose is certainly ample enough to generate a reproductive advantage of 2 percent in a population critically at risk for rickets and osteomalacia.

Another long-standing criticism holds that lactase sufficiency among Europeans could not have been crucial for obtaining calcium from milk since it is easy to convert milk into substances which break down lactose into simpler sugars. Cheese, yogurt, and fermented milk, for example, are calcium-rich dairy products which do not produce unpleasant symptoms among lactose-intolerant individuals. But the conversion of milk to cheese, yogurt, or fermented milk means that lactose will not be available to facilitate the absorption of calcium. (The degree to which lactose converts to the simple sugar, galactose, in soured milk products depends on the length and temperature of incubation. At high ambient temperatures most of the lactose in yogurt is "auto-digested" in a few hours.) Lacking solar and dietary sources of vitamin D, individuals who obtained their calcium from these milk products would still have been at a disadvantage with regard to satisfying their calcium needs as compared with the lactose-tolerant individuals who were able to drink their milk with the lactose unmodified. The way natural selection operates is through slight differences in reproductive success accumulating over many generations. Since lactose enhances the absorption of calcium, lactose-tolerant drinkers of fresh milk would still enjoy a reproductive advantage over the lactose-intolerant drinkers of fermented milk, cheese, or yogurt, and the frequency of the gene for prolonging lactase sufficiency after childhood would still increase and spread, provided of course that the population was critically at risk for rickets and osteomalacia.

The logic of this explanation can be extended to provide an understanding of why many populations with a long history of dairying and milk consumption such as Jews, Italians, Arabs, and people from southern India exhibit intermediate frequencies of lactose tolerance. In each of these cases one would expect selective pressure for lactose tolerance to vary in relation to the number of sources of calcium other than raw milk which environment, technology, and economic practices make available. In India, for example, outside of the traditional northwest pastoral zones, the frequency of lactose tolerance is intermediate or low, although the population has probably been consuming milk products for at least four thousand years. The explanation for this is that the southern Indians have been subjected to only mild selective pressure for obtaining calcium from milk. Southern Indian agriculture provides dark green leafy vegetables and legumes—good sources of calcium—which are chopped up and served in spicy "dals." There is also abundant sunshine so that the need to protect against skin cancer outweighs the need to obtain vitamin D, and the skin color of South Indians is quite dark. With selection stress at intermediate levels, milk is consumed primarily in the form of yogurt. Yet yogurt can retain a considerable amount of lactose if it is not thoroughly fermented—and this is the characteristic form in which it is consumed in southern India. So individuals who are lactase-sufficient continue to derive more calcium from milk than those who are lactase deficient and will have a slight advantage over individuals who are lactase insufficient, resulting in medium to low levels of the genes for lactase sufficiency.

And this brings us back at last to Lowie's "astonishing fact." Upon learning about the geographic distribution of lactose intolerance, the answer to why the Chinese and others in eastern and Southeast Asia spurn milk seems deceptively self-evident. They spurned milk because they were lactase-deficient and could not digest it. But the explanation of why people in the Orient spurn milk cannot be just that. The Chinese did not spurn milk because they are lactose intolerant; they are lactose intolerant because they spurned milk. Or more precisely, they maintained the gradient of lactose intolerance from infancy to adulthood that is normal for our species in the absence of any significant advantage to be derived from drinking milk. This means that in the Far East people were never obliged by their habitat or mode of subsistence to depend on milk for their calcium or for any other nutrient.

Why was China different from India in this respect? The Oriental lands which spurned dairying practice a form of intensive irrigation agriculture which depended less on animal plowing then India's agricultural system. As discussed in the chapter on the sacred cow, India's monsoon climate sharply differentiates wet from dry seasons, and obliges farmers to deploy large numbers of ox-drawn plows for the preparation of fields before the rains begin. In China, where less stringent conditions of soil and climate prevail and where irrigation agriculture is much further advanced than in India, preparations of fields for planting can be achieved by manpower alone or with smaller numbers of animal-drawn plows. Furthermore, unlike India, China was not com-pelled to raise traction animals in the zones of dense human settlements since China has always had access to animals raised by pastoralists who inhabited the vast grasslands of the inner Asian frontier. This opportunity was foreclosed to India, which was cut off from inner Asia by the Hindu Kush and Himalaya mountain chain, the highest in the world. Without India's need to breed large numbers of work animals in or near their villages, the Chinese had no reason to keep large numbers of cows to breed oxen and therefore never were motivated to use milk as a by-product of their use of animals for plowing. The Chinese were also under no economic obligation to raise sheep or goats for dairying. On the contrary, the density of settlement weighed against any substantial diversion of resources to these smaller ruminants as a source of animal food. The Chinese and other eastern Asians have long displayed an exceptional ability to build irrigation terraces and raise plant foods on hillsides which, among less intensive agriculturists, are best exploited by grazing and browsing ruminants. In all of these respects, China not only contrasts with India, but even more so with Europe, which is a region of rainfall agriculture and, until recently, of low population density.

Rather than depend on ruminants for their principal animal food supply, the Chinese turned instead to the pig. For millennia the Chinese, unlike the people of India and the Middle East, have made the pig an integral part of their agricultural system. They succeeded in doing this by placing the pig in pens adjacent to their farmhouses and feeding it on household garbage. This has proven to be an extraordinarily successful arrangement, as the prominence of pork in Chinese cuisine testifies.

If the Chinese had ever been under pressure to develop the art of stealing mammary secretions from their domestic animals, the ever-present handy family sow and not the distant and less numerous ruminants would have been their most likely target.

So why didn't the Chinese (or anybody else) ever milk their pigs? The answer is that the pig's mammary glands are not suitable for milking. The whole physiology of the pig reflects a strategy of nursing that is different from that of the ruminants. Cows, sheep, and goats have capacious reservoirs—udders—in which milk secreted by the lactation glands is collected. This arrangement permits the ruminant mother to continue to move about and feed while being suckled by its nurslings. Pigs give birth to large litters of helpless piglets. The sow builds a den where it leaves them while it forages for food. The sow has no reservoir for storing milk in advance of nursing. The sucking piglets stimulate the production of milk, which is released in short bursts in relatively small amounts. After about fifteen minutes the sow needs to feed itself again. Not even the Chinese, with all their genius for thrifty foodways, could get milk out of a sow's teats (at least not enough to make sow's milk a valuable by-product of raising pigs for meat).

But regardless of whether pigs could have been bred to give milk, the fact is that the Chinese, unlike Europeans, were under no nutritional pressure to make use of milk. A considerable portion of the Chinese diet has long consisted of various cabbages, varieties of lettuce, spinach, and other dark green, leafy vegetables which are chopped into small pieces, combined with small morsels of animal flesh, and stir-fried. The use of large amounts of dark green, leafy vegetables for human consumption inevitably generates large quantities of partially decomposed leaves and stems, which make excellent pig food. The householders supplemented this with various by-products of soybeans, another prominent Chinese specialty. I have already indicated that dark green, leafy vegetables are a rich source of calcium; now I have only to add that soybeans are also rich in calcium and that the Chinese climate allows for plenty of sunny days in order to make clear why the Chinese were under no selective pressure to milk their pigs or any other domestic animals. With neither reproductive nor economic advantage to be gained from dairying, the frequency of the genes for lactase sufficiency among the Chinese remained at the low levels that are common among the great majority of the members of our species. Those occasional Chinese who were lactase-sufficient and who experimented with milk drinking gained no reproductive advantage over their lactase-deficient neighbors. When some rash lactase-deficient individuals decided to experiment with milk drinking, they were rewarded with Dr. Ahmed's complaint, thereby laying the basis for a general and, for them, well-founded belief that the mammary secretions of animals are a loathsome abomination.

While the risk of bone disease was the paramount source of selection pressure for lactase sufficiency in Europe, one should not lose sight of the fact that milk is a source of calories and high-quality protein as well as of calcium and lactose. Any population which has to depend on milk consumption as the primary source of its calories and proteins as well as of its calcium can be expected to show genetic effects of selection pressure against lactase insufficiency. This, then, is the explanation for why certain dark-skinned pastoral nomads in Africa who have no lack of solar-activated vitamin D have levels of lactase sufficiency that match those of Scandinavia. Unlike the Chinese, individuals in these groups who were lactase-sufficient and able to consume copious quantities of fresh milk without manifesting Dr. Ahmed's complaint would have had higher rates of reproductive success than lactase-insufficient individuals. This advantage would persist even if milk were normally consumed in fermented form or as cheese or yogurt. Studies of East African pastoral groups who subsist almost entirely on milk supplemented by small amounts of blood and meat show that during the driest part of the year as well as during droughts, reserves of cheese and dried milk products dwindle and people are obliged to consume fresh or only partially soured milk. Dr. Ahmed's complaint would be even more devastating to camel nomads such as the Bedouin, who are obliged to depend on fresh camel's milk when traversing the deep desert.

Two final points: first, lactase-deficient populations in central Africa, the entire New World, and all of Oceania never had any chance to develop a tolerance for milk drinking simply because neither they nor their ancestors ever raised or even saw a milkable domestic animal. So unlike the Chinese and other Far Easterners, these people never developed an active distaste for milk. Since there is nothing encoded in their cultural experience to warn them that milk is not good to eat, and that they would be better off getting their calcium from bones or plant foods, they are peculiarly vulnerable to the ethnocentric Western conceit that "milk is good for every body."

Second, I must warn that the kinds of genetic variation which are involved in the explanations of why some populations are lactophobes and others are lactophiles are not pertinent to the solution of the other puzzles in this book. The "coevolution" of lactophilia with the genetic basis for lactase sufficiency is highly instructive in this regard precisely because it is so different from the evolution of most foodways. There is no evidence that similar genetic changes accompanied or facilitated the evolution of vegetarianism, the pork and beef taboos, the preference for all-beef hamburgers, or the rise and fall of hippophagy. And for the remaining puzzles as well as for the vast majority of variations in regional and natural cuisines, the most important, the most distinctive, the most shocking differences have absolutely no basis in *genetic variations* (which of course does not mean that they do not have a biological basis). There is, for example, no genetic variation that can explain the disgust which most Americans experience at the prospect of eating certain small creatures which are elsewhere a source of gastronomic delight. It is to the riddle of these small things that I now turn.

CHAPTER EIGHT

SMALL THINGS

ASK EUROPEANS or Americans why they don't eat insects, and you can count on the answer: "Insects are disgusting, and full of germs. Ugh!" The object of this chapter is not to try to change anyone's feelings about eating insects. All I want to do is to offer a better explanation. I think we have the whole thing backward. The European and American rejection of insects as food has little to do with insects as disease carriers or their association with dirt and filth. The reason we don't eat them is not that they are dirty and loathsome; rather, they are dirty and loathsome because we don't eat them.

Back in the days when I was teaching introductory anthropology at Columbia College, I used to pass around open cans of Japanese fried grasshoppers to get students in the mood for thinking about cultural differences: "Don't be greedy. Take some but leave a few for your neighbor." I thought it was a great way to identify potential field-workers until my chairman pointed out that if anyone got sick they could take me and the whole university to court. Given the large number of students who did show signs of impending illness, I had to accept the advice. Groans of disgust gave way to hostile glares and an evident lack of interest in the point I was trying to make. Pressed for their reaction, they didn't mince words: "I don't care what you say. Anyone who would eat these things isn't normal. It's unnatural to want to eat insects."

But one thing I'm sure of is that none of us has an instinctive aversion to eating small invertebrates, be they insects, spiders, or earthworms. First of all, if our ancestry is a guide to our nature, we have to accept the fact that we are descended from a long line of insect eaters. I gave some evidence for this in the chapter on meat hunger. Most living species of contemporary great apes and monkeys eat significant quantities of insects. Even monkeys which do not actively pursue insects as prey consume them in copious amounts in the form of adventitious or sought-after bonuses wrapped up in leaves or buried inside fruit. Monkeys also spend a good part of the time searching each other's hair for lice, not altogether as an expression of pure altruism; the searchers get to eat all the lice they want, as well as an assurance that the little rascals have been sent to a place where they can do no further harm.

Chimpanzees—our closest relatives among the great apes—pursue insect game as avidly as they pursue baby bushpigs and baboons. In their eagerness to dine on termites and ants they even manufacture a special tool—a strong, supple twig stripped of leaves. To catch termites, they insert the twig into the ventilation shafts of a termite mound. They wait a few seconds for the residents to swarm over the twig, then they pull it out and lick off the prey with their tongue. In "fishing" for a species of aggressive driver ants which can inflict painful bites, the procedure is similar but requires greater skill and determination. Upon finding the ants' subterranean nest, the chimps insert their special tool into the entrance. Hundreds of infuriated ants swarm up the twig. William McGrew tells what happens next: "The Chimpanzee watches their progress and when the ants have almost reached its hand, the tool is quickly withdrawn. In a split second the opposite hand rapidly sweeps the length of the tool—catching the ants in a jumbled mass between thumb and forefinger. These are then popped into the open, waiting mouth in one bite and chewed furiously."

All this insectivory among monkeys and apes is to be expected given the likelihood that the whole primate order probably evolved from a primitive shrew which belonged to the mammalian order known as the insectivores. In shaping humankind's primate ancestry, natural selection favored precisely those traits which were useful for the pursuit and capture of insects and other small invertebrates in tropical arboreal habitats. An animal that subsists by hunting for insects on the limbs, branches, or leaves of trees needs a special set of traits: keen stereoscopic vision rather than a keen sense of smell; an agile body; fingers that can grasp and pick up tidbits and bring them close to its eyes for inspection prior to putting them in the mouth; and, above all, a complex, alert mind capable of monitoring the movements of prey amid the light-dappled, wind-blown, rain-spattered arboreal canopy. In this sense, insectivory laid the basis for the further evolution of manual dexterity, differentiation of hands from feet, and the extra braininess that define *Homo*'s distinct place in the great chain of being.

With insectivorous ancestors so prominent in our family tree, we should not be surprised that the abomination of insects and other small invertebrates by Europeans and Americans is the exception rather than the rule. Franz Bodenheimer, father of entomology in modern Israel, was the first scholar to document the extent of humankind's appetite for insects. (He is also known for his demonstration that the manna from heaven of the Old Testament was a crystalized excretion of surplus sugar from a species of scale insect that inhabits the Sinai Peninsula.) Bodenheimer presents evidence of insectivory on all the inhabited continents. People around the globe seem to be especially fond of locusts, grasshoppers, crickets, ants, termites, and the larvae and pupae of large moths, butterflies, and beetles. In some societies insects rival vertebrates as a source of animal protein and fat.

Before there were European settlements in California, for example, the native peoples lacked agriculture or domesticated animals other than dogs, and depended heavily on insects for their basic subsistence. They especially sought the young, fat larvae of bees, wasps, ants, crane flies, and moths. In late summer the pupae of a small fly (*Ephydra hians*) washed ashore along the beaches of California and Nevada's brackish lakes, forming windrows which made it easy for the Indians to harvest huge numbers at a time. They also caught copious quantities of locusts by beating the ground and driving hordes of these insects in a contracting circle onto beds of hot coals. To capture pandora moth caterpillars the Indians built smudge fires under the pine trees and waited for the two-and-a-half-inch creatures to become stupefied and plop to the ground. Women, children, and old men killed and dried these caterpillars in a bed of hot ashes. They also laid tons of dried locusts and moth larvae aside for the winter months when even insects became scarce.

Many indigenous peoples of the Amazon basin seem to be especially keen on insect fare. According to a study carried out among the Tatuya Indians who live near the border of Colombia and Brazil, about twenty different species of insects are consumed. The comprehensiveness of this study is unique, but I only have permission to cite the quantitative results in preliminary form. Almost 75 percent of the insects were consumed in their fat larval stage; the rest were divided between winged sexuals—also fat in preparation for flight and mating—plus the soldier castes of ants and termites whose large heads make tempting tidbits if you can bite them faster than they can bite you (remember the chimpanzees chewing furiously). An important finding is that insect consumption is more significant for women than for men. This fits in nicely with the generalization I have already drawn attention to, that women in Amazonia have less access than men to animal food. In the case of the Tatuya, women seem to make up for some of this disparity by eating more insects proportionate to fish and meat. At certain times of the year, insects counted for about 14 percent of the women's average per capita protein intake from all sources.

But I don't want to give the impression that only band and village peoples find small things good to eat. Many of the world's most sophisticated civilizations consume insects as part of their daily fare. The Chinese, for example, until recently at least, ate silkworm pupae, cicadas, crickets, giant water beetles (*Letho-cerus indicus*), stinkbugs, cockroaches (*Periplaneta americana* and *P. australasie*), and fly maggots. China's insectivorous foodways may have stemmed in part from a gourmet interest in exotic dishes. But the biggest consumers of insects were the poor and destitute classes who lacked alternative sources of animal proteins and fats. The peasants of traditional China did not participate in the great haute cuisine of the gentry and the imperial court. Instead they were noted for making "judicious use of every kind of edible vegetable, and insects as well as offal." In keeping with their frugal dietary regimen, China's peasants consumed large quantities of silkworms, especially in the silk-producing prov-inces. The young women who unwound the cocoons dropped each silkworm into a pot of hot water, kept at the ready for the unreeling, thereby assuring themselves a supply of freshly cooked food throughout the day. "They seem to eat off and on all day long since they work rapidly for long hours at a stretch, and the cooked morsels are constantly before them. One gets a pleasant odour of food being cooked, when passing through a reeling factory." In several silkworm districts farmers cropped their silk-worm cocoons during the busy spring planting season, but had to wait until the summer before they had enough time to unwind the silk. To kill the pupae and preserve the silk, they either baked the cocoons or pickled them in brine. After they unwound the cocoons, the farmers dried the salted worms in the sun to preserve them for the leaner months. When the time came for them to be eaten, they were soaked in water and taken out and fried with onions or mixed with eggs, if the farmer had laying hens.

In contemplating the enjoyment of insect foods by non-West-erners, the extreme lack of animal proteins and fats in the diet of preindustrial peasant population must be kept in mind. Coolies in the nineteenth century in north China, for example, ate "sweet potatoes three times a day, every day, all through the year with small amounts of salted turnips, bean curd, and pickled beans." For these unfortunate souls, cockroaches and water bugs were luxuries.

The peoples of Southeast Asia rivaled the Chinese in their intense insect-eating foodways. Laotians, Vietnamese, and Thais all seem to have gone in for giant water bugs. In addition, the Laotians ate fried cockroach eggs and several species of large spiders (not insects of course, but equally small and ill-reputed as food among Westerners). In the early 1930s W. S. Bristowe gave a detailed account of Laotian foodways, insisting that the people ate insects and arachnids as well as other arthropods such as scorpions not merely to ward off starvation but because they liked the taste. I see no contradiction here: people might very well be expected to acquire a taste for something that wards off starvation. Bristowe himself tried eating spiders, dung beetles, water bugs, crickets, grasshoppers, termites, and cicadas and found:

> none distasteful, a few quite palatable, notably the giant waterbug. For the most part they were insipid, with a faint vegetable flavour, but would not anyone tasting bread, for instance, for the first time, wonder why we eat such a flavourless food? A toasted dungbeetle or soft-bodied spider has a nice crisp exterior and soft interior of soufflé consistency which is by no means unpleasant. Salt is usually added, sometimes chili or the leaves of scented herbs, and sometimes they are eaten with rice or added to sauces or curry. Flavour is exceptionally hard to define, but lettuce would, I think, best describe the taste of termites, cicadas and crickets; lettuce and raw potato that of the giant *Nephila* spider, and concentrated Gorgonzola cheese that of the giant waterbug (*Lethocerus indicus*). I suffered no ill effects from the eating of these insects.

More about those spiders. Bristowe describes how he went spider hunting with a Lao companion and in one hour collected six *Melpoeus albostriatus* weighing a total of half a pound. Other notable spider eaters include New Caledonians, the Kamchatka, the San of the Kalahari, the Caribs of the West Indies, and the inhabitants of Madagascar. The Guaharibo and Piaroa Indians of South America display a special fondness for tarantulas.

Before the invention of soap and insecticides, lice afflicted humans much as they afflict other primates; family members picked them out one by one from each other's hair and cracked their bodies between their teeth. Many human lice-pickers solve the problem of making sure that the elusive creatures will not reinfest them by cracking the lice between their teeth and swallowing them, monkey-style. Bodenheimer cites a nineteenth-century naturalist's account of lice eating among the nomadic Kirghiz (whom we have already met as great horsemeat lovers). "I was witness of a touching, if barbarous scene of wifely devotion. Our host's son was deep in sleep. . . . Meanwhile his affectionate and devoted wife profited the opportunity to clean his shirt of the vermin [lice] swarming in it. . . . She systematically took every fold and seam in the shirt and passed it between her glistening white teeth, nibbling rapidly. The sound of the continuous cracking could be heard clearly."

In brief, my personal observation and my reading of available accounts of insect eating, supplemented by inquiries addressed to anthropological colleagues, convinces me that the overwhelming majority of human cultures until recent times regarded at least some insects as good to eat. But I cannot attest to the true extent of insectivory in the world today because the loathing in which insectivory is held by Europeans and Americans has been communicated to the food experts of less developed countries, and this has made them reluctant to study the contribution of insects to national diet, or even to admit that their compatriots eat any insects at all. A further complication is that insectivory may actually be on the wane in countries like China and Japan. But even if this is the case, it does not diminish the puzzle of why insectivory should ever be spurned since it was or still is an accepted foodway in hundreds of cultures.

Another thing is clear: the majority of the world's cultures still do not share the loathing expressed toward insects in European and Euro-American foodways. What makes this loathing particularly interesting is that not so long ago (anthropologically speaking) Europeans themselves practiced insectivory. Aristotle, for example, was familiar enough with the consumption of cicadas to state that they tasted best in the nymph stage before the last molt and that among the adult forms "first males were better to eat, but after copulation the females, which are then full of white eggs." Aristophanes calls grasshoppers "four winged fowl" and implies that they were eaten by the poorer classes of Athens. Pliny's *Natural History* attests to the fact that the Romans also ate insects; especially a bark-dwelling grub called *cossus*, which was served in what Pliny called "the most delicate dishes." From medieval times onward, aside from a few references to German soldiers in Italy eating fried silkworms, or gourmets consuming the larvae of the cockchafer beetle—rolled in flour and bread crumbs—even the French abstained from insect fare. In fact, during the nineteenth century, while some scientists and men of letters were trying to get the French to eat horsemeat, others were trying with less success to get them to eat insects. At least one elegant insect banquet was held at a fancy Paris restaurant in the 1880s (shades of the horsemeat banquets a few years earlier) whose *pièce de résistance* was white cockchafer larvae. During an 1878 debate in the French parliament over a law aimed at eradicating insect pests, a member of the Senate, M. W. de Fonvielle, published a recipe for making soup out of maybugs. Meanwhile the vice-president of the Insect Society of Paris illustrated a lecture on his "absorption" theory of insect control by swallowing a handful of maybugs accompanied by "signs of high satisfaction."

Like the advocates of horsemeat, some European insectivory enthusiasts embraced their cause in the name of providing cheap meat to the working classes. Outraged by insects that ate up "every blessed green thing that do grow," the English squire V. H. Holt, for example, published a book in 1885 entitled "Why Not Eat Insects?" If farm laborers would diligently collect wireworms, leather jackets, maybug larvae, and chafergrubs, not only would the wheat crop be twice as big, but children would be kept out of mischief, and the poor would no longer have to complain that they can't afford to eat meat. "In these days of agricultural depression we should do all we can to alleviate the suffering of our starving labourers. Ought we not to exert our influence towards pointing out to them a neglected food supply?" This sounds like a rational proposition, but it was doomed to failure.

From a nutritional standpoint, insect flesh is almost as nourishing as red meat or poultry. One hundred grams of African termites contains 610 calories, 38 grams of protein, and 46 grams of fat. By comparison 3.5 ounces (100 grams) cooked medium-fat hamburger contains only 245 calories, 21 grams of protein, and 17 grams of fat. An equal portion of moth larvae contains almost 375 calories, 46 grams of protein, and 10 grams of fat. By dry weight, locusts range from 42 percent to 76 percent protein and from 6 percent to 50 percent fat. Lowly housefly pupae contain 63 percent protein and 15 percent fat while bee pupae when dried consist of over 90 percent protein and 8 percent fat. The only unfavorable comparison that one could make between insects and red meat, poultry, or fish concerns the quality of their protein as measured in terms of the essential amino acids, but some insects have amino acid scores that are almost as good as beef or chicken. Like other flesh foods, insects are rich in lysine, which tends to be the amino acid in shortest supply in most grains and tubers. Most importantly, perhaps, the combination of high fat content with high protein has the "protein-saving" effect, which is nutritionally desirable for people who are faced with chronic shortages of both proteins and calories. In this regard, insects would seem to be a better food bargain than high-protein, low-fat arthropods such as shrimp, crabs, lobsters, and other crustaceans (which are close relatives of insects) and of low-calorie, low-fat clams, oysters, and other molluscs. One would have to eat 7.3 pounds (3,300 grams) of shrimp versus a mere 1.1 pounds (500 grams) of winged termites to satisfy daily calorie needs.

A possible drawback of insects is that they are covered with a hard substance known as chitin, which humans cannot digest. The thought of having to crunch through the chitinous spiny legs, wings, and bodies of creatures like grasshoppers and beetles alarms those not accustomed to insectivorous foodways, but the indigestibility of chitin cannot be used to explain the Euro-American rejection of insects as food any more than one could explain a reluctance to eat lobster or shrimp because of the indigestibility of their "shells" which, as it happens, are also made of chitin. The solution to the chitin problem is quite simple: eat insects in their pupal and larval stages before they grow legs and wings and before their skin gets thick and hard; or pull off the legs and wings of adult forms and consume only the softer parts. True, even the soft, immature forms contain a small amount of chitin, but this might even be advantageous since the chitin acts as roughage which, as I pointed out in the meat hunger chapter, is in short supply in other kinds of meat.

This brings us to the number one rationalization given by Euro-Americans for their loathing of insect flesh: bugs carry and transmit dreadful diseases. No one would deny that insects carry or harbor fungi, viruses, bacteria, protozoans, and worms which can adversely affect human health. But as I pointed out in the chapter on the pig taboo, in the absence of scientific sanitary animal husbandry, so do cattle, sheep, pigs, chickens, and every other familiar barnyard animal. There is usually a simple solution to the problem of contaminated flesh: cook it. And since there is no reason why insects cannot be cooked, the same advice applies to the problem of contaminated insect flesh. Humans probably do not usually eat insects raw any more than they usually eat meat raw. With the exception of the honey ant, whose honey-swollen abdomen is bitten off and swallowed whole, or an occasional locust, grub, or similar tidbit, most insects are fried or roasted, which rids them of hairs and spines and gives them a crisp exterior. Adult forms may also be roasted or boiled, making it easy to detach and winnow the offending wings and legs. Giant water bugs, roaches, beetles, and crickets are boiled and then soaked in vinegar. The object is not to gulp them down raw, but to pick them apart cooked, with slivers of bamboo, much as one picks meat out of a boiled crab or lobster. Actually, it is not as morsels of food that insects endanger human health. Even roaches or houseflies—to take the worst cases—are far more dangerous crawling over plates, utensils, and foods that are ready to be served, than boiled in a soup or fried in oil.

Scientists have recently discovered that some beetles and cockroaches may produce or contain carcinogens and that some people have allergic reactions to cockroaches, meal moths, flour beetles, rice weevils, and grain borers. But scientists have also recently discovered that everything from mushrooms to charcoal-broiled steak presents carcinogenic risks, and as for allergic reactions, wheat, strawberries, and shellfish contain some of the most potent allergens known.

One might at this point wish to resort to a bad-to-think argument. Granting that insects can be eaten without harmful effects, nonetheless the fact remains that many creeping, crawling creatures are associated with dirt and filth, which in turn are associated with disease. It is this mental association, whether true or false in the actual case, which makes insect eating so unappetizing for most Euro-Americans. But why should anyone associate dirtiness with clean-living locusts, beetle larvae, silkworms, termites, moth larvae, and hundreds of other insect species which spend their lives in the great outdoors, far from humans, eating grass, leaves, and wood? If anything, most insects are as clean as most products of fields and barnyards. Was not European agriculture historically based on raising crops fertilized with the excrement of cows, horses, pigs, and other animal droppings? If all it takes for a food species to fall into ill repute is an association with dirt, humankind would have starved to death long ago. Besides, the European pattern of rejecting insects as food was already firmly established long before disease was linked to dirt and before the lack of sanitation came to be seen as a danger to public health.

The only way we can get the principled answer we are looking for is to examine the comparative costs and benefits of eating insects or other small things. We have to begin by viewing insects as alternative sources of nourishment within whole systems of food production. While insects are among the most abundant creatures on earth and a rich and wholesome source of protein and fats, they are nonetheless inherently among the least efficient and least reliable sources of these nutrients in the entire animal kingdom. From the standpoint of time and energy costs per harvested unit, most insects are far outclassed by ordinary domesticated animals and many wild vertebrates and invertebrate fauna. It is this aspect of utilizing insects for human food which provides the basic key to understanding why insects are sometimes avoided and sometimes preferred and why when insectivory is practiced certain species are eaten more than others.

Ecologists have given a good deal of thought to questions like these with regard to the diets of nonhuman foraging animals—animals that must search for their foods. Contrary to what most people may imagine, such nonhuman foragers as monkeys, wolves, or rodents do not eat everything edible they encounter in their natural habitat. They are very much like humans in this regard. Of the hundreds of species they could eat and digest, they collect, pursue, capture, and eat only a small number, even though they may come in frequent contact with the spurned items. To account for this picky behavior, ecologists have developed a set of principles known as optimal foraging theory. This theory not only predicts that foragers will select the best cost/benefit food "bargains" available to them, but it provides a method for calculating at precisely what point a particular food item will become too costly to warrant its collection or capture.

Optimal foraging theory predicts that hunters or collectors will pursue or harvest only those species which maximize the rate of caloric return for the time they spend foraging. There will always be at least one species that will be taken upon encounter, namely the one with the highest rate of caloric return for each hour of "handling time"—time spent in pursuing, killing, collecting, carrying, preparing, and cooking the species after it is encountered. The foragers will take a second, third, fourth, etc., species when they encounter them only if by doing so it raises the rate of caloric return for their total effort. To illustrate, suppose that there are only three species in a particular forest: wild pigs, anteaters, and bats. Suppose further that in four hours of searching through this forest, a forager can expect to encounter one wild pig, and that the "handling" (pursuit, killing, cooking, etc.) of a wild pig costs two hours while its caloric value is twenty-thousand calories. If the handling time for an anteater is also two hours, but its caloric return is only ten-thousand calories, should the hunter stop to pursue an anteater when he encounters one or should he hold out for a wild pig? In four hours of searching, if he takes wild pig and nothing but wild pig, the hunter's rate of caloric return will be:

$$\frac{20,000 \text{ calories}}{4 \text{ hrs.} + 2 \text{ hrs.}} = \frac{20,000}{6} = \frac{3,333 \text{ calories}}{1 \text{ hr.}}$$

If he stops to take an anteater, his rate of return will be:

$$\frac{20,000 + 10,000 \text{ calories}}{4 \text{ hrs.} + 2 \text{ hrs.} + 2 \text{ hrs.}} = \frac{30,000}{8} = \frac{3,750 \text{ calories}}{1 \text{ hr.}}$$

He should not pass up anteaters since 3,750 is greater than 3,333. What about bats? Suppose that for bats "handling time" is also two hours but caloric return is only five hundred calories. Should he stop for a bat?

$$\frac{20,000 + 10,000 + 500 \text{ calories}}{4 \text{ hrs} + 2 \text{ hrs.} + 2 \text{ hrs.} + 2 \text{ hrs.}} = \frac{30,500}{10} = \frac{3,050 \text{ calories}}{1 \text{ hr.}}$$

No. If he stopped for a bat instead of holding out for an anteater or a wild pig, he would be "wasting time."

Optimal foraging theory predicts, in other words, that foragers will continue to add items to their diet only as long as each new item increases (or does not diminish) the overall efficiency of their foraging activities. This prediction is especially interesting with regard to the question of how the abundance of a food item—such as an insect species—influences its position on or off the optimal diet "list." Items which lower the overall rate of caloric return will not be added to the list no matter how abundant they become. Only the abundance of the higher-ranked items influences the breadth of the list: as a high-ranking item becomes scarce, items previously too inefficient to be on the list get added.

The reason for this is that since more time must be spent before the high-ranking item is encountered, the average rate of return for the whole list shifts downward so that it is no longer a waste of time to stop for items that have a low rate of caloric return.

These relationships can be grasped intuitively if we imagine a forest in which someone has fastened twenty-dollar bills and one-dollar bills to the upper branches with clothespins. Should you climb up to get the one-dollar bills? Obviously, the answer depends on how many twenty-dollar bills there are. If there are only a few twenties in the whole forest, you would settle for taking ones. But if there were many twenties, you would be making a bad mistake to go after the ones, even if there were a lot of them. Yet no matter how few twenties there are, you would never pass up a twenty if you came across one.

In a study of the actual rates of caloric return among the Aché Indians of eastern Paraguay, Kristen Hawkes and her associates found that only sixteen species were taken upon encounter during foraging expeditions. The average rate of return after encounter of the sixteen resources ranged from 65,000 calories per hour for collared peccaries to 946 calories per hour for a species of palm fruit. As predicted, despite the fact that each item was decreasingly efficient measured in terms of postencounter calories per hour, its inclusion in the diet raised the overall efficiency of the Achés' foraging system. For example, if the Aché were to take only the top two species—collared peccaries and deer—their overall foraging efficiency would be only 148 calories per hour, since despite their high caloric return, these species are scarce and seldom encountered. By adding the third- and fourth-ranked items—pacas and coatis—overall foraging efficiency increases to 405 calories per hour. As each of the remaining less valuable species is added, the overall average rate of return continues to rise but in smaller and smaller increments. The list ends at a species of palm fruit which, as I said, only yields 946 calories an hour. Presumably, the Aché do not add additional species because they have found by trial and error that there are none available which would not lower their overall foraging efficiency (about 872 calories an hour for all sixteen items). Now, what about insects?

On their foraging expeditions the Aché stop to harvest only one insect—the larvae of a species of palm beetle. Large numbers of these larvae live in clumps of rotting palm logs. The Aché harvest them by hacking chunks out of the logs and breaking the soft wood apart with their hands. At an average rate of return of 2,367 calories per hour after encounter, palm larvae rank eleventh—just below white-lipped peccaries and just above fish. Adding them to the diet raises the Achés' overall foraging efficiency ratio from 782 to 799 calories per hour.

Optimal foraging theory therefore offers an explanation for what must otherwise seem to be an utterly capricious gustatory indifference on the part of many societies to thousands of edible species of plants and animals in their habitat. It also presents a predictive framework for possible past and future changes in the list of products consumed by foragers based on fluctuations in the abundance of the higher-ranked food sources. If, for example, collared peccaries and deer were to become increasingly abundant, the Aché would soon find it to be a waste of time to gather palm fruits; eventually, they would give up eating palm larvae, and if encounter rates with deer and collared peccary rose to a point where stopping to take anything else lowered the overall rate of return, they would take nothing but deer and collared peccaries. Going the other way, if deer and collared peccaries became decreasingly abundant, the Aché would never cease to capture them on encounter, but they would no longer find it a waste of time to stop and harvest resources—including insects— which they now spurn.

Optimal foraging theory is particularly exciting when applied to insects and other small things because it helps to explain why people on skimpy diets may nonetheless pass up items like insects and earthworms which are very abundant in their habitat. It is not the commonness or rarity of a food item which predicts whether it will be in the diet, but its contribution to the overall efficiency of food production. An efficient but rare item will be part of the optimal mix, while an inefficient but abundant item may not be utilized.

Unfortunately I cannot cite additional quantitative data to test these predictions with regard to small things—but in a rough qualitative sense the theory seems to be applicable to the problem of why insectivory was abandoned in Europe. While insects may be easy to capture, and have a high calorie and protein return per unit of weight, the benefit from catching and preparing insects is very small for most insect species compared with large mammals, fish, or even smaller vertebrates such as rodents, birds, rabbits, lizards, or turtles. One can predict therefore that those societies which have access to the fewest large vertebrate species can be expected to have the broadest diets and to engage in the most intensive consumption of insects and other small things. This is part of the explanation of why some of the most diligent insect eaters live in tropical forest habitats where, as I explained in discussing the occurrence of meat hunger in the Amazon, large animals are seldom encountered and game in general can quickly be depleted by even small groups of hunters. Going toward the opposite end of the spectrum, one can see why insect eating dropped out of European cuisines and never became a significant part of meat-rich Euro-American diets. To return to Fernand Braudel's characterization of postmedieval Europe as the "world center of carnivory," if horsemeat could be spurned because there was an abundance of pork, mutton, goat, poultry, and fish, who needed insects?

The principles of optimal foraging theory not only suggest the conditions under which a culture will abandon insectivory but also provide a means for predicting which insects will be preferred when insectivory is practiced. The trouble with most insects as a source of human food is that although they exist in vast numbers, they are small and widely dispersed. The most avidly consumed insects have the opposite characteristics: they are large-bodied and can be harvested not one by one, but in concentrated swarming masses. Locusts, which can measure up to three inches in length and whose swarms consist of billions of individuals, are

the paradigmatic case. One swarming species, the desert locust
(*Schistocera gregaria*), invades sixty-five countries from Mauri-
tania to Pakistan, and gets eaten in all of them. Locusts ordinarily
exist in a solitary phase as grasshoppers. Swarms develop from
the simultaneous hatching of eggs, which have lain dormant in
the soil until moistened by heavy rains. When a generation matures, overcrowding triggers the gregarious flight response. A
medium-sized swarm may contain 40 billion locusts and cover an
area of two hundred square miles. Swarms may travel thousands
of miles and reach altitudes as high as ten thousand feet above
the earth. When the whirring plague passes overhead, vast
numbers fall to the ground and are easily captured as they
attempt to gorge themselves on crops and natural vegetation.
During a swarm people scoop up locusts by the hundreds
from clothing, walls, and plants; collect them in nets and
baskets; and throw them into boiling water or onto a bed of
hot coals.

Since locusts are responsible for devouring crops and natural
pasture, they alter the availability of higher-ranked items—crops
and domesticated animal products—and assure themselves a place
in the optimal diet. Confronted with the destruction of both plant
and animal resources, the only alternative for the afflicted is to
broaden their diet and eat the eaters. This principle of eating
the eaters may also apply in the case of nonswarming
species. For example, the giant water bugs which are much
appreciated in China and Southeast Asia are harvested
individually, but they share two traits with locusts: they are
large and they eat what humans eat, in this case the hatch-
lings of the fish which peasants raise in their irrigated rice
fields and which is for them an important source of animal
protein.

An interesting consequence of the locust's special attributes—
its large size, huge swarms, and devastating effect on crops and
pasture—is that it was exempted from the ban on insect eating
found in the Book of Leviticus ("beetles" are also exempt, but
their species identity is unclear).

These may ye eat: the locust after his kind; the bald locust after his kind; and the beetle after his kind, and the grasshopper after his kind.

The practical significance of insect eating for the Israelites was tested by John the Baptist, who survived in the wilderness on nothing but locusts and honey. Incidentally, optimal foraging theory has implications for the entire list of prohibited birds and other inefficient animals tabooed in Leviticus. Given the abundance of efficient species such as cattle, sheep, and goats, the banning of species such as sea gulls, pelicans, and bats would not be irrational, even if the Israelites encountered large numbers of some of these creatures in their homelands.

But back to locusts. Despite the permission or encouragement of Old and New Testaments, Europeans never acquired a taste for locusts. Caprice? I doubt it. If one inspects a map showing the maximum recorded invasions of *Schistocera gregaria*, virtually all of Western Europe with the exception of the southern fringe of the Iberian Peninsula lies outside the northern limits of the swarms. European farmers were not entirely free of other species of locusts, but the European species seldom caused the widespread destruction of crops and pasture characteristic of the regions where locust eating was often the only alternative to starvation.

Termites and ants probably rank next to locusts in quantities of "small things" consumed around the globe. Termites and ants are small, but they are good energy bargains because they occur in dense colonies and swarm by the millions and billions. Some species build subterranean nests from which human foragers harvest them exactly as chimpanzees do—by inserting a twig into the nest and pulling it out. A more common mode of procuring ants and termites is to attack the hills and mounds in which they nest and which dominate the landscapes in many tropical habitats. Traditionally, in West Africa, people fumigate the nests to drive the inhabitants into the open. But the best time to harvest ants and termites is at the beginning of the rainy season, when after sprouting wings and putting on extra fat, they swarm forth voluntarily. In the aftermath of a heavy rain, all the termites in a neighborhood sometimes leave their nests on the same day, forming huge, whirring clouds that rise as high as five hundred feet and blot out the sun. To capture the winged forms, women and children of the Ivory Coast place cone-shaped straw brooms over the exit holes. When the insects have massed on the brooms, they are shaken off into waiting pots of water, their wings wetted so they can not fly off. Elsewhere, people cover all the exit holes but one and collect the swarms in ingenious traps made from leaves and baskets.

In the tropics, as is well known, insect life is far more abundant than in temperate areas such as Europe. Most of the animal biomass in Amazonia, for example, consists of insects and earthworms. Compared with the tropics, Europe—like all temperate regions—has far fewer species of insects, an absence of giant forms, and a relative lack of species which swarm or exist in concentrated and easily harvested masses. To be sure, as in the case with locusts, Europe has its share of ants and termites, but not the kind that build nests as big as houses and that swarm in numbers sufficient to blot out the sun. Europe is not noted for three-and-a-half-inch-long water bugs which weigh in at half an ounce apiece like *Beostoma indica*, nor for creatures like the Yukpa Indian's dobsonfly, which has a six-inch wingspan, nor for its clumps of rotted palm trees teeming with giant palm grubs.

What I am suggesting boils down to this: If a habitat is rich in insect fauna—especially large and/or swarming species—*and* if it is at the same time poor in large wild or domesticated vertebrate animal species, diets will tend to be highly insectivorous. But if a habitat is poor in insect fauna—especially large and/or swarming species—*and* if it is at the same time rich in domesticated or wild species of large vertebrates, diets will tend to exclude insects. Actually, there are four rather than just two types of situations which should be kept in mind. A simple "two-by-two" square shows what I mean:

	Large Vertebrates Absent	Large Vertebrates Present
Swarming Insects Present	1	2
Swarming Insects Absent	3	4

Cell 1 represents the situation in which the consumption of "small things" is likely to be most intense, as in Amazonia or in the tropical forest area of Africa: lots of swarming insect species, few large vertebrate species. Cell 4 represents the situation in which the eating of "small things" is likely to be least intense, as in Europe or the United States and Canada: few swarming insects and lots of large vertebrates. Cells 2 and 3 represent two different situations, each likely to be associated with intermediate levels of the consumption of "small things": lots of both large vertebrates and swarming insects; and a paucity of both large vertebrates and of swarming insects.

One loose end remains: the peculiar loathing which accompanies the European and American rejection of insects as food. The interesting fact is that most Westerners not only refrain from insectivory but the mere thought of eating a grub or a termite—not to mention a roach!—makes many people sick to their stomachs. And to touch an insect—or worse, to have one crawl on you—is itself a disgusting event. Insects, in other words, are to Americans and Europeans as pigs are to Moslems and Jews. They are pariah species. The standard claim that insects *are* dirty and disgusting makes no more sense than the standard claim of Jews and Moslems that pigs *are* dirty and disgusting. I have already formulated a theory (in the chapter on the pig) for predicting when a species that is not good to eat will become a pariah or a deity. Let me apply it here.

A species will be apotheosized or abominated depending on its residual utility or harmfulness. A Hindu cow not eaten provides oxen, milk, and dung. It is apotheosized. A horse not eaten wins battles and plows fields. It is a noble creature. A pig not eaten is useless—it neither plows fields, gives milk, nor wins wars. Therefore it is abominated. Insects not eaten are worse than pigs not eaten. They not only devour crops in the field, they eat the food right off your plate, bite, sting, make you itch, and suck your blood. If you don't eat them, they'll eat you. They're all harm and nothing good. The few useful species such as insects that eat other insects or that pollinate plants do not compensate for the uncountable hosts of noxious cousins.

To make themselves even more loathsome to Westerners, insects lead a furtive existence in close proximity to humans; they penetrate houses, closets, and cabinets, hiding during the day and emerging only at night. Small wonder many of us react phobically to them. Since we don't eat them we are free to identify them with the quintessential evil—enemies who attack us from within—and to make of them icons of dirt, fear, and loathing.

My theory of residual utility will no doubt strike a certain class of animal lovers as false and impious. Have I forgotten that Americans and Europeans deliberately keep a certain class of animals about the house which are not good to eat and which have no use whatever?

CHAPTER NINE

DOGS, CATS, DINGOES AND OTHER PETS

FRIENDS OF MINE recently moved to a house on a five-acre suburban lot to indulge their passion for raising horses. I was working on the horsemeat chapter for this book when they invited me to a party. As we looked through the picture window at two geldings and a fat mare grazing on the front lawn, I remarked as casually as I could, "I know a man who wants to open a chain of fast-food horseburger restaurants." When my host calmed down enough to treat me as a dumb anthropologist rather than as a potential horse thief, he stammered out: "Eat horses? We couldn't think of anything like that. They're our pets."

"Don't people eat pets?" I wondered (to myself, of course . . . I had no desire to risk any further misunderstanding). Europeans, Americans, and New Zealanders of European descent (my friend was born in New Zealand) think it self-evident that pets are not good to eat. Yet, as an anthropologist, I see nothing self-evident about it. Animals that are treated in a very petlike manner may nonetheless end up inside their owner's stomach (or with the owner's consent, in someone else's stomach).

Just what is a pet anyway? To begin with I would say that pets are animals which people feel friendly toward, feed and groom, and voluntarily live with. Pet species are the logical opposites of pariah species. We do not feed or groom pariah species. Instead we try to exterminate them (like roaches or spiders) and banish them from human company. In contrast, rather than banish pets from human company, we draw them close to us; rub, scratch, decorate, and "pet" them; invite them into our homes, treat them like members of the family, and allow them to come and go as they please.

Before continuing, I should point out that the distinction between pariah and pet species is subject to a certain amount of individual variation among the members of particular cultures. A minority of Americans feels hostile to cats and dogs; and a small percentage of Americans feels friendly toward boa constrictors, tarantulas, and roaches. Yes, in Gale Cooper's *Animal People*, Geoff Alison describes how his pet three-inch-long giant Madagascar hissing cockroaches enjoy crawling on his fingers: "They have a great time going under, over, and around." Every society has people who deviate from the norm. This accounts for the fact that some pet stores sell pariah species as pets. Yet, if pet stores had to make a living from selling only snakes and giant Madagascar hissing cockroaches, they would soon close their doors. Why these deviations occur is an interesting subject, but not one that I can investigate here.

The question before us is whether an animal that is part of a people's regular cuisine can still be a pet. Most American pet owners would probably agree with my horse-owning friends, but anthropologists know that extremely petlike relationships can exist between humans and animals that are good to eat. In this book's meat hunger chapter, I pointed out how strongly the peoples of New Guinea and Melanesia crave pork. The flesh of swine is so good that they feel obliged to share it with their ancestors and their allies. Yet in other respects, they treat pigs in what Americans would regard as a very petlike manner. Let me provide some details. Since the care and feeding of pigs is women's work, while the task of slaughtering pigs falls to men, New Guinea women have more opportunity to develop an affectionate relationship with pigs. Among highland groups, women and children eat and sleep in the same hut not with their men but with their pigs. The men live apart in exclusive male clubhouses. If a piglet has been separated from a sow, the women do not hesitate to nurse it at the breast along with a human baby. And they carry the piglet as they carry their own children back and forth to their distant yam and sweet potato gardens. As the piglet matures, they hand-feed and groom it and they worry about it when it gets sick as they worry about their own children. Only after the piglet has grown to considerable size do the women restrict its movements within the house by building a pen for it next to their own sleeping quarters. Margaret Mead once offered the observation that New Guinea "pigs are so petted and cossetted that they assume all of the characteristics of dogs—hang their heads under rebuke, snuggle up to regain favor, and so on." To this I would add, "and they get eaten like New Guinea dogs, too." For the time will come when even the most favorite pig will be eaten in a village pig feast or traded to another village to help make someone else's ancestor happy.

East Africa is another region well known for its petlike treatment of animals that are good to eat. The Dinka, Nuer, Shilluk, Masai and other pastoralists who live in the Nilotic Sudan and northern Kenya pet and cosset their cattle as if they were New Guinea pigs. Only it is the men rather than the women who tend cattle and who grow more intimately attached to these animals. The men give each calf a name and gradually cut and twist its horns into shapely curves. They talk and sing about their oxen and cows, groom them, decorate them with tassels, wooden beads, and bells. Among the Dinka, men build large thatched reed-and-grass cattle houses to protect their cattle from mosquitoes and predators. As in New Guinea, Dinka husbands and wives sleep apart; but in this case the husband sleeps inside his cattle house, amid his cattle, while his wives and children sleep in separate huts nearby. Like most pastoralists, the Nilotic cattle lovers derive the principal portion of their animal food from milk and milk products. But they have a well-developed taste for beef, which they indulge on the natural death of an older animal and at feasts commemorating important events such as funerals, marriages, and the change of seasons.

In his classic study of the Nuer, anthropologist Evans-Pritchard noted that "whilst Nuer normally do not kill their stock for food, the end of every beast is in fact, the pot, so that they obtain sufficient meat to satisfy their craving and have no pressing need to hunt wild animals." To be eaten, Nuer cattle, like New Guinea pigs, must be ritually slaughtered and shared with the ancestor gods. "Desire for meat is shown without shame on these occasions," and "Nuer recognize that some men sacrifice without due cause." At some ceremonies "there is a general scramble for the carcass" and in the rainy season young men may "join together at a homestead with the purpose of slaughtering oxen and gorging themselves with meat."

What these examples suggest is that being a pet is not an either/or state of being. People may treat animals in a more or less petlike fashion. Rather than argue over whether a pet store boa constrictor or a New Guinea pig or a Nuer cow is a genuine pet, we ought to identify the degree to which the human-animal relationship in particular cultures displays strong or weak petlike qualities. A relationship to a species that is a pariah to almost everyone but its owner may be petlike in other respects but cannot rank high by objective criteria of petdom, no matter how fondly owner and animal regard each other. Pariah species like boas and tarantulas fail at least one other test of "petness." While they can live under the same roof with their eccentric human friends, they have to be kept behind bars or glass; they cannot roam about the house at will. Domesticated animals such as Dinka or Nuer cattle or New Guinea pigs score higher on this petness test: they are not only brought into the house but people actually sleep with them. Their fond owners' craving for meat, however, severely lowers their status as pets. While they are drawn close to the bosom of the family, they are also murdered and drawn into its stomach, a form of togetherness from which human members of the domestic group (even among cannibals—see next chapter) are usually exempt. Continuing on to still higher levels of petdom, we encounter the much-beloved Hindu cow and Anglo-American horse. Spiritual communion absolutely nullifies any thought of dining on beef or horseflesh, yet physical communion falls short of the ideal. The critters are too big to join the family inside the house and must be enjoyed outdoors or through the living room window. This petness checklist shows why in Western eyes the supreme paragons of petdom are cats and dogs: we feed and groom them, they live inside our houses and sleep in the same room, or even the same bed, with us; and our mutual fondness is never disturbed by a craving for their flesh (a restraint which seems generally to be reciprocated).

An animal that is good to eat can neither reach the depths of abomination nor the heights of petdom. These extremes are reserved exclusively for forbidden flesh. One can say therefore that at the highest level of petdom, pets are not good to eat. But this does not mean, as my horse-owning friends would have it, that we don't eat animals because they are pets. Petdom is never an independent determinant of foodways. Why a species is not eaten and why it becomes a pet and not a pariah still depends on how it fits within a culture's overall system for producing food and other goods and services.

Let me demonstrate this with the case of the dog. Westerners refrain from eating dogs not because dogs are their most beloved pets, but essentially because dogs, being carnivorous, are an inefficient source of meat; Westerners have a great abundance of alternate sources of animal foods; and dogs render many services alive which far outweigh the value of their flesh and carcass. In contrast, dog-eating cultures generally lack an abundance of alternative sources of animal foods, and the services which dogs can render alive are not sufficient to outweigh the products they can provide when dead. For example, in China, where perennial shortages of meat and the absence of dairying have produced a long-standing pattern of involuntary vegetarianism, dogflesh eating is the rule, not the exception. An oft-told tale of Chinese and English dog lovers illustrates this sharp cultural difference. As the story goes, there is a reception at the English ambassador's residence in Peking. The Chinese minister of foreign affairs admires the ambassador's female spaniel. The ambassador tells the minister that the bitch is about to be bred and that he would be honored if the minister would accept the gift of one or two of the pups. Four months later a basket containing two puppies is delivered to the minister's house. A few weeks go by and the two men encounter each other at a state function. "How do you like the puppies?" asks the ambassador. "They were delicious," replies the minister.

The events depicted may not have actually occurred, but there is nothing apocryphal about the fundamental difference between Chinese and Euro-American attitudes toward dogflesh. As reported in *Newsweek*, the Peking municipal government has instituted strict rules against the rearing of dogs in urban households. In two years, the government "exterminated" 280,000 dogs. I don't know how many of these went into the pot, but one restaurant in Peking reports that it uses an average of thirty dogs per day. With meat generally in scarce supply and insects good to eat, dogflesh is a welcome addition to the Chinese menu. Traditionally the Chinese raised their dogs in the countryside, letting them scavenge for humanly inedible barnyard refuse and garbage. The ban on Peking dogs suggests that the Chinese are not yet affluent enough to raise dogflesh in city apartments. Unlike their urban counterparts in the West, city dogs in China have few residual utilities to balance out the cost of feeding them. With low crime rates, few markets for stolen goods, and neighborhoods organized for political surveillance, people don't need watchdogs to protect their property. And as for the service dogs render elsewhere as companions, the one thing you get plenty of in a country with one billion people is companions. But more about this aspect of modern-day petdom later on.

First, I'd like to test my explanation of the difference between dog eaters and non–dog eaters with two outstanding studies of the role of dogs in non-Western cultures. One, carried out by Katherine Luomala of the University of Hawaii, concerns the people and dogs of Polynesia; the other, carried out by Joel Savachinsky of Ithaca College, concerns the people and dogs of Arctic North America.

Three major Polynesian groups, the Tahitians, Hawaiians, and

Maori of New Zealand, possessed dogs prior to being visited by European sailing ships. (Dogs were also present on the Tuomotus, but little is known about how they were used.) Virtually all Polynesian dogs ended their lives as part of a human meal. The Polynesians sheltered some of their dogs inside their houses; they kept others in special huts, surrounded by fences, or under a protective tree. They let most dogs scavenge for their food, but they fed others systematically on cooked vegetables supplemented by fish scraps. They force-fed some dogs to fatten them up quickly, holding them down on their backs and stuffing them with fish and vegetable paste. Vegetable-fed dog meat was admired for its delicate flavor. To prepare a dog for cooking, they tied its muzzle shut and strangled it with their bare hands or with pressure applied with a stick; sometimes they strangled it by pressing its head into its chest. The dog was then disemboweled, washed, singed to remove its hairs, basted with blood caught in a coconut shell, and baked in an earth oven. Polynesian dogs were so good to eat that people had to share them with the deities. This was done in Tahiti and the Hawaiian Islands by priests who sacrificed large numbers of dogs on important public occasions. While a small portion of sacrificed dogs went uneaten, the priests generally either consumed the dogflesh themselves or took the less sacred parts home to share with their wives and children. Only the Hawaiian and Tahitian priests and aristocrats were normally allowed to enjoy dogflesh. Women and children were not supposed to eat dog, but after a sacrifice, Tahitian commoners "secretly carried home leftovers to their families." During pregnancy, if a Maori wife craved dog meat, her husband had to provide some.

All of these groups—Hawaiians, Tahitians, and Maori—regarded dogs as prize possessions and standards of value. Hawaiians paid fees, rents, taxes, and tolls with dogs. And to discover who was responsible for the magic that caused a man's death, they had to give tens and sometimes hundreds of dogs to diviners. The Polynesians valued their dogs for hair, skins, teeth, and bones, as well as for flesh. Dogskin cloaks were the Maori chief's most prized heirlooms. Hawaiians adorned themselves with dogteeth anklets and bracelets made from hundreds of matched sets of fangs fastened to netting. Dog fangs were also placed in rows in the open mouths of the wooden images of the Hawaiian gods, while Tahitian warriors trimmed their breastplates with white doghair and made combs and fishhooks out of dog teeth and jawbones.

This preoccupation with dogflesh and the services and by-products of dead rather than living dogs accords well with the outstanding fact about Polynesia's system of food production: they had no domesticated herbivores. Dogs were actually the only domesticated species possessed by the Maori. True, Hawaiians and Tahitians had pigs and chickens in addition to dogs, and given a choice, both Hawaiians and Tahitians preferred to eat pork over dog meat, but their islands were densely populated, and they lacked sufficient low-altitude forests for pigs to forage in, nor did they possess a crop suitable for pig fodder. The energy staple of Hawaiian and Tahitian cuisine was poi, a starchy mass made by cooking, pounding, and kneading the roots of the taro plant. The trouble with taro is that in a raw state its roots contain a high level of oxalic acid, which pigs find unpalatable. So to feed pigs, taro had to be cooked first, making pork as much a luxury as dog meat (whose diet also depended on cooked vegetables). As for chickens, they thrive best on worms and grains or as barnyard scavengers of the leftovers from threshing or milling. But the Polynesians had no grains—no rice, wheat, maize—and chicken was even scarcer than dog meat.

While they were especially useful dead as a source of valuable animal flesh, Polynesian dogs were not especially useful alive as a source of valuable products or services. Most importantly, neither the Hawaiians nor the Tahitians used dogs to hunt with, the reason being that there were no large huntable animals—neither predators nor prey—in their island habitat. While the Maoris did use dogs for hunting, the dogs were not very good at it. Dog prey consisted mostly of kiwis, a flightless bird, and certain species of caterpillars which lived among the leaves of the sweet potato vines. While this shows that Maori dogs were useful in the hunt, from an optimal foraging perspective, the hunting of worms also shows how hard up the Maoris were for animal food— a subject to which we will return in the next chapter. There is also a possibility that Maori dogs were trained to attack strangers and enemies in battle. But as the lone domesticated animal in New Zealand, dogs would have had to render far weightier and more decisive services in order to avoid being considered good to eat.

James King, a companion of Captain Cook, had a chance to observe the Hawaiians before their customs changed. He wrote in 1779 that he could not "recollect one instance in which a dog was made a companion in the manner we do in Europe." King was not prepared to accept the possibility that petness was a variable quality. He regarded the custom of eating dogflesh as "an insuperable bar to their admission into society; and as there are neither beasts of prey on the island, nor objects of chase, it is probable that the social qualities of the dog, its fidelity, attachment and sagacity, will remain unknown to the native." Yet, despite their taste for dogflesh, the Polynesians treated their dogs in a petlike manner. Hawaiian women nursed puppies at their breast just as women in New Guinea nursed piglets. "Dogs sometimes became such pets that their nurses surrendered them with reluctance and great sorrow." But surrender them they did, for the Hawaiians considered dogs fed on human milk to be the tastiest of all. Maori men could also be quite affectionate to their dogs, taking them along on canoe trips and on other extended journeys, and Hawaiians likewise expressed attachment to their dogs by carrying them in their arms or on their backs to social and religious gatherings. Isn't it clear, then, that what prevented the dog from becoming as much of a pet in Polynesia as in Europe was its importance as a source of food and not any lack of capacity or desire on the part of the Polynesians to treat dogs as pets?

Now let me turn to the case of a people who inhabit a much harsher environment and who keep more dogs per capita than the Polynesians, but who avoid dogflesh as assiduously as any modern-day Euro-American dog lovers. Fifty miles north of the Arctic Circle near Colville Lake in Canada's Northwest Territories there is a group of Hare, an Athabaskan-speaking people, who make their living from hunting and trapping. The Hare's aversion to dogflesh accords well with the proposition that if an animal is more valuable alive than dead, it will not be eaten. During the eight months of the arctic winter, the Hare continually travel from one small bush camp to another in pursuit of caribou, moose, marten, mink, fox, beaver, muskrat, ermine, and freshwater fish, including trout, whitefish, and pike. Dogs are not used to stalk and corner certain prey animals such as caribou or fish, but they provide an indispensable means of getting from one hunting area to another. Writes anthropologist Savachinsky:

> Travel between the village and their bush camps, the process of setting, checking, and extending traplines; the hauling of wood, fish, meat, and equipment; the movement to caribou areas; and the periodic trips to the settlement to trade furs and replenish supplies—these were some of the absolutely essential tasks that require the use of a dog team.

During the course of a single winter and spring a hunter—and his dogs—travel as much as twenty-four hundred miles. In this arduous life-style, each family has to have at least one dog team—and each dog team has to have a minimum of four to six adult dogs. The seventy-five members of the Colville Lake community keep 224 dogs, a ratio of three dogs for every person. This means that as much time has to be spent in providing meat and fish for the dogs as for the people. But it is far better to feed dogs and hunt and travel with them than to eat dogs and hunt and travel without them. Unlike Polynesian dogs, the Arctic Indians' dogs help their masters to produce a surplus of meat which both dogs and humans share.

The Hare are not only horrified by the thought of eating dogflesh, they experience enormous difficulty in killing sick, lame, or useless dogs, even though they make their living by routinely killing other animals. The people at Colville Lake are so reluctant to kill their infirm and uselsss dogs that they try to pay others to shoot them. Often these offers are refused. "Me, I just can't look at that dog and shoot it," was the typical response. If visiting Mounties are present, desperate owners may turn the dog loose in the hope that the police will fulfill their duty and shoot it as a stray. When all else fails, an overaged dog may be left to freeze at a hunter's bush camp. But this is a form of "triage," to which in former times humans were also subject when a band as a whole faced the choice of dying along with an ailing campmate or of leaving him or her to perish and moving on to save the group.

As compared with Polynesia, native North Americans in general were not fond of dogflesh. According to one study, out of a sample consisting of 245 native North American cultures only 75 were dog eaters. Yet like the Polynesians, native North Americans lacked domesticated herbivores—they even lacked the pig (although they had one or two partially domesticated fowl, namely turkey and duck). The reason they were less tempted than the Polynesians to dine on dogflesh is that in general they had access to a much broader variety of wild game. Where dogs made a vital contribution to hunting, as among the Hare, there was little reason to eat them. Most of the 75 dog-eating cultures fell into a kind of intermediate category: either the dog was not essential for the hunt or huntable animals were relatively scarce. On the great plains, for example, from southern Canada to Texas, buffalo were the most important food source. Dogs are of little help in locating or killing such large animals, but the dog was not entirely useless. Prior to the spread of the European horse, dogs rendered a service in helping women haul tipis and other possessions from camp to camp. The plains Indians therefore had mixed feelings about eating dogs, and many of them regarded dogflesh primarily as a food that they would consume only during a famine or other emergency. Dog meat had greater appeal for the Indians of central California, who did not have access to large game and whose diets consisted mainly of seeds and acorns with a liberal sprinkling of lizards, rabbits, and insects. More avid consumers of dogflesh were to be found among groups which depended upon maize and other domesticated plants rather than on hunting. Twelve out of 75 North American dog-eating cultures deliberately raised or fattened dogs for eating. Michael Carroll of the University of Western Ontario has shown that almost all North American dog meat enthusiasts were either primarily agriculturalists or primarily gatherers of wild plants.

By far the greatest center of dog meat eating in North America and perhaps in the world was to be found in pre-Columbian Mexico precisely where the conditions which inhibited dog eating among the Hare were completely reversed. In central Mexico, for example, as in Polynesia, large huntable land animals were virtually nonexistent. While the Mexicans did not need dogs for hunting, they sorely needed them for meat since, like other native North Americans, the only domesticated animals they possessed were dogs and turkeys. Can it be a mere coincidence that in addition to being famous for dog meat eating, pre-Columbian Mexico is even more famous for a well-developed taste for human flesh? (That's what the next chapter is about.)

In a moment I shall attend to the question of the residual utilities which render dogs and cats and other pets unfit for the cuisines of modern industrial societies. But first let me dispose of a tenacious myth about an allegedly useless canine pet that is kept by the native peoples of Australia. The dingo (*Canis antarticus*) is a semiwild species of dog that has intrigued me ever since Robert Lowie cited it as another one of his prime examples of "capricious irrationality." In Lowie's words: "The Australian kept his dog, the dingo, without training it to catch game or render any service whatsoever." Many observers concur that the Australian Aborigines neither ate the dingoes nor used them to hunt or kill game. The Aborigines were extremely fond of their dingoes. Native women were as keen to nurse dingo pups as Hawaiian women were to nurse the pups of Polynesian dogs. Until they reached maturity, dingoes were treated much like children. The Aborigines rubbed the same mixture of fat and red ochre on them that they rubbed on humans, and with the same purpose—to make their bodies strong and resistant to disease. They gave each a name, kissed them on the muzzle, murmured endearments to them, and carried them about to "protect their tender paws from prickles and burrs." But after all this tender loving care there would come a time when the dingoes felt an urge to depart from human company. They wandered off into the bush, never to return. And the Aborigines never tried to stop them. In fact older dingoes were unwanted and considered a nuisance around camp. People no longer fondled them nor fed them on tidbits, and their departure was not lamented in the least. I should also point out that the Aborigines kept infants of other animal species around camp as children's playthings in the usual manner of hunter-gatherer societies, but unlike dingoes these other "pets" quickly ended up in the cooking fire. Dingoes were also in fact eaten. True, they were not a mainstay of the Aborigines' diet, but virtually all Aborigines ate dingoes in times of scarcity. And at least some groups were as likely to eat dingo as any other meat available. One scientific report written early in this century listed dingoes under the heading "native foods" and stated that they "are keenly hunted and eaten; they are usually speared at a waterhole." A late nineteenth-century report states "whilst they domesticate the dingo and make a pet of it, they also eat it, about which there can be no doubt." For reasons that are about to become clear, the Aborigines preferred not to eat the dingoes that were their pets. But in times of scarcity, they would indeed eat their canine campmates, down to the puppies if things got bad enough.

The failure to hunt with the aid of dingoes seems particularly mystifying, in view of the importance of game animals in the Aborigines' diet. Certainly there was no dearth of small- and medium-sized species toward whose capture dogs can make an important contribution. The proof of the presence of species that dogs could hunt is that upon the introduction of European hunting breeds, the Aborigines enthusiastically adopted various hybrid crosses between dingoes and European dogs for hunting purposes. They used dingoes crossed with greyhounds, wolfhounds, or elkhounds to hunt several kinds of kangeroo. And for hunting smaller game, they used hybrids that were a cross between dingoes and corgis.

Now while it is true that the Aborigines did not use dingoes to hunt the way they used European hunting dogs, they did use them to hunt in another way. As feral dingoes pursued their own animal quarry in the bush, the Aborigines hastened after them, cued on by the loud barking. Arriving on the scene just after the dingo had made its kill, the hunters easily drove it off and appropriated the kill for themselves.

The dingo also rendered service as a sentinel. In times past the Aborigines were quite warlike and much given to ambushes, raids, and sneak attacks carried out by enemy shamans. Hidden in the bushes, these shamans targeted their victims with pointed bones that could penetrate the body and destroy its soul like a primitive death ray. Today the Aborigines no longer practice warfare, yet one of the main reasons they give for keeping a large number of dogs around their camps is that their violent barking warns of the approach of strangers and of invisible harmful spirits. The Aborigines must have valued the dingoes as sentinels even more in the past when warfare was still practiced.

Dingoes rendered another service by helping to keep the Aborigines warm at night. Like other arid regions, the interior of Australia is hot during the day and cold at night. The Aborigines slept huddled together with all the dingoes they could find—one explorer counted two women and fourteen dingoes under a single blanket. Body heat may also have figured in the Aborigines' penchant for carrying dingoes from place to place. Women frequently wore them wrapped around the waist; forepaws and nose grasped in one hand, hind legs and tail in the other, as if the animals were portable heating pads.

Some additional information will help lay the myth of the useless dingo to rest once and for all. We must keep in mind that the dingo was not a fully domesticated creature. As I mentioned, the Aborigines were very fond of dingo puppies and juveniles, but as the animals got older the Aborigines stopped feeding them.

At mealtime, adult dingoes had to keep their distance, and many a hapless dingo was probably forced to subsist almost entirely on human feces. Since dingoes sooner or later departed from human company, unlike fully domesticated dogs, the dingoes did not reproduce while living with humans. How then did the Aborigines get their canine campmates? Not by breeding them but by hunting them. "A mother dog would be tracked to her den and speared [and eaten] during the pupping season, and some of her puppies would be taken back to camp to become temporary pets."

All of these bits and pieces of dingo lore fit together to form a highly practical system of human-animal relationships during what is best regarded as an incipient or rudimentary phase of canine domestication. The dingo is brought as a puppy into protective human custody, serves for a while as body warmer, sentinel, companion, and emergency meat supply, and then is let loose to reproduce in the wild, thereby stocking the habitat with a game animal that is particularly easy for humans to capture and eat (if its barking does not lead them to larger game). The fact that the Aborigines quickly developed an entirely different system of rearing and using dogs when they obtained European hunting breeds suggests that the limitations of the previous system were dictated by genetically determined constraints on the extent to which the dingo could be used as a fully domesticated species, not by the stupidity or sentimentality of the Aborigines. Unlike the presumed ancestors of the common dog, the dingo hunts alone or in pairs rather than in packs. This characteristic probably explains the dingo's regular return to the wild state. Not adapted to hunting cooperatively in adulthood, dingoes pass from a higher to lower intensity of social interaction as they mature. Unable to train and trust them when they became full grown, the Aborigines could not use dingoes as other human groups used fully domesticated dogs. But this is a far cry from saying that they kept dingoes as completely useless pets.

Although the evidence I have presented strongly suggests that the residual utility of a pet determines whether it will be eaten or not, this finding is certain to be hotly contested by modern-day pet owners. Most Americans believe that the essential condition of petdom is uselessness, not utility. Even the dictionary says so: "*pet*: A domesticated animal kept for pleasure rather than utility." But there is obviously something seriously wrong with this definition, isn't there? (I am not referring to the strange misconception that pet store guppies and parakeets are domesticated animals.) Since when are pleasure and utility opposites? Does a Hindu cow which gives copious quantities of useful milk give less pleasure to its owner than a dry and barren cow? Or, to return to the Hare and their wonderfully useful sled dogs, if a team exhibits great stamina and intelligence, does it diminish its owner's pleasure? On the contrary, the faster and farther a team of sled dogs can go, the more its owners find pleasure in them, not only in the furs and meat they help provide, but in simply looking at them and boasting to others about how good they are.

The denial of useful functions to pets is totally at odds with the evolutionary history of the most popular pet species. Dogs, cats, and horses would not have been domesticated were it not for the services they rendered in relation to hunting, protection of property, rodent control, transportation, and warfare. In addition to these more obvious utilities, pets have also rendered a number of other services, many of which still must be considered as tangible benefits to be weighed against the costs of modern-day pet keeping.

The idea that pets are useless stems from the animal-keeping customs of aristocratic classes. Imperial courts of the ancient world from China to Rome maintained zoological gardens where exotic birds and animals were put on display as a source of amusement and as symbols of wealth and power. Egyptian royalty was partial to cats, especially cheetahs, while Roman emperors posted pet lions outside their bedroom chambers. To regard these animals as useless is to ignore the great value of imperial pomp and luxury for displaying and validating power and authority. Commoners could not fail to be impressed by the ability of their rulers to keep man-eating lions and tigers as pets, especially since these animals were fed on disobedient slaves and prisoners of war. Exotic animals along with gold and jewels also served as instruments of foreign relations. They were among the most precious gifts exchanged between potentates seeking to form alliances. In a closely related practice, aristocratic Egyptian women wore live snakes around their necks just as modern women of wealth (or pretenders to wealth) wear dead minks around their shoulders. During medieval times in Europe, all sorts of animals were taken into royal households and pampered by women while their husbands collected and pampered human dwarfs and freaks. In the seventeenth century fashionable ladies carried little dogs in their bosoms, sat with them at the dinner table, and fed them on sweets. But ordinary people could not afford to keep pets that were not also useful for protection, hunting, herding, or catching rats. With the rise of mercantile or capitalist classes, keeping pampered pets therefore became an important means of showing that one was no longer a commoner. Yet keeping pets for such a purpose is scarcely a useless activity since it is through prestigious consumption that one gets to be received into affluent and powerful circles. With increased democratization of income, the keeping of expensive pets has ceased to be as valuable for social contacts as it once was, although there are still many advantages awaiting those who have gained admission to their local "horse and doggy set."

From very early times to the present, pets have also been useful as entertainers. Modern-day household pets can't match the entertainment value of lions attacking elephants (or people) in the Roman circus, but cats chasing imaginary mice or dogs retrieving bouncing balls can be at least as amusing as the late-night movie, not to mention the more kinky opportunities afforded those whose taste in pets runs toward carnivorous South American fish or lizards that won't eat anything but live crickets.

A rather thin line has always separated the amusement of pet keepers from their edification. Anthropologists report that people who depend on hunting for animal food invariably keep a number of young wild animals around the camp or village as pets. In

addition to obtaining decorative hair or feathers from these animals, hunters also probably acquire a considerable amount of
information about animal physiology and behavior—information
that is useful in tracking and killing the adults of the species.
This educational function lingers on as a motive for keeping pets
in modern societies, where parents often explain that pets are
needed to familiarize their children with copulation, pregnancy,
birthing, nursing, and death, given the restricted opportunities
for urban children to observe human examples of these "facts of
life."

Finally there is a connection between the use of pets for amusement and their use for sport. When hunting ceased to be primarily
a means of subsistence, it retained its utility as an elite sport in
which dogs and horses continued to play a valuable role. With
democratization, elite aspects of hunting are less prominent today, but some of its former importance as a subsistence activity
has been restored. Furthermore, as modern sports, both hunting
and riding have acquired a new health-care function because of
the alternative they offer to sedentary urban life-styles.

But I have yet to come to the two most important useful functions of modern-day pets. When a random sample of cat and dog
owners in a Minnesota suburb were asked to check off a list of
"advantages" of pet owning, the most commonly selected alternatives were in rank order: (1) companionship, 75 percent; (2)
love and affection, 67 percent; (3) pleasure, 58 percent; (4) protection, 30 percent; and (5) beauty, 20 percent. Some of the other
perceived advantages were: educational value of cats and dogs
for children (11 percent) and use for sports (5 percent). Only 1
percent of respondents indicated that they thought there were
no advantages to owning a cat or a dog. Item 1, "companionship,"
and item 2, "love and affection," refer essentially to the same
function; item 3, "pleasure," to repeat my previous objections
about the opposition between pleasure and utility, is not an independent function but a consequence of all the other items;
while 5, "beauty," refers to a quality which is too vague to be
distinguished from "pleasure." This leaves "companionship" and

"protection" far in the lead over the other useful functions of dogs and cats. Let me consider "protection" first.

The Minnesota study was undoubtedly biased in the direction of underestimating the protection utility of dogs, since it lumped cat owners and dog owners together and was carried out in a low-crime suburban setting. A study of dog owners excluding cat owners in Melbourne, Australia, obtained substantially different results: 90 percent of the respondents felt that their dogs gave them companionship while 75 percent felt a need to be physically protected by a dog. A study carried out in Gothenburg, Sweden, gave similar results: 66 percent of respondents reported feeling a need to be physically protected by their dogs. Dogs deter crimes against persons and property by acting as sentinels and by barking and frightening off would-be burglars and other attackers. This is a service which modern homeowners and apartment dwellers find particularly useful because they have valuable movable possessions, must leave their houses and apartments unattended for many hours each day, and are frequently the sole permanent occupant of the premises.

According to *Money* magazine, the purchase price of a medium-sized dog plus initial shelter, equipment, and veterinary expense is about $365. If we amortize this sum over a ten-year life span and add $348 yearly for feeding, grooming, occasional veterinary care, and boarding, such a dog costs its owner about $385 in cash per year. About a half hour a day is needed for grooming, walking, and feeding. I shall not assign a monetary cost to this factor since it usually does not involve any cash outlays, nor does it involve "foregone income"—income which would be earned if the dog owner did not use the time for dog care. Besides, the exercise is good for them. I cannot say how many crimes a dog deters during its lifetime, but it would only have to scare off one or two burglars in ten years to be worth the investment of $3,850. Over the same period $3,850 spent on gates, fences, latches, locks, keys, bolts, electronic sensors, light fixtures, flood lamps, and electricity also would not be unusual, and no one can say exactly how many crimes these devices actually deter either (computerized sentry systems alone cost about $1,750 plus repairs and maintenance).

Even without adding in the value of the other services rendered, one can see that dogs remain highly useful in a practical sense. Cats and most other pets, however, have no crime-deterrent value, and the explanation of their status hinges on assigning a practical value to "companionship." This is not difficult.

The practical value of companionship is rooted in human nature. Numerous experiments have shown that nonhuman primates are intensely social creatures born with a need to associate with each other in order to mature. Monkeys deprived of companionship develop severe life-threatening neuroses. They sit in their cages, stare fixedly into space, circle in a repetitive stereotyped manner, clasp their heads in their hands and arms, and rock back and forth for long periods of time. While we do not have experimental evidence about humans reared in isolation, behavioral scientists generally agree that humans are also born with an innate need for close, supportive, and loving relationships.

The companion value of all kinds of pets provides the key to their ever-growing popularity in urban industrial societies. Companionship is so central to their use in such societies that some professional animal caretakers have stopped calling pets "pets" and have taken to calling them "companion animals" instead. For example, the clinic at the small animal hospital of the University of Pennsylvania's School of Veterinary Medicine calls itself the Companion Animal Clinic. Some animal rights activists advocate dropping the term *pet*. Michael Fox of the Humane Society, for example, writes: "I hope that in the future, the term 'pet' will fall from general usage and be replaced by 'companion animal' which is kept not by a 'master' but by a 'human guardian.' "

Modern societies have solved many problems related to human needs such as the need for shelter, for an adequate food supply, and the prevention and cure of disease, but they have failed miserably by not providing high-quality, mutually supportive companionship. Band and village peoples used to live (some still do) in large families surrounded by neighbors—who not only knew each other but who were related by ties of descent and marriage. Companionship was not an urgent problem for them. While animals may have provided companionship in some degree, the value of this service could not have been as great as it is today.

The specific conditions responsible for making companionship the salient utility of contemporary petdom are closely related to the conditions which make dogs so useful in the deterrence of crime. People live apart, isolated from friends and family, in one- or two-person households, lacking friendly neighbors, in communities where they have no roots, and which are in any event communities in a geographical but not an interactive sense. Increasingly, young people postpone marriage or don't get married at all. When they get married, they have one or two children, and many couples have none. Divorce rates continue to rise, and single-parent households are increasing faster than any other kind. Meanwhile, people are living longer, and the "empty nest" syndrome now occurs earlier, enduring for most of a lifetime. Equally important is the quality of relationships. Competition for grades, college admissions, jobs, promotions, and business deals undermines trust and confidence. As a victim of a computer programming fraud explained to the *Wall Street Journal*: "If you're in business you don't trust anybody. The ones you trust are the ones who'll get ya." Except for a fortunate few, most people have jobs which depend on obeying and being respectful toward bosses, managers, executives, foremen, and other "superiors," and this inevitably results in episodes of humiliation, wounded pride or self-doubt.

Companion animals partially compensate for all of these unsatisfactory human relationships. The overriding utility of pets in contemporary society is that they can substitute for people in satisfying our specific cultural lack of warm, supportive, and loving relationships. Neither "pet" nor "companion animal" objectively conveys the centrality of this function. We would not be so quick to think that the essence of petdom is uselessness if we identified today's pets for what most of them really are: proxy humans. It is because they are proxy humans that pets help us to overcome the anonymity and lack of social community engendered by big-city life. As proxy humans, they can "stir the dead air" of empty apartments, and give countless single people someone to go home to. It is because they are proxy humans that they can stand in for absent or unsatisfactory husbands or wives or children, fill the empty nest, and ease the burden of loneliness which old age so often brings in hyperindustrial cultures. And they can do all this without imposing the suspicions and penalties characteristic of real humans caught up in highly competitive, stratified, and exploitative relationships.

One might suppose that to substitute for humans, pets would have to communicate like humans. Alas, they cannot really carry on a conversation. But as Freudian analysts and Catholic priests have long recognized, levels of frustration and anxiety can be lowered merely by having someone listen or even appear to be listening to you. Pets make excellent substitutes for such listeners. The Companion Animal Clinic at the University of Pennsylvania found that 98 percent of pet owners talked to their animals, 80 percent talked to them "as a person," not "as an animal," and 28 percent confided in their pets and talked about events of the day. A nonrandom survey by *Psychology Today* magazine found that 99 percent of pet owners talked to their pets, using baby talk or confiding in them. I wish that I could cite comparative data from societies that are less troubled by the problem of companionship to see if they also talk to pets as persons. The horse nomads of Asia sang *about* mares in their love songs, and the Nuer sang songs of praise *about* cattle, but I doubt that they talked *to* horses and cattle as they talked to people about the events of the day. Why should they when they were always surrounded by real human listeners?

Psychiatrists, veterinarians, and social workers are just beginning to realize the implications of the fact that in the United States and similar societies, pets can serve as proxy humans. They are rapidly creating a whole industry of pet-assisted therapies based on the principle that animals can provide supportive companionship for people who are deprived of security, warmth, and love in their experiences with real humans. They are bringing pets into psychiatric wards and finding that patients who will not talk to people will talk to dogs, cats, and fish, and that once this breakthrough is achieved, patients become more responsive to their doctors and eventually talk to them, too. Pet-assisted therapies are also making their mark in nursing and retirement homes where loneliness, depression, boredom, and withdrawal are acute problems. After acquiring a pet, nursing home residents interact more with staff and other patients. Outpatients with various kinds of health problems report that pets help them to laugh, cope with loneliness, and become more active physically. Pets are also being introduced into prisons in order to improve morale and to stop the inmates from fighting with each other.

Experimental evidence indicates that when people pet their pets, heart rate and blood pressure readings of both humans and animals decline. Just staring at fish in a home aquarium lowers blood pressure to a clinically significant extent. Other studies show that where victims of heart attack are divided into two groups—those who have pets at home and those who don't—only 72 percent of the non–pet owners were alive one year after hospitalization as compared with 96 percent of the pet owners. Naturally, other variables played a role in promoting survivorship, but owning a pet accounted for more of the difference than any other factor.

Supposedly useless American pets, like supposedly useless Hindu cows and Australian dingoes, turn out on closer inspection to be quite a bargain. They don't make agriculture possible, but they make urban industrial society a lot more livable. As proxy humans, one or two pets can take the place of a whole army of human service workers. They can entertain us like stand-up comedians, educate us like biology teachers, exercise us like gym coaches, relax us like wives or husbands, love us like children, listen to us like psychiatrists, confess us like priests, and heal us like physicians. And all for a few hundred dollars a year. But we must not lose sight of the other side of the equation. Dogs, cats, horses, rats, mice, hamsters, goldfish, and, yes, even giant Madagascar hissing cockroaches all have one thing in common: compared with cows, pigs, and chickens, they are highly inefficient sources of animal food. In optimal foraging theory terms, it is the abundance of the higher-ranking ruminant species that knocks them off our optimal diet, not the fact that they are pets.

And this brings us to an intriguing question. If proxy humans are good or bad to eat depending on the balance between their residual utility and the relative abundance of more efficient converters of plants to animal foods, what about *real* humans? Do the principles that apply to the flesh of dogs, cats, dingoes, and other pets apply to the eating of human flesh as well?

CHAPTER TEN

PEOPLE EATING

THE PUZZLE of cannibalism concerns the socially sanctioned consumption of human flesh when other foods are available. I am not going to explain the practice of people eating when the only food available is human flesh. That kind of people eating occurs the world over from time to time regardless of whether the eaters and the eaten come from societies that approve or disapprove of the practice. There is no puzzle as to why they do it. Sailors adrift in lifeboats, travelers snowbound in alpine passes, and people trapped in besieged cities sometimes must eat each other's corpses or die of starvation. Our puzzle is not concerned with such emergencies but with people eating each other when they have access to alternative sources of nourishment.

In order to explain the preference for or against nonemergency consumption of human flesh, a further distinction must be made. One must recognize that, as in every puzzling foodway, production precedes consumption. Before we can understand why some cultures prefer and others detest human flesh, we must confront the question of how people eaters supply themselves with their human repast. Basically, there are just two ways to obtain an edible corpse; either the eaters forcibly hunt, capture, and kill the eaten, or the eaters peacefully acquire the body of a relative

who has died a natural death. Peaceful acquisition and consumption of bodies or parts of bodies is an aspect of mourning
rituals; the acquisition of bodies through violent means is an
aspect of warfare. These two modes of cannibal production have
entirely different sets of costs and benefits and hence cannot be
subsumed under a single explanatory theory. (Note that I have
ruled out the peaceful acquisition of the bodies of strangers through
purchase. Corpses are seldom for sale. Diego Rivera's claim that
he thrived on cadavers bought from the Mexico City morgue
when he was an anatomy student should probably be taken with
a grain of salt—the great painter was much given to what his
biographer called "myth making.")

Although the mortuary customs of many band and village societies called for the consumption of portions of the remains of
dead relatives, only the ashes, carbonized flesh, or ground-up
bones of the deceased were generally ingested. These vestiges
were not a significant source of proteins or calories (although in
tropical habitats ashes and bones could have been an important
means of recycling scarce minerals). Consumption of the ashes
and bones of a deceased loved one was a logical extension of
cremation. After the body of the deceased had been consumed
by the flames, the ashes were often collected and kept in containers to be finally disposed of by ingesting them—usually mixed
in a beverage (which seems to be a lot tidier than scattering them
in the Ganges or, as recently proposed, rocketing them into outer
space). Another common mode of disposing of the dead was to
bury the corpse and wait for the flesh to be cleaned off (which
would not take more than a few days in tropical soils). Some or
all of the bones would then be exhumed with loving care
and reburied inside the family house or put in baskets and
hung from the rafters. As a final step the bones would then
be pulverized, mixed with a beverage, and mournfully
consumed.

Here is an anthropologist's eyewitness description of mortuary
cannibalism among the Guiaca, a village people of the upper
Orinoco River in South America:

We ourselves have observed several instances of the cremation of the deceased in the village plaza on the day of his
death, the careful collection of the half-carbonized bones
from the ashes, and the grinding of these bones in a wooden
mortar. The resulting powder was poured into little cala-
bashes and given to the dead person's closest relatives who
kept them near the roof of their hut. On ceremonial occasions
. . . the relatives would put some of this powder into a large
calabash half full of plantain soup and drink the mixture
accompanied by lamentations. The family was very careful
not to spill any of it. . . .

Travelers, missionaries, and scientists report that Amazonian groups
practiced a number of interesting variations on this basic theme.
The Craquieto, for example, roasted a dead chief over a slow fire
until the corpse was entirely dry, wrapped the mummified remains in a fresh new hammock, and hung it in the chief's abandoned hut. After several years the relatives held a big feast,
burned the mummy, and drank the ashes mixed with *chicha*, a
fermented beverage made from maize. Several cultures buried
their corpses, exhumed them after a year, and drank the powder
made from the burnt bones with *chicha* or some other fermented
beverage. Some groups waited as long as fifteen years before
exhuming the bones and grinding them up. Some groups ate the
ashes. The Cunibo burned only the hair of a dead child and
swallowed the ashes with food or fish broth. Although reports of
people consuming roasted portions of the flesh of the deceased
also exist, they are far less common than the reports of the consumption of ashes or ground-up bones and lack authentic details
concerning the degree of carbonization of the flesh.

I believe that this indifference to the potential food value of
peacefully acquired corpses (as opposed to bodies violently acquired through warfare) partially reflects the inefficient and health-
threatening nature of such food resources; inefficient because
most natural deaths are preceded by a considerable weight loss
leaving too little flesh to justify the expense of cooking the corpse;
and health-threatening because of the likelihood that the de-

ceased succumbed to or was weakened by a communicable disease. (In contrast, individuals killed or captured through warfare are likely to have been well nourished and in good health before meeting their fate. In this regard, Diego Rivera's account has an air of authenticity. He claims that he and his companions only ate the bodies of persons who had died of violence—"who had been freshly killed and were not diseased or senile.") The burial and carbonization of bodies of the dead reflect, it seems to me, a cultural recognition through trial and error of the physical dangers of disposing of the dead by eating them or by keeping their decomposing remains near the living. This cannot be the whole explanation, since, as I have argued with respect to insects, pork, and dead cows and horses, vigorous cooking greatly reduces their health-threatening qualities. There would be social danger as well. Cannibalism practiced on the whole fresh corpse of a relative might easily fan the flames of suspicion and mutual mistrust. In fact or fancy there would be members of the local group who seemed all too eager to make a meal of the sick and dying. (Band and village peoples—in fact almost all premodern groups—lack a concept of natural death and attribute the death of a relative to malevolent forces and witchcraft.) Carbonization of the fresh body, or burial, reduces the suspicions that are at peak level just after the loved one has died at the same time that it reduces the exposure to disease. In situations in which significant nourishment was obtained from a relative's corpse, the eaters were probably under considerable stress from protein-calorie malnutrition so that the benefits of eating the body without carbonizing it or leaving it buried until the bones were clean outweighed the risks of disease or accusations of sorcery.

This at least appears to be the explanation for corpse eating by relatives among the Foré of highland New Guinea. D. Carleton Gajdusek received the Nobel Prize in medicine in 1976 for relating the Foré's practice of eating their relatives to a disease caused by a "slow virus"—a type of pathogen previously unknown but since linked to many other diseases, including cancer. As among other New Guinea highlanders, Foré mortuary rituals obliged female relatives of the deceased to bury the corpse in a shallow grave. Traditionally, after an interval of unknown duration, the women exhumed the bones and cleaned them but did not eat any of the flesh. During the 1920s the women changed this practice, possibly to compensate for a decline in the rations of meat they were able to obtain from their menfolk. They exhumed the corpse after only two or three days and began to eat the entire body cut from the bones and cooked in bamboo cylinders along with fern leaves and other greens. (Because of the high altitude at which the Foré live, boiling was not an effective defense against contaminated food.) Three decades later the Foré began to make headlines as the victims of a previously unknown fatal "laughing disease," called "kuru." In the advanced stages of kuru the victims—mostly women—lost control of their facial muscles, creating the impression that they were laughing themselves to death. The research for which Gajdusek received the Nobel Prize revealed that kuru was caused by a "slow virus" probably transmitted as a consequence of the Foré's unusual mortuary rituals—the handling of the partially decomposed corpse and the consumption of its flesh.

Since neither Gajdusek nor other anthropologists who have lived with the Foré actually witnessed the eating of human flesh, the suggestion has been made that the virus was spread merely by contact with the corpse rather than by consumption of infected morsels. Yet Foré women themselves freely told several researchers that they had previously engaged in mortuary cannibalism. Their decision to consume the corpse's ripe flesh may very well have had a nutritional motivation. Although no study of the diet of the Foré at the time they adopted mortuary cannibalism was ever made, later studies show that the usual pattern of unequal distribution of animal foods among men and women probably prevailed. In Gajdusek's time, after the suppression of cannibalism, daily consumption of protein by females was only 56 percent of recommended allowances, and virtually all of it was of plant origin. As among many South American groups, men appropriated the flesh of large animals for themselves, leaving frogs, small game, and insects for the women and children. And as expected, the Foré have a very high level of witchcraft accusations against women. Presumably, similar adverse effects upon health and social cohesion often accompanied attempts by other cultures to consume the bodies of relatives and neighbors in conjunction with mortuary rituals, helping to limit the popularity of such practices. Let me turn now to the explanation of the more common of the nutritionally significant forms of people eating, namely, cannibalism practiced on forcibly acquired bodies.

Powerful sanctions everywhere prevent adult members of primary groups from killing and eating each other. In fact the taboo against killing and eating one's relatives is the most fundamental precondition if people are to live together and cooperate on a daily basis. This taboo automatically means that if cannibalism is to be practiced on forcibly acquired bodies, such bodies must be obtained from socially distant individuals—from strangers or from outright enemies. In other words, they can only be acquired as a result of some variety of armed conflict. Since warfare aptly characterizes most of the armed conflict leading to the forcible acquisition of human bodies, I shall refer to this variety of cannibalism as "warfare cannibalism."

We owe one of the earliest and most complete eyewitness accounts of warfare cannibalism to Hans Staden, a shipwrecked German naval gunner who was taken captive by the Tupinamba Indians of Brazil. Staden spent nine months in 1554 in a Tupinamba village before escaping and making his way back to Europe. What Staden saw with his own eyes was the ritual torture of prisoners of war, their dismemberment, and the cooking, distribution, and consumption of their flesh. Staden does not specify exactly how many cannibal incidents he witnessed, but he does describe three specific occasions on which he watched people being cooked and eaten, adding up to a total of at least sixteen victims. Here is his general description of the fate of Tupinamba prisoners of war:

When they first bring home a captive the women and children set upon him and beat him. Then they decorate him with grey feathers and shave off his eyebrows, and dance around him, having first bound him securely so that he cannot escape. They give him a woman who attends to him and has intercourse with him. . . .

They feed the prisoner well and keep him for a time while they prepare the pots which are to contain their drink. . . . When all is ready they fix the day of his death and invite the savages from the neighbouring villages to be present. The drinking vessels are filled a few days in advance, and before the women make the drink, they bring forth the prisoner once or twice to the place where he is to die and dance around him.

When the guests have assembled, the chief of the huts bids them welcome and desires that they shall help them to eat their enemy. . . . they paint the face of the victim, the women singing while another woman paints, and when they begin to drink they take their captive with them and talk to him while he drinks with them. After the drinking bout is over they rest the next day and build a hut on the place of execution, in which the prisoner spends the night under close guard. Then, a good while before daybreak on the day following, they commence to dance and sing before the club [that the executioner will use], and so they continue until day breaks. After this they take the prisoner from his hut. . . . they place stones beside him which he throws at the women, who run about mocking him and boasting that they will eat him. These women are painted, and are ready to take his four quarters when he is cut up, and run with them around the huts.

Then they make a fire about two paces from the prisoner which he has to tend. After this a woman brings the club . . . shrieking with joy, and running to and fro before the prisoner so that he may see it. Then a man takes the club and standing before the prisoner he shows it to him. Meanwhile he who is going to do the deed withdraws with fourteen or fifteen others, and they all paint their bodies grey with ashes. Then the slayer returns with his companions, and the

man who holds the club before the prisoner hands it to the
slayer. At this stage the [headman] approaches, and taking
the club he thrusts it once between the slayer's legs which
is a sign of great honour. Then the slayer seizes it and thus
addresses the victim: "I am he that will kill you, since you
and yours have slain and eaten many of my friends." To
which the prisoner replies: "When I am dead I shall still
have many to avenge my death." Then the slayer strikes
from behind and beats out his brains.

The women seize the body at once and carry it to the fire
where they scrape off the skin, making the flesh quite white,
and stopping up the fundament with a piece of wood so that
nothing may be lost. Then a man cuts up the body, removing
the legs above the knee and the arms at the trunk, where-
upon the four women seize the four limbs and run with them
around the huts, making a joyful cry. After this they divide
the trunk among themselves and devour everything that can
be eaten.

When this is finished they all depart, each one carrying
a piece with him. The slayer takes a fresh name. . . . He
must lie all that day in his hammock, but they give him a
small bow and an arrow so that he can amuse himself by
shooting into wax, lest his arm should become feeble from
the shock of the death blow. I was present and have seen
all this with my own eyes.

Before I try to explain the cost/benefit basis of Tupinamba
people eating and of warfare cannibalism in general, let me confront the issue of whether or not Staden's description is truthful.
In his popular book, *The Man-Eating Myth*, anthropologist William Arens claims that Staden's account, like all other accounts
of cannibalism (except for emergency cannibalism) is a tall tale.
Arens advances three arguments to discredit Staden's account.
Staden could not have translated verbatim the words of his Tupinamba captors right from the first day of his captivity because
he didn't speak Tupi-Guarani, the native language; Staden re-
constructed cannibal events in impossibly precise detail nine years
after they allegedly took place; and Staden relied on John Dryan-

der, a German doctor, to help him fake the manuscript. Another anthropologist, Donald Forsyth, has refuted these claims. Staden was in fact a member of an expedition led by the Spanish captain Diego de Sanabria, which set sail from Seville in the spring of 1549. Two of the expedition's three ships made it to a Brazilian harbor near modern-day Florianópolis. The larger of the two vessels sank in the harbor. For two years Staden and his ship-wrecked companions kept themselves alive by trading salvaged items from their ships with Tupi-Guarani–speaking villagers in exchange for food. When the salvaged items were used up, the survivors split into two groups. Staden's group took the small ship north along the coast. After another shipwreck, Staden and his companions reached the Portuguese settlement of São Vicente—the colonial forerunner of the modern-day port of Santos—in January 1553. For the next year Staden worked as a gunner for the Portuguese and was in close contact with at least one Tupi-Guarani–speaking native whom he described as his "slave" and who accompanied Staden on hunting expeditions. Staden was also well acquainted with other Tupi-Guarani–speaking residents of the Portuguese settlement.

In January 1554 a Tupinamba raiding party captured Staden and brought him back to their village. Staden spent the next nine months in constant fear of being killed and eaten. In September 1554 he eluded his captors, made his way to the coast, and was rescued by a French ship. The ship docked in Honfleur, Normandy, on or about 20 February 1555. On reaching his native Marburg, Germany, Staden quickly sought the help of Dr. John Dryander, a distinguished scholar and friend of Staden's family. Staden's motive in going to Dryander is clear from what Dryander says in the introduction to Staden's book. Staden wanted someone of high repute to serve as a character witness and to vouch for his account:

I have known [Staden's] father for upwards of fifty years, for he and I were born and taught in the same town, namely Wetter. Both in his home and in Hombert in Hesse where he now lives, he [i.e. the father] is looked upon as an upright, pious, and worthy man not unversed in the arts. . . . I believe that Hans Staden has faithfully reported his history and adventures from his own experience and not from the account of others, that he has no intent to deceive and that he desires no reward or worldly renown, but only the glory of God, in humble praise and faithfulness for his escape.

Staden's book was finished at the latest in December 1556, less than two years after his return to Europe and less than three years after the date of his capture, although it was not actually published until early 1557. Forsyth has checked all of the principal facts, dates, and names by cross-reference to specific individuals mentioned by Staden as being at certain places and specified dates. From this resume it is clear that Staden spoke Spanish and Portuguese as well as German and had ample opportunity during the five years (1549 to 1554) which *preceded* his capture, to have learned Tupi-Guarani, that he did not delay nine years in writing down his experiences but two at the most; and that he asked for and received Dryander's help not to invent and embellish a tall tale, but to assure the reader that he was a pious and honest man.

Other sixteenth-century accounts independently corroborate the fundamental pattern of warfare cannibalism as practiced by the Tupinamba. Jesuit missionaries to Brazil wrote hundreds of pages of letters and reports about the practice. Most of these Jesuits spent years traveling among and visiting Tupinamba villages and almost all of them had learned to speak Tupi-Guarani. Father José de Anchieta, for example, who mastered Tupi-Guarani sufficiently to compose the first grammar of that language, had this to say about cannibalism in 1554:

If they capture four or five of their enemies, they [immediately] return [to their village] to eat them at a great feast . . . such that not even the [prisoners'] nails are lost. They are proud all their lives because of this singular victory. Even the prisoners feel that they are being treated in a noble and excellent manner, asking for a glorious death, as they see it,

for they say that only cowards and weaklings die and are
buried and go to hold up the weight of the earth, which they
believe to be extremely heavy.

Anchieta was no armchair ethnographer. He not only obtained
information from talking with the Tupinamba but from traveling
among and living in their villages where he recorded specific
events, as in his account of the slaughter on 26 June 1553 of an
enemy "slave."

But in the afternoon when they were all full of wine, they
came to the house where we were lodging and wanted to
take the slave to kill [him]. . . . Like wolves the Indians
pulled at him [the slave] with great fury; finally they took
him outside and broke [open] his head, and together with
him they killed another one of their enemies, whom they
soon tore into pieces with great rejoicing, especially the
women, who went around singing and dancing, some [of the
women] pierced the cut off members [of the body] with sharp
sticks, others smeared their hands with [the victim's] fat and
went about smearing [the fat on] the faces and mouths of
others, and it was such that they gathered [the victim's] blood
in their hands and licked it, an abominable spectacle, such
that they had a great slaughter on which to gorge themselves.

Another Jesuit father, Juan de Aspilcueta Navarro, wrote about
a direct encounter with cannibalism in 1549 in a village near what
is the modern-day city of Salvador.

. . . upon my arrival they told me that they had just finished
killing a girl and they showed me the house, and when I
entered it I found that they were cooking her to eat her,
and the head was hung on a timber; and I began to chide
and decry such an abominable thing and so against nature.
. . . And afterwards I went to other houses in which I found
the feet, hands, and heads of men in the smoke.

In a letter dated 28 March 1550, Navarro gave this additional
eyewitness account:

One day many [of the men] from the villages where I teach went to war, and many of them were killed by their enemies. In order to avenge themselves, they returned [to the war] well prepared and treacherously killed many of their enemies, from which they brought much human flesh. Such that, when I went to visit one of the villages in which I teach . . . and upon entering the second house I found a pot like a large earthen jar in which they had human flesh cooking, and when I arrived they were taking out arms, feet, and heads of humans, which was a dreadful thing to see. I saw seven or eight old women who could barely keep themselves standing up dancing around the pot and stirring the fire, so that they looked like demons in hell.

Another Jesuit eyewitness of Tupinamba cannibal rituals was Father Antonio Blasquez. Writing in 1557, after being in Brazil for four years, Blasquez stated that the Indians find "their happiness by killing an enemy and afterwards, for vengeance, to eat his flesh . . . there is no other meat they like better." Again, Blasquez was no armchair observer:

Six nude women came into the square singing in their manner and making such gestures and shaking that they seemed like devils; from their feet to their heads they were covered with something [that looked like] beetles [made] of yellow feathers; on their backs they had a bunch of feathers that looked like a horse's mane, and in order to enliven the festivity they played flutes which are made of the shin bones of their enemies when they kill them. With this garb they walked [around] barking like dogs and mimicking speech with such grimacing that I don't know what to compare them to. All of these inventions they do seven or eight days before killing them. Because at that time there were seven [prisoners to be killed], they made [the prisoners] run and throw stones and oranges, while their women held them prisoner with cords tied to their necks; even if [the prisoner] doesn't want to, they make him throw oranges, challenging him to do so. . . . The [captives] are persuaded that in [participating] in those ceremonies, they are brave and strong, and if out

of fear of death, they refuse to [participate], they call them
weak and cowardly; and therefore to flee is, in their view,
a great shame. They [i.e., the captives] do things when they
are about to die which if you hadn't seen it, you wouldn't
believe. . . .

Naturally the Jesuits tried to stop the slaughter of prisoners.
Again and again they relate how they personally confiscated cooked
or smoked human flesh or whole bodies that were about to be
cooked, and rescued or baptized prisoners who were about to be
killed and eaten. If the Tupinamba did not in fact practice cannibalism, the Jesuits were not merely gullible consumers of nasty
rumors, they must have been consummate liars. I refuse to believe Arens's claim that they lied to each other, lied to their
superiors in Rome, and lied in this manner continuously for over
fifty years without a single word of protest from a single honest
man among them.

Many eyewitness accounts attest to the existence of a similar
complex of torture, ritual execution, and eating prisoners of war
among other native American peoples, especially in northern
New York State and southern Canada. For example, in 1652 the
explorer, Peter Raddison, witnessed the consumption of one of
his comrades: "They cut off some of the flesh of that miserable,
broiled it and eat it." Another explorer, Wentworth Greenhalgh,
recorded the capture of fifty prisoners on 17 June 1677 near the
Iroquois village of Cannagorah. On the next day Greenhalgh
witnessed four men, four women, and one boy being tortured to
death: "the cruelty lasted about seven hours, when they were
almost dead, letting them loose to the mercy of the boys, and
taking the hearts of such as were dead to feast on."

As in the case of the Tupinamba, Jesuit missionaries provided
the most detailed eyewitness accounts of Iroquois and Huron
cannibalism. In a famous incident related by a Christianized Huron, the Iroquois tortured two missionaries to death and ate their
hearts. The Jesuit superior, Father Regnaut, to whom the Huron
had told the story, states that he himself had witnessed similar

acts of torture and cannibalism. "I do not doubt all which I have just related [the Huron's story] is true, and I would seal it with my blood, for I have seen the same treatment given to Iroquois prisoners whom the Huron savages have taken in war. . . ."

The longest and most detailed eyewitness account of torture and cannibalism concerns the treatment of an Iroquois captive in the year 1637. Three missionaries were present—Father Paul le Jeune, Father Garnier, and the narrator, Father François le Mercier. The account begins with the prisoner entering the village singing and escorted by a crowd of people. He was "dressed in a beautiful beaver robe and wore a string of porcelain beads around his neck." For two days his captors took good care of him, cleaned his wounds, and gave him fruits, squash, and dog meat to eat. In the evening they took him to the council's long house:

> The people gathered immediately, the old men taking places above, upon a sort of platform, which extends, on both sides, the entire length of the cabins. The young men were below, but were so crowded that they were almost piled upon one another, so that there was hardly a passage along the fires. Cries of joy resounded on all sides; each provided himself, one with a firebrand, another with a piece of bark, to burn the victim. Before he was brought in, the [chief] encouraged all to do their duty, representing to them the importance of this act, which was viewed, he said by the Sun and by the God of war. He ordered that at first they should burn only his legs, so that he might hold out until daybreak; also for that night they were not to go and amuse themselves in the woods [have sex].

The prisoner was then made to run a flaming gauntlet from one end of the long house to the other:

> . . . each one struggled to burn him as he passed. Meanwhile, he shrieked like a lost soul; the whole crowd imitated his cries, or rather smothered them with horrible shouts. . . . The whole cabin appeared as if on fire; and, athwart the flames and the dense smoke that issued therefrom, these barbarians—crowding one upon the other, howling at the top of their voices, with firebrands in their hands, their eyes

flashing with rage and fury—seemed like so many Demons who would give no respite to this poor wretch. They often stopped him at the other end of the cabin, some of them taking his hands and breaking the bones thereof by sheer force; others pierced his ears with sticks which they left in them; others bound his wrists with cords which they tied roughly, pulling at each end of the cord with all their might. Did he make the round and pause to take a little breath, he was made to repose upon hot ashes and burning coals. It is with horror that I describe all this to your Reverence, but verily we experienced unutterable pain while enduring the sight of it.

On the seventh round of the cabin the prisoner became un-conscious. The chief then tried to revive him, poured water in his mouth and gave him corn to eat. When he was able to sing again the torture resumed.

They hardly burned him anywhere except in the legs, but these, to be sure, they reduced to a wretched state, the flesh being all in shreds. Some applied burning brands to them and did not withdraw them until he uttered loud cries; and, as soon as he ceased shrieking, they again began to burn him, repeating it seven or eight times—often reviving the fire, which they held close against the flesh, by blowing upon it. Others bound cords around him and then set them on fire, thus burning him slowly and causing him the keenest agony. There were some who made him put his feet on red-hot hatchets, and then pressed down on them. You could have heard the flesh hiss, and have seen the smoke which issued therefrom rise even to the roof of the cabin. They struck him with clubs upon the head, and passed small sticks through his ears; they broke the rest of his fingers; they stirred up the fire all around his feet.

Finally, the prisoner lapsed again into unconsciousness, and this time was killed and dismembered and eaten:

They so harassed him upon all sides that they finally put him out of breath; they poured water into his mouth to strengthen his heart and the [chief] called out to him that he should take a little breath. But he remained still, his mouth open, and almost motionless. Therefore, fearing that he would die otherwise than by the knife, one cut off a foot, another a hand, and almost at the same time a third severed the head from the shoulders, throwing it into the crowd, where some one caught it to carry it to the [chief] for whom it had been reserved, in order to make a feast therewith. As for the trunk, it remained at Arontaen, where a feast was made of it the same day. We recommended his soul to God and returned home to say Mass. On the way we encountered a Savage who was carrying upon a skewer one of his half roasted hands.

I have quoted the Jesuits' eyewitness accounts of cannibalism at length in order to refute Arens's mischievous contention that "the collected documents of the Jesuit missionaries often referred to as the source for Iroquois cruelty and cannibalism, do not contain an eyewitness description of the latter deed." It is true that the Jesuits' eyewitness accounts of torture and cannibalism among the Iroquois and Huron provide more information regarding torture than the cooking and chewing part of the proceeding. But I think the reason for this is obvious. As eyewitnesses whose culture prohibited cannibalism, the Jesuits were revolted by the consumption of human flesh; but as men who were not accustomed to watching people being tortured (even though their European countrymen used torture on a larger scale than the Indians), they were far more appalled and revolted by the way the victims were killed than by how they were cooked.

Let me pause at this point to make some preliminary estimates of the costs and benefits of warfare cannibalism. If we regard warfare as a form of hunting organized to obtain meat, the costs far exceed the benefits. Humans are big animals, but it takes an immense effort just to capture a few of them. The hunted are as alert, evasive, and as well-informed about hunting as the hunters. And as a prey species, humans have another unique feature. Unlike tapirs, fish, or locusts, humans become less attractive as prey the more their numbers exceed the numbers hunting them. This is because they are the most dangerous prey in the world and are just as likely to kill some of their pursuers as to be killed by them. On the basis of optimal foraging theory, one would seldom expect hunters to take humans on encounter. They would be better off to pass them by in favor of palm grubs and spiders.

But warfare cannibals are not hunters of human flesh. They are warriors involved in the process of stalking, killing, and torturing their fellow humans as an expression of intergroup politics. The main expenditures and risks incurred in procuring and killing cannibal victims therefore cannot be charged to hunting; rather, it must be charged to warfare. The Tupinamba, Huron, or Iroquois did not go to war to obtain human flesh; they obtained human flesh as a by-product of going to war. Their consumption of the flesh of prisoners of war was therefore quite rational from a cost/benefit perspective. It was the nutritionally prudent alternative to letting a perfectly good source of animal food go to waste, and one for which there were no penalties, as in the Foré case. As an extra source of animal food, prisoners' flesh must have been especially welcomed by those who normally received small shares in meat distribution, especially the women, who were often more "meat hungry" than their men. And this accounts for the prominent role played by the Tupinamba and Iroquois women in the rituals accompanying the cannibalistic feast.

Among the Iroquois and Huron, warfare "paid the bill" not only for capturing enemy men and women, but for bringing them home to the captors' village in order to torture them. And torture itself had its own gruesome economy entirely separate from the costs of eating human flesh. Warlike societies such as the Iroquois and the Huron used torture to train their youth to be relentlessly aggressive toward the enemy. The prisoner's living body was undoubtedly a more effective training device than modern-day sand-filled dummies and plastic targets. Torture purged the village youth of the last vestige of pity for the enemy and inured them to the sights and sounds of combat. And it not only prepared young men for their own pain in combat, but it warned them of a dreadful fate if their courage failed and they let themselves be captured by the enemy.

I cannot say very much about the numbers of prisoners whom the Iroquois and Huron brought back to their villages to be tortured and eaten. The Jesuit accounts give the impression that the number of such prisoners was not very large. Moreover, the Iroquois and Huron were not as stressed for animal food as the Tupinamba, since their temperate forest habitat was well endowed with large game species such as deer, moose, and bear. I find it difficult therefore to attach much nutritional significance to the practice of eating of prisoners brought back to the village. Even though the costs were minimal (after discounting the war-related portion), the benefits were trivial. But the Iroquois and Huron did not confine their cannibalism to prisoners brought back to the village. They appear to have consumed a much larger quantity of human flesh while away from the village in the aftermath of the pitched battles which they fought with their enemies. These were occasions when the victims were stressed for food of any kind and when the bodies of the slain enemy represented a vital contribution to their combat rations. For example, after a battle fought against the French near Schenectady on 19 January 1693, Peter Schuyler, the mayor of Albany, reported that his Iroquois Indian allies "after their natural barbarity did cutt the enemy's dead to pieces, roast them, and eat them." This report was confirmed and elaborated by historian and governor of New York Cadwallader Colden who interviewed Schuyler about the incident. Colden wrote:

> The Indians eat the bodies of the French that they found . . . Schuyler (as he told me himself) going among the Indians at that time, was invited to eat broth with them, which some of them had ready boiled, which he did, till they putting the ladle in the kettle to take out more, brought out a French man's hand, which put an end to his appetite.

Since the Mohawk were allies of the English against the French, neither Colden nor Schuyler could have been interested in emphasizing the "savagery" of Iroquois customs.

The French for their part were no less open about their Huron allies' use of human flesh as combat rations. The governor of New France, Jacques Devonville, reported that after a battle with the Seneca in 1687, the Huron ate the fallen enemy. "We witnessed the painful sight of the usual cruelties of the savages who cut the dead into quarters, as in slaughter houses, in order to put them in the pot; the greater number were opened while still warm, that their blood might be drank."

Consumption of fallen enemy warriors to supplement combat rations seems to have been a common practice among village societies in many different parts of the world. The well-documented case of the Maori of New Zealand provides some important details. Maori war parties deliberately carried little food, living off the land wherever possible in order to increase their mobility and the element of surprise. On the march "they looked forward to the human source of supply and talked of how sweet the flesh of the enemy would taste." The Maori cooked both the battlefield dead and most of their captives shortly after battle. If there was more flesh than they could consume, they deboned the meat and packed it in baskets for the return journey. Occasionally prisoners were kept alive so that they could carry these baskets and afterward serve as "slaves" until being killed and eaten in a cannibal feast. While I cannot supply any details concerning the overall contribution of human flesh to Maori subsistence, the nutritional significance of cannibalism on war expeditions cannot be denied. According to anthropologist Andrew Vayda, "Regardless of whether the Maoris believed that they were acquiring revenge, manna, aliment or pleasure through the process of digestion, the fact was that human flesh served for nutriment. This fact made cannibalism a useful practice in war."

The incorporation of enemy bodies into the battlefield commisariat, while nutritionally practical, was not always militarily feasible. For a victorious military force to be able to make camp, collect the enemy's bodies, light fires, and cook and eat a cannibal meal implies that the enemy has been so totally crushed that no counterattack is feasible. To consume their cannibal meals, the victors must feel secure against any possibility that the enemy will be able to regroup or summon up the assistance of allies and return to the fray. This kind of security implies in turn a scale of military operations that could not be managed by groups like the Tupinamba. Their military operations consisted of stealthy attacks against villages where everyone was asleep. The typical response of the victims was to run into the forest and, after a few moments of butchery, the engagement—more aptly described as a raid than a battle—was over. The victors at once turned around and headed for home because they feared that the dispersed enemy could regroup, summon allies, and return to the fray on more favorable terms.

The same military contingencies meant that the victors could only bring a small number of prisoners back home with them in order not to reduce the mobility of the raiding party. These military considerations also explain why many band and village societies only managed to bring back token pieces of the enemy—heads, scalps, fingers—rather than whole bodies or live prisoners. In other words, the practice of warfare recurrently led to a taste for human flesh on the battlefield, back home, or in both places, which was probably fulfilled wherever cannibalism was compatible with military strategy and military logistics.

If what I have just said is true, then one would expect that as the military capability for taking prisoners and eating them on the battlefield or bringing them back home increased, the intensity and scope of warfare cannibalism would also increase. As we will see in a moment, this prediction holds to a certain point in the development of societies which were chiefdoms. But with the rise of state forms of political organization, warfare cannibalism ceased to be practiced rather abruptly. From antiquity to modern times, virtually every society that has been organized as a state has condemned the consumption of human flesh more forcefully than it has condemned the consumption of any other kind of animal food. Yet states have a military capacity to capture and eat enemy soldiers that is ten thousand times greater than that of the Tupinamba or Iroquois. It is one of the great ironies of history that for the last five thousand years the people who fought the bloodiest battles with the most combatants and the highest levels of destruction—who fought wars so staggering in scope and ferocity as to be unimaginable to any poor cannibal— are to this day horrified by the thought of consuming the remains of even a single human being. (The one great exception was the Aztecs, a subject to be discussed ere long.)

I wish I could say that the reason cannibalism was rejected was because states and empires like Sumeria, Egypt, Han China, Rome, or Persia had "higher" religious and moral values than the Tupinamba, the Maori, the Iroquois, and other peoples who lacked central governments or standing armies. I wish I could say that Christians, Moslems, Jews, and Hindus became too "civilized" to eat each other. Unfortunately, it makes as little sense to offer this kind of explanation as to say that we have become too "civilized" to eat insects or horses. The great French essayist Michel de Montaigne long ago deflated the ethnocentric puffery of Westerners who would make cannibalism the ultimate measure of moral depravity. Upon learning about Tupinamba people eating from an acquaintance who had spent twelve years in Brazil, Montaigne emphatically rejected the notion that the Indians were on that account more savage than his own countrymen.

> I am not so much concerned that we should remark on the horrible barbarity of such acts, as that, whilst rightly judging their errors, we should be so blind to our own. I think there is more barbarity in eating a live than a dead man [this refers to a Frenchman who had cut off a piece of his enemy's body and eaten it in public], in tearing on the rack and torturing the body of a man still full of feeling, in roasting him piece-meal and giving him to be bitten and mangled by dogs and swine (as we have not only read but seen with fresh memory, not between old enemies but between neighbors and fellow citizens, and what is worse, under the cloak of piety and religion), than in roasting and eating him after he lies dead. . . . We may therefore call those people [the Tupinamba] barbarians in respect to the rules of reason, but not in respect to ourselves, who surpass them in every kind of barbarity.

To this it is my sad duty to add that nothing has changed in the four hundred years since Montaigne wrote his essay. Our so-called civilization has not deterred us from burning, blasting, and dismembering unprecedented numbers of fellow human beings as a means of resolving intergroup conflicts. If anything, when it comes to warfare, we have sunk lower than any of our predecessors: before the nuclear era, no two enemies ever planned to wage a war that would annihilate the whole world, friends, foes, and bystanders alike, in order to settle their own differences. And as for cruelty, according to Amnesty International, one-third of the countries of the world still use torture against enemies at home and abroad. No, I regret to have to say that human flesh became bad to eat for essentially the same reasons that the Brahmans stopped eating beef and Americans won't eat dogs: the costs and benefits changed. More efficient sources of animal food became available, and the residual utility of prisoners of war increased, making them more valuable alive than dead. Let me explain how these changes came about.

There are three basic differences between states and bands or village-level societies: state societies have more productive economies enabling their farmers and workers to produce large surpluses of food and other goods; state societies have political systems which can place conquered territories and populations under a single government; and state societies also have a governing class whose political and military power depends on the flow of tribute and taxes from commoners and vassals. Since each farmer and worker in a state society can produce a surplus of goods and services, the larger a state's population grows, the greater the amount of surplus production, the bigger the tax and tribute base, the more powerful the governing class becomes. In contrast, band and village societies are incapable of producing large surpluses. And band and village societies lack a military and political organization that is capable of uniting defeated enemies under a central government or a governing class that stands to benefit from taxation. For band and village societies the military strategy that most benefits the victors therefore is to kill or disperse the population of neighboring groups in order to lower the pressure of population on resources. Because of their low productivity, band and village societies cannot derive long-term benefits from capturing enemy personnel. Since captives cannot produce a surplus, bringing one home to serve as a slave simply means one more mouth to feed. Killing and eating captives is the predictable outcome; if captive labor cannot yield a surplus, captives are worth more as food than as producers of food. In contrast, for most state societies, killing and eating captives would thwart the governing class's interest in expanding its tax and tribute base. Since captives can produce a surplus, far better to consume the products of their labor than the flesh of their bodies, especially if the meat and milk of domesticated animals (not available to most band and village people) is part of the surplus.

The abandonment of warfare cannibalism had additional payoffs for rulers who sought to create ever-larger imperial systems. They gained a great psychological advantage by assuring the enemy that surrender would not lead to being killed and eaten. Armies marching under the pretext of spreading higher "civilization" encounter less resistance than those marching under the banner of "we have come to kill and eat you." In sum, a renunciation of warfare cannibalism was part of the general evolution of moral and ethical systems distinctive of imperialistic states, an evolution which ultimately led to the rise of universalistic religions emphasizing the unity of humankind and the worship of merciful gods who value love and kindness.

Let me anticipate a skeptical reaction. After battle many bodies would be strewn over the battlegrounds. Why prevent the victors from eating them? If the taboo against cannibalism were restricted only to the enemy who remained alive, could not the victorious soldiers obtain extra combat rations without jeopardizing the labor value of the living captives? A similar objection could be raised concerning the origin of the taboo on horseflesh. As we saw earlier, with the development of the taboo on horseflesh, even dead horses littering the battlefield were not good to eat. A similar solution seems appropriate for the two cases. The strongest taboo is one that admits of no exceptions. The greater the temptation to violate a taboo, the stronger it has to be. In order to protect live prisoners of war or live war-horses from being killed and eaten, human flesh or horseflesh must be equally taboo, alive or dead. I should also point out that the temptation to consume forbidden flesh could not have been as great among officers and aristocrats as among commoners. It was easier for the elites to renounce human flesh just as it was easier for them to renounce horseflesh. In the aftermath of battle, the captives were marched off to work for the benefit of the elites, not for the benefit of the commoners. And as always, officers and aristocrats enjoyed a privileged abundance of alternative animal foods. Meat-hungry commoners faced a less satisfactory prospect; they could neither enjoy an abundance of alternative animal foods, nor could they profit from the labor power of conquered peoples. Since they had nothing to gain from keeping former enemies alive, they had to be indoctrinated with powerful general sentiments against cannibalism in any form. They had to be taught a loathing for human flesh so strong that even the thought of eating battlefield dead (human or equine) would make them feel ill. Meat-hungry commoners might still creep into the fields and clandestinely eat the unthinkable; but the owners of living horses and living men could sleep more easily knowing that "civilized" people did not eat either men or horses, dead or alive.

Incidentally, one can see why the practice of eating the corpses of dead relatives also does not occur among state-level societies, even in token form. Any deviation from the ban on consuming human flesh would weaken the commitment of the state to the eradication of warfare cannibalism. States could not very well permit people to eat dead relatives, while preventing them from eating dead enemies. And so in the Old World it came to be understood of humans as it came to be understood of horses, be they alive or dead, friend or foe, they were not good to eat, no matter how good they might be to kill.

The theory I have been outlining predicts that the practice of warfare cannibalism should increase in scope and intensity with the development of chiefdoms and then rapidly wither away in the transition from chiefdom to state. Oceania provides a particularly interesting test. When first contacted by Europeans, the peoples of New Guinea, northern Australia, and most of the islands of Melanesia such as the Solomon Islands, the New Hebrides, and New Caledonia practiced some degree of warfare cannibalism. Most of these groups were organized on a band or village basis; none had gone beyond the level of small-scale chiefdoms. The major exception was Fiji, where armies of powerful paramount chiefs fought pitched battles with each other for hegemony over a dense population without yet achieving a semblance of centralized government. And it is precisely on Fiji that warfare cannibalism reached a pitch of ferocity unmatched in the rest of Oceania. Early nineteenth-century eyewitness accounts indicate that prisoners captured outside a Fijian chiefdom or drawn from rebellious subjects within a chiefdom were sacrificed and eaten under the ritual supervision of priests at important events such as the dedication of a temple, the construction of a chief's house, the launching of canoes, and the visits of allied chiefs. "All enemies killed in battle are, as a matter of course, eaten by the victors, the bodies being previously presented to the spirit." The Fijians believed that human flesh was the food of the gods. They regarded the sacrifice and eating of human beings as a form of communion in which gods and mortals shared a meal (just as the Veda, Israelites, and Teutons sacrificed cattle and shared beef with the gods). In connection with wars waged in the early nineteenth century, Fijian "cannibalism was frequent and sometimes orgiastic." One missionary estimated that "during a five-year period in the 1840's, not fewer than 500 people had been eaten within fifteen miles of his residence." The limits of the number of people who could be eaten after the sacking of large towns was probably near three hundred. One chief commemorated his cannibal repasts by setting out a stone for each victim. At the end of his life he had laid out 872 stones.

Although Fiji's chiefdoms were bigger and better organized than most Melanesian political groupings, there were frequent periods of drought and nutritional stress. November through February was a season of hunger when the supply of yams and taro ran low. While the Fijians possessed domesticated pigs, they were unable to raise them in substantial numbers, and their diet was notably poor in animal foods. The fact that the Fijians ate their captives only after participating in elaborate rituals presided over by priests does not diminish the nutritional significance of the ingested flesh any more than the rituals practiced by the Aryans and Israelites during the sacrifice of cattle and the consumption of beef diminish the nutritional significance of beef. The consecration of captives to the major war god by chief or priest "freed the other bodies taken for more general consumption." Yet it would be incorrect to say that the Fijians went to war in order to eat human flesh; rather, as in other cases of warfare cannibalism, having gone to war, they increased their material gains by eating as well as killing the enemy.

In contrast to the Melanesians, most of the peoples of Polynesia, another great island culture area of the Pacific, did not engage in warfare cannibalism. This accords well with the development in Polynesia of native political organizations based on rudimentary forms of taxation and labor conscription. In Hawaii, for example, villages were grouped into districts, and districts into island-wide kingdoms. District chiefs collected "gifts" of tapa cloth, fishing gear, and food from the villages and passed them on to the king. If a proper quantity of "gifts" were not forthcoming, the king's warriors would plunder the uncooperative villages. The kings used their revenue to support personal retainers and warriors as well as craftsmen and workers who helped to enlarge the irrigation ditches and construct ponds for raising fish. When storms damaged these facilities, the king and his subchiefs distributed emergency food and supplies kept in their storehouses. With their highly productive irrigation agriculture, their fish ponds, and their deep-sea fishing canoes, the Hawaiians, like the Tongans and Tahitians, enjoyed a secure and abundant food supply that was relatively rich in animal products (including, of course, their poi-stuffed "pet" dogs).

To repeat, not all of the Polynesian islanders refrained from warfare cannibalism. The major exceptions were the Maori, the Marquesans, and possibly the Samoans. But these islands lacked the centralized political organization found on Tonga, Tahiti, and Hawaii. The political organization of the Maori resembled the fragmented chieftaincies of Melanasia, while the political organization of Marquesas islanders and the Samoans was no more centralized than that of Fiji. All three of the Polynesian groups that practiced warfare cannibalism also lacked the highly productive agriculture and fisheries which characterized the politically centralized Polynesian Islands. To sum up. In Oceania at least, the predicted relationship between warfare cannibalism and level of political organization seems to hold up: with the rise of centralized governments, prisoners of war became more valuable as taxpayers and peasants than as meat for a meal.

As I mentioned earlier, the Aztecs of Mexico are the one great exception to the rule that state societies everywhere suppress warfare cannibalism. Perhaps there are other exceptions, but if so, historians have never described them, and they have gone undetected by archaeologists. I fear that my explanation of why state societies kill people but do not eat them will remain unconvincing unless I can explain why the Aztecs continued to eat people as well as kill them.

When contacted by Hernando Cortés's expedition in 1519, the Aztecs had not only failed to repress the eating of enemy dead, they were practicing a state-sponsored form of human sacrifice and cannibalism on a scale never rivaled before or since. Estimates of the number of victims who were put to death and consumed each year range from a low of 15,000 to a high of 250,000. Most of them were enemy soldiers recently captured on the battlefield or temporarily in service as household slaves. The Aztecs also sacrificed and ate female captives and slaves. A small number of victims were children and infants expropriated from or donated by commoner families. As in prestate forms of warfare cannibalism, the Aztecs followed a highly ritualized procedure laden with symbolic significance in killing their victims and distributing their flesh. Like the Fijians they believed that human flesh was the food of the gods. But the Aztecs staged their sacrifice rituals against a backdrop of monumental plazas and temples and before daily throngs of spectators. Teams of butcher-priests dispatched the victims at the tops of the stepped pyramids which rose from the center of the Aztec's capital, Tenochtitlán. In front of the stone statues of the principal gods, four of these priests seized the victim, each one pulling on a limb, and spreadeagled him or her backward over a low, rounded stone. A fifth priest then hacked open the wall of the chest, wrenched out the beating heart, and pressed it against the statue while the attendants pushed the victim's body gently down the pyramid's steps. When it reached the bottom other attendants severed the head and delivered the rest to the house compound of the "owner"—the captain or nobleman whose warriors had captured the deceased. On the following day, the body was cut up, cooked, and eaten at a feast attended by the owner and his guests, the favorite recipe being a stew flavored with peppers, tomatoes, and squash blossoms. Some doubt exists as to what happened to the trunk and its organs. According to one of the chronicles, the Aztecs threw the trunk to the animals in the royal zoo. But another chronicler refers to whole bodies minus only head and heart being delivered to the owner's compound. All chroniclers agree that the head was usually pierced by a wooden shaft and placed on display on a latticework structure or "skull rack" alongside the heads of previous victims. The largest of these skull racks was located in the main plaza of Tenochtitlán. One eyewitness counted the number of poles and shafts and concluded that it contained 136,000 skulls. A modern skeptic has recalculated this total based on the maximum height of the trees available to the Aztecs and the average width of a skull and come to the conclusion that the skull rack in question actually could have contained no more than 60,000 skulls.

But this was not the only skull rack in the Aztec capital. In the same plaza there were five additional, if smaller, racks, and there were also two tall towers made of an uncountable number of skulls and jaws held together by lime. These skulls did not accumulate at a steady pace. Although there were regular feast days throughout the year at which as many as 100 prisoners were sacrificed at a time, the priests killed much larger numbers at intervals to commemorate major historical events such as military victories, the coronation of a new king, or the building or enlargement of pyramids or temples. For example, the Aztecs enlarged and rededicated the main pyramid in Tenochtitlán at least six times. Native accounts state that the priests sacrificed 80,400 prisoners in four days and nights at the rededication which took place in 1487—the last before the Spanish conquest. By allotting two minutes per sacrifice, historian and demographer Sherburne Cook concluded that no more than 14,000 prisoners could have been dispatched. But Francis Robicsek, a cardiovascular surgeon familiar with the history of pre-Columbian Mexico, holds that an experienced surgeon would have needed only twenty seconds per victim. That would put the killing capacity of the highly experienced surgical teams at the tops of the pyramids back up to 78,000. An important point is whether the prisoners cooperated or not. A majority of Aztec scholars follow the lead of Mexico's tourist agency and try to cover up the monstrous nature of Aztec religion by claiming that the prisoners were eager to submit to the knife because they believed it was an honor to be eaten by the gods. This propensity to sentimentalize cruelty in the name of cultural relativism is totally at variance with the reported facts. The most important historical document concerning the Aztecs, Bernadino de Sahagun's *Florentine Codex*, states that the masters of captive slaves "pulled them and dragged them by the hair to the sacrificial stone where they were to die." And in Motolinia's sixteenth-century *History of the Indians of New Spain*, we find the following warning:

> Let no one think that any of those who were sacrificed by being slain and having their hearts torn out or being killed in any other way, suffered death voluntarily and not by force. They had to submit to it, feeling great grief over their death and enduring frightful pain.

Against attempts to downscale the number of cannibal victims, I would point out that contingents of Aztec priests accompanied the Aztec armies into combat and performed sacrificial rituals immediately after a battle was won. There is also some evidence that under duress, the Aztecs may have eaten bodies left on the battlefield. Taking into consideration the possibility that sacrificial victims such as those dedicated to the rain god may not always have been eaten, and allowing for the tendency of both the Spaniards and the Aztecs to exaggerate the number of victims available for cannibal feasts, we are still left with the fact that the Aztecs practiced warfare cannibalism on an unprecedented scale. No one can deny that the Aztec state and Aztec religion encouraged rather than banned its practice.

How can one explain the unique failure of the Aztec state to repress warfare cannibalism? I think the same costs and benefits apply to this exception as to the rule. As in other state societies, the Aztec elite had to strike a balance between the nutritional benefits provided by human flesh and the political and economic costs of destroying the wealth-producing potential of human labor power. The Aztecs chose to eat the human equivalent of the golden goose. The reason they made this unique choice was that their system of food production was uniquely devoid of efficient sources of animal foods. The Aztec had never succeeded in domesticating a single large herbivore or omnivore. They possessed neither ruminants nor swine. Their principal domestic animals were the turkey and the dog. Turkeys are good converters of grain to flesh; but they can be used on a large scale for meat production only when a human population can afford the 90 percent energy loss incurred by eating the meat instead of the grain. Similarly, the dog is scarcely the kind of creature one would want to mass-produce as an animal food. Dogs themselves thrive best on meat. Why feed meat to a dog to get meat for people? Although the Aztecs did try to develop breeds of dogs that put on weight from eating cooked corn and beans, they would have been better off sticking to turkeys, which can at least eat uncooked plant food. In no way could either dogs or turkeys have furnished more than a token quantity of meat per capita even if they were eaten only by the Aztec elites.

Perhaps I need to emphasize at this point that the overall degree of poverty and hunger was not the crucial difference between the Aztec subsistence system and the subsistence systems of state societies which successfully repressed cannibalism. The peasants of India and China probably lived no better than the Aztec peasants. The pinch did not occur on the mass level but on the level of the military and religious elites and their followers. By repressing warfare cannibalism, Old World elites obtained significant improvements in their wealth and power. By preserving the lives of their captives, they could intensify the production of luxury goods and animal foods for their personal consumption and for redistribution to their followers. Perhaps the commoners also benefited to some extent, but that was not crucial. Among the Aztec, the practice of warfare cannibalism probably did little to improve the condition of the peasantry. It continued because it continued to benefit the elites; repressing it would have diminished rather increased their wealth and power.

The link between the Aztecs' unique failure to repress cannibalism and their lack of domesticated herbivores was formulated by anthropologist Michael Harner in 1977. The storm of denunciation which greeted Harner's modest proposal is to me far more remarkable than the Aztec's taste for human flesh. No one has come forth to deny that the Aztecs waged incessant warfare far and wide throughout central Mexico; nor has anyone sought to protect the Aztecs from being depicted as the world's number one practitioners of human sacrifice. Most scholars even accept the fact that the Aztecs were great cannibals. But what has driven normally mild-mannered scholars into a frenzy is the proposal that the Aztecs went to war, built pyramids, and sacrificed thousands of prisoners, as one critic put it, "as a way the Aztecs had for getting some meat." This immodest proposal is entirely a product of prejudice and misinformation and has nothing whatsoever to do with the nutritional explanation of Aztec warfare cannibalism that I have just presented. It embodies a view that is directly contrary to the cost/benefit approach that I have been following—since it charges the full cost of warfare, the building of the pyramids, and the sacrifice of prisoners to the production of human flesh, whereas everything that I have said about why warfare cannibalism occurs at all is premised on the assumption that warfare cannibalism is a by-product of warfare and that its costs can be written off almost entirely as costs of war which would have been incurred whether or not the combatants ate each other.

Proceeding on their entirely different and quite erroneous assumptions, critics of the theory that Aztec cannibalism reflects a peculiar nutritional situation have attempted to show that the Aztecs suffered from no dearth of good, wholesome, proteinaceous and calorific foods. Anthropologist Ortiz de Montellano, for example, has diligently collected information on the extraordinary variety of foods consumed by the Aztecs in order to prove that meat hunger could not have motivated their cannibalism. It is indeed true that in addition to their staples—corn, beans, chia, and amaranth—the Aztec ate a wide variety of tropical fruits and vetetables. And although turkeys and dogs were their only domesticated sources of animal food, it is also true that they hunted and ate a broad spectrum of wild animal species. As enumerated by Montellano, these include deer, armadillo, thirty varieties of waterfowl, pocket gophers, weasels, rattlesnakes, mice, fish, frogs, salamanders, fish eggs, water flies, corixid beetles, beetle eggs, dragonfly larvae, grasshoppers, ants, and worms. Another expert on Aztec food habits adds quail, partridge, pheasant, tadpoles, molluscs, rabbits, hares, opossum boars, tapirs, crustacea, and *tecuitutl*, a "green lake scum" formed by waterfly eggs from which "the people made a bread which was cheese-like in flavor." The breadth of this diet is truly remarkable, but it leads to a conclusion entirely contrary to what Montellano intends to prove. Montellano is correct: "the Aztecs consumed a greater variety of foods than we do." But so did the meat-hungry warfare cannibals of Amazonia. If the Aztecs ate everything from deer to water beetle eggs and green lake scum, why should anyone be surprised that they also ate people? Once again let me refer to the basic principles of optimal foraging

theory: "small things"—insects and worms and fly larvae—are
highly inefficient resources. Their prominence in the Aztec's diet
cannot be used as evidence that the Aztecs enjoyed an abundance
of animal food. On the contrary, what the breadth of their diet
shows is that higher-ranking species such as deer and tapir were
in extremely short supply. Because of the exorbitant amount of
time needed to collect and process the Aztec's lower-ranking
forageable species, and because of the energetic inefficiency of
their domesticated animals, animal foods could only have made
up a small fraction of the Aztec diet. Despite the impression that
animal foods were abundant, when shared on an annual per capita
basis among the million or so people who lived within a twenty-
mile radius of the Aztec capital, the daily intake of meat, fish,
and fowl was almost certainly no greater than a few grams per
day. In view of the absence of efficient alternative sources of
animal food, any attempt to prevent military commanders from
using human flesh as a means of rewarding their followers would
have met a far greater degree of resistance in the Aztec case than
was true of the generality of Old World states and empires,
every one of which possessed several domesticated ruminant
species.

At the same time that the lack of efficient alternative sources
of animal food raised the value of the enemy as "meat on the
hoof," it lowered the value of the enemy as serf, slave, and
taxpayer. It did this in two ways. First, the absence of domesticated ruminants and swine meant that even if the conquered
populations were preserved instead of eaten, there was no way
their labor power could be harnessed to the task of improving
the supply of animal food. With the population of wild species
already depleted by too much hunting and collecting, additional
labor devoted to foraging would have brought meager returns.
Secondly, the absence of large domesticated herbivores which
could serve as beasts of burden diminished the value of the enemy
as producers of plant food. Lacking cattle or horses, the Aztecs
were obliged to rely on human porters to transport the harvest
of tributary provinces to their capital. Human porters have the

distinct disadvantage of needing to be fed a large portion of the crops they transport in order to be able to carry their burdens. As compared with cattle and equines, which can subsist on humanly inedible plants, human beasts of burden are a costly mode of moving a grain harvest from one region to another. One can see therefore why the Aztecs' captives were worth more to them dead as meat than alive as serfs and slaves. The Aztecs were unusually ill supplied with meat and other animal products; and the tribute populations were unusually unrewarding as a source of subservient labor: they could not relieve the Aztecs' meat hunger; and they themselves ate up much of the grain surplus while carrying it to their masters. The Aztec solution was grim but cost-efficient: they treated their captives the same way Midwestern cornbelt farmers treated their hogs. They walked the grain harvest to Tenochtitlán on the hoof.

Because they ate as well as taxed a considerable proportion of their able-bodied population, the Aztecs never succeeded in establishing a stable system of imperial rule. As soon as a province had restored its manpower, it tried to rebel against the oppressors. The Aztecs then returned and laid the basis for the next rebellion by marching a new crop of prisoners back to Tenochtitlán.

I hope I have made it clear that I do not believe that cannibalism among the Aztecs was impelled by a "protein shortage" or that Aztec "cannibalism arose out of necessity" or that Aztec cannibalism was "a response to dietary insufficiency" or that "protein starvation" among the Aztec was an "impelling force to Cannibalism" (all of these upside-down notions appeared in a single article by Ortiz de Montellano). Rather, my point is that the practice of warfare cannibalism was a normal by-product of prestate warfare and that the question that has to be answered is not what impelled state societies to practice it but what impelled them not to practice it. The scarcity of animal food among the Aztecs did not compel them to eat human flesh; it simply made the political advantages of suppressing cannibalism less compelling by leaving the residual utility of prisoners of war more or less where it had been among societies like the Tupinamba and the Iroquois.

I suspect that the reason so many scholars turn this relationship on its head is that they themselves are members of state societies that have suppressed warfare cannibalism for thousands of years, and therefore find the notion of people eating abhorrent. This leads them to assume ethnocentrically that there must be some great compelling reason for people to do such a horrible thing as to eat human flesh. They fail to see that the real conundrum is why we who live in a society which is constantly perfecting the art of mass-producing human bodies on the battlefield find humans good to kill but bad to eat.

Imagining that his task was to prove that the Aztecs did not go to war "to get some meat," Ortiz de Montellano also studied the relationship between the seasonal occurrence of food shortages and the months when the greatest numbers of prisoners were sacrificed. He discovered that the hungriest time of the year was the time of the year when the fewest prisoners were eaten. Since "the biggest consumption of human meat took place . . . in the middle of the corn harvest," he concluded that the whole sacrificial complex had nothing to do with meat hunger but was merely "an expression of gratitude and communion," a gesture of "thanks and reciprocity to the gods." But the overlap between the season of sacrifice and the season of harvest is exactly what one would expect if the Aztecs did not go to war to eat prisoners but ate prisoners as a by-product of going to war. The hungry season is the time of winter rains in the basin of Mexico; the harvest season is the dry season. Armies, even modern armies, avoid rainy-season campaigns; not only is it easier to get around when the ground is dry, but the ripening crops in the enemy's fields make it possible to live off the land. The crops also provide tempting spoils of war to be transported home on the heads and backs of prisoners. Montellano's "gesture of thanks and reciprocity" still stands, but it in no way contradicts the nutritional significance of the rituals. Who would not thank the gods for the gift of corn and meat? All state-level religions render such thanks at harvest time. The only thing different about the Aztecs is that the meat was human meat. Saying it was part of their religion to eat human meat gets us nowhere. It is like saying that Hindus abhor beef because their religion forbids cow slaughter or that Americans don't eat goats because goats don't taste good. I shall never be satisfied with that kind of explanation.

CHAPTER ELEVEN

BETTER TO EAT

THERE IS a common misunderstanding of optimization theories
which I now need to discuss. To say that a foodway represents
an optimization of costs and benefits is not to say that it is an
optimal foodway. Optimization is not the same as optimal (optimal
foraging theory, strictly speaking, is a misnomer—it should be
optimization foraging theory).

A number of years ago during the debate over the useful functions of the Hindu taboo on cattle slaughter, John Bennet of
Washington University in St. Louis accused me of making "such
a convincing case for the effectiveness of the present system that
one is encouraged to accept it as the best India has to offer." My
reply, which seems a bit hysterical in retrospect, was to declare
myself "innocent of this barbarity." I then coined the phrase (or
at least I think I was the one who coined it): "Panglossian func-
tionalism," to set myself apart from people who, like Dr. Pangloss
in Voltaire's *Candide*, believed that even disasters such as earth-
quakes and flood were "all for the best in the best of all possible
worlds." I am no Dr. Pangloss. Not only do I reject the notion
that this is the best of all possible worlds, but I believe we all
have the obligation to try to make it a better world. But if we do
not understand the causes of existing systems, it seems unlikely
that we can devise better systems to replace them. Or, as I told

235

Bennet, it would be convenient if India's cattle complex could be regarded as a completely harmful product of silly superstitions and ignorant mismanagement. Then anything that would work at all would be better than the present system. But if in fact the sacred cow embodies a form of practical cost accounting, innovators must be held responsible not merely for introducing a workable system, but for one that works better.

Many well-intentioned experts do not realize that different kinds of betterment strategies flow from the assumption that foodways are dominated by irrational thoughts as opposed to the assumption that they are dominated by practical costs and benefits. If foodways are largely emanations of ignorant, religious, or symbolic thoughts, then it is what people think that needs to be changed. If, on the other hand, what seem like harmful religious or symbolic thoughts are actually themselves embodied in or constrained by practical circumstances surrounding the production and allocation of food resources, then it is these practical circumstances that need to be changed. Failure to understand the practical basis for food preferences and aversions therefore can seriously impede attempts to make good to eat better to eat. It can lead not only to ineffective remedies but to dangerous ones. I touched on this issue in discussing the use of milk in international aid programs, and it lurks in the background of the meat hunger and sacred cow chapters. But I have yet to bring this issue to center stage. Let me do that now by briefly taking up two final puzzles which are directly concerned with problems of malnutrition in Third World countries. The first concerns a peculiar pattern of restraints placed on the diets of pregnant and lactating women; the second concerns a dreaded nutritional disease which causes blindness. Let me take them up in turn.

Since pregnancy and lactation place extra nutritional demands on women, one would expect that Third World families would try to give their expectant and nursing mothers extra amounts of high-quality foods. Yet I have long been baffled by the fact that throughout much of the Third World there are customs and beliefs which seem to be aimed at lowering rather than raising the nutritional status of pregnant and lactating women. To quote from a popular textbook, "protein needs increase during pregnancy, yet repeatedly we have found taboos, superstitions, and prohibitions that serve to eliminate or reduce potential sources of protein from the diet of the menstruating, pregnant, or lactating women."

India is notorious for having these seemingly bizarre food beliefs. A study carried out in the state of Tamil Nadu found that there were over a hundred foods which women said were not good to eat when they were pregnant or were nursing a baby. The forbidden items include meat and eggs, many kinds of fruits, and several types of nutritious seeds, pulses (legumes), and grains. And despite the generally poor nutritional status of the Tamil Nadu mothers, they abstained from all solid foods for the first few days after childbirth and from all meats and fish for at least a week. The author of the study holds that these taboos reflect purely arbitrary cultural values and religious beliefs and that they are the cause of critical nutritional deprivations. But I hold that it is irresponsible to let the matter rest at this point.

As in previous cases, there is a need for additional data. The study does not tell us what foods women eat before, during, and after pregnancy and childbirth. To recall the lesson of previous chapters, nobody eats everything. Diets cannot be judged by what people don't eat; it's what they do eat that counts. So what we need to know is exactly how different the normal female diet is from the pre- and postpartum diet. Even if we accept the premise that pregnant and lactating women actually eat only the kinds of foods they say they eat, it does not necessarily mean that they thereby condemn themselves to a diet that is any worse than normal. A lot depends on *how much* they eat, doesn't it? In Tamil Nadu, as in other parts of India, milk and milk products are normally the most important source of animal proteins. Over 57 percent of Tamil Nadu women approved of the consumption of milk during pregnancy. And among those Tamil Nadu women who normally ate meat, fish, and eggs, 87 percent said it was all right to continue to eat fish. Did they actually consume more, less, or the same amount of milk and fish during pregnancy? If

they gave up eating an occasional morsel of meat but ate more
fish and drank more milk, they would be better off, not worse
off. The same reservations pertain to the other Tamil Nadu taboos.

Fruits figure prominently among foods to be avoided. Yet the
only fruits commonly said to be spurned were pineapple and
papaya. Did those who spurned pineapples and papaya eat them
when they weren't pregnant? And how about their consumption
of other fruits? Did it go up or down? There was a high consensus
for avoiding sesame seeds. But many other seeds were not forbidden. The most commonly to-be-avoided grain is *Setari italica*.
But the Tamil Nadu regard this as a "poor man's" millet, and
most people prefer not to eat it anyway. Similarly, the most to-
be-avoided pulse (legume) is horsegram (*Dolichos biflorus*), another insignificant "poor man's food." Finally, the author of the
study writes that "restrictions on other cereals and pulses were
extremely rare." Potentially, at least, this seems to trivialize the
whole list of tabooed items since what women normally eat are
the "other cereals and pulses."

Turning to the immediate postpartum period, Tamil Nadu
women say they follow an even more comprehensive set of taboos
than during pregnancy. Yet faithful compliance with the list of
items-to-be-avoided would still not necessarily result in the lowering of nutritional standards. For the first "few days" only liquid
foods must be eaten, but these liquids could be quite nourishing
since they include milk, rice water, soups, and coffee with sugar.
While the majority of women said they avoided nonvegetarian
food for at least a week only 6 percent of nonvegetarians said
they became pure vegetarians for one month or more. In any
event, within "a few days" bread, legumes, vegetables, and rice
can be added to the liquid diet. Hence, despite the restricted
list of edibles, nursing women need not interrupt their normal
diet of rice and legumes supplemented by milk, milk products,
meat, and fish. And again, we do not know if there are changes
in the quantities of the foods that are permitted and actually
consumed. The most disturbing question of all is whether one

can obtain a reliable picture of what people eat merely by asking them. Perhaps Indian women actually eat what they say they don't; or perhaps they eat something else that is as good as or better than the tabooed item.

I can cite another study of pregnancy and lactation taboos in which marked discrepancies of both kinds come to light. In a Malayan fishing village called Ru Mada, anthropologist Christine Wilson asked fifty women to tell her what kinds of foods they would and would not eat after childbirth. The women said they must abstain from all fruits except bananas and durian, all fried foods, several species of fish, and all curries, gravies, and sauces. These restrictions were said to be in force for forty days. As for what they *should* eat during the same period, the women specified rice, small lean fish, European bread rolls, eggs, bananas, coffee with sugar, plain biscuits, yeast, and turmeric and black pepper as seasonings. The anthropologist then had the opportunity to record what two Ru Mada mothers actually consumed during one day of their forty-day postpartum food taboo period. In just this one day of observation per mother, the women ate three items—fried fish, soy sauce, and curry—which they were explicitly not supposed to eat. They also consumed another six items—tea, coconuts, chiles, margarine, fortified milo-chocolate drink, and condensed milk—which were not on the ideal lying-in diet. I think it is especially significant that three of these additions—margarine, milo, and condensed milk—are expensive, prestigious, and normally not consumed by Southeast Asian peasants. They obviously represent an attempt to supplement rather than deplete the lactating mother's diet.

According to anthropologist Wilson, the diet of the two lactating mothers was nonetheless inadequate as judged by prudent medical standards. But I am very uncomfortable with this conclusion. Ru Mada women severely restrict their activity while lying in. During the forty-day period of dietary restrictions, they give up all strenuous tasks such as carrying heavy baskets or chopping wood. Instead they spend two to five hours each day lying on their beds with a warming fire under them. To some extent this lower rate of physical activity may compensate for the extra calories needed to produce mothers' milk. I am not suggesting that the diet is adequate, but merely that there are grounds for suspecting that it is an improvement over what women normally eat. Wilson's conclusion that "the severe restrictions to the postpartum diet [are] inimical to the women's health" is unsubstantiated. Certainly she presents no evidence that the lying-in diet was inferior to the diet of nonpregnant and nonlactating women as a *consequence* of postpartum dietary restrictions.

A far more likely explanation of substandard diets during pregnancy and lactation, especially in poor, underdeveloped, and overpopulated places like Tamil Nadu and Ru Mada is that families can't afford the recommended daily allowances. Pregnancy and lactation often lead to a marked reduction in the woman's contribution to the earning powers of her family, and this exacerbates the strain on her husband, older children, and other relatives to maintain their own nutritional standards. Such families, and their women in particular, face some excruciating choices. They must balance the demands of pregnancy, lactation, and the newborn infant for extra rations against the normal ongoing needs of husband, older children, and working adults. In other words, where endemic food shortages exist, extra rations diverted to pre- and postpartum women and unborn or newly born infants may be a "luxury" which cannot be achieved without adversely affecting someone else.

One of the reasons Westerners are so quick to leap to the conclusion that Third World foodways are dominated by ignorance and irrational religious beliefs is that we do not have to make the difficult choices which extreme poverty obliges others to make. It is difficult for affluent Westerners to understand the narrow range of alternatives open to Third World low-income families in allocating family income to food. The more family income depends on hard physical labor, the more important it becomes to make sure that the principal wage earner gets fed well enough to go to work, even if this means that other family members are hardly fed at all. Another anthropologist, Daniel

Gross, who has studied the nutritional choices of impoverished peasant families in northeast Brazil, coined the phrase "bread-winner effect" to designate this phenomenon. I had the chance to observe an interesting manifestation of the "breadwinner effect" in India. The streets of Trivandrum, capital of Kerala State, are lined with a remarkable number of small restaurants or "tea houses," which are patronized primarily by manual laborers. Among the patrons who regularly take their meals at these establishments are mothers from some of the poorest and most desperate families in the neighborhood. Why do these mothers eat out so often, alone, and away from their children? It so happens that in Kerala, lower-caste women are obliged to find employment in extremely arduous jobs. They break stones for roadbeds, stoop over for hours at a time planting rice seedlings, and carry eighty-pound loads of rock or as many as twenty bricks at a time on their heads along narrow dikes and up precarious ladders. Leela Gulati, who studied the lives of some of these mothers, reports that they spend as much as two rupees a day out of a salary of only seven rupees on restaurant meals for themselves, although they ac-knowledge that the same food would cost much less prepared at home. My interpretation of this apparent extravagance is that as the family's principal and sometimes sole wage earner, it is ab-solutely essential that these women eat well enough to meet the heavy demands placed on their bodies. Eating at home would be cheaper, but it would mean eating larger portions and higher-quality foods right in front of the other family members without sharing any of it with them—an unthinkable prospect. It simply is not possible for these women to hold onto their jobs and eat at home.

All this leads me to suggest that nutritionally adverse preg-nancy and lactation taboos are not emanations of arbitrary beliefs and superstitions. Rather they probably represent an attempt to rationalize a situation in which cruel circumstances often dictate that a woman nourishes her embryo and child literally out of her own flesh and blood. These taboos may also exemplify the dietary advantages which men seek for themselves at the expense of women and which I have alluded to in discussing the distribution of animal foods. Perhaps they more accurately represent a mixture of self-exploitation by women as well as exploitation of women by men. In line with this possibility, another study carried out in Tamil Nadu reports that 74 percent of female respondents said that it is better for a pregnant women to eat no more than or even less than what she normally eats. Do women really believe this, or have they simply learned that because of the breadwinner effect, men expect pregnant women not to make additional demands for food which cannot in any event be satisfied?

An even more intriguing issue related to this line of inquiry is why so many southern Asian women say they believe that it is better to have a small baby than a big baby despite the fact that Western medical statistics show that the lighter a baby is at birth, the worse its chances of survival. One possibility is that in undernourished populations, small babies, small children, and small adults may actually have a better chance of survival since they tend to require disproportionately less food than bigger babies, children, and adults. Or does this belief simply reflect the fact that small, undernourished mothers have less painful and less dangerous deliveries with small rather than large babies? Or is it again simply a matter of mothers giving in to the inevitable and recognizing that they and their unborn children must share the uncertainties imposed by poverty? I do not know the answers to these questions, but it is far more intriguing to ask them than to accept the view that pregnancy and lactation taboos exist because women like to think irrational thoughts. Moreover, to return to my main point, the two approaches lead to entirely different perspectives on what should be done to improve the nutritional status of women and infants in Tamil Nadu and Ru Mada, and other Third World cultures. If diets are impaired primarily by irrational thoughts, then the prime remedy must be to change how people think. This suggests that what Third World women need most is to be educated about scientific principles of nutrition. But if practical reason already prevails, what they need most is a rise in their family's disposable income.

Anthropologists Kathleen Dewalt and Gretl Pelto make this point in their study of a rural Mexican village. They concluded that the quickest way to get dramatic improvements in nutritional standards is to increase the resources poor families have to work with. I would only add that the slowest way to get people to eat better is to tell them what they ought to eat when they can't afford what they ought to eat.

Now for the second example of the danger of favoring explanations that attribute apparently harmful foodways to arbitrary cultural values and beliefs. This case involves the relationship between a widespread food aversion and a disease of the eye that leads to blindness and which afflicts millions of children, especially toddlers of two to three years in less developed countries. The disease is called xerophthalmia (pronounced zeer-ahf-thalmeea), literally, "drying of the eye." Between four hundred thousand and five hundred thousand preschool-age children in Indonesia, India, Bangladesh, and the Philippines develop an active form of this disease each year. Although precise figures are not available, on a worldwide basis nearly a million preschool children a year display symptoms associated with xerophthalmia, and of these 30 percent to 50 percent will become blind in both eyes. The proximate cause of xerophthalmia has been known for many years. It results from a deficiency of vitamin A. In the absence of this vitamin, the mucus-secreting cells at the cornea of the eye cease to produce moist lubricants and deposit instead a hard, dry protein called keratin. Deprived of its lubricating and protective moisture, the eye becomes covered with keratin, and this leads to the ulceration of the eyeball and its eventual obliteration. If treated before deep ulceration occurs, the pathological course can be reversed and partial or even complete vision restored. In severe cases massive injections of vitamin A are needed, but an increase in the consumption of dietary sources of vitamin A will prevent the disease from occurring as well as cure it during its early stages.

Vitamin A is a readily available nutrient. Almost any diet that includes animal liver, animal fat, or whole milk is likely to supply enough vitamin A to prevent xerophthalmia. But even if people are too poor to consume animal foods, there are plenty of cheap viamin A–rich plants which can perform the same function. Yellow, orange, and dark green fruits and vegetables which contain carotene pigments are a good source of the precursor of vitamin A. It seems paradoxical therefore that xerophthalmia occurs so widely in tropical countries where such fruits and vegetables are easily cultivated. All a normal Indonesian or Indian child would need in order to satisfy recommended standards for vitamin A is about thirty grams per day of leafy vegetables like amaranth, spinach, or kale. Unfortunately, it would appear that the aversion to consuming dark green, leafy vegetables—an aversion which manifests itself in the United States in the legendary struggle of child against spinach—also occurs in the tropics. This has led many nutritionists to regard xerophthalmia as a prime case of a harmful and irrational food aversion. In the oft-quoted words of nutritionist Donald McLaren: "Xerophthalmia is a disease that really gives the lie to the common belief that nutritional deficiencies are due to food shortages. Pro–vitamin A carotenoids occur in abundance in the green leaves that on all sides greet the visitor to the typical village in the monsoon tropics. The curse is that rice, the staple food in these areas, is devoid of carotene and the people do not realize the importance of the green leaves."

The fact that xerophthalmia can be prevented and cured in normal children by eating dark green, leafy vegetables is not at issue. But doubts exist as to whether xerophthalmia is primarily due to arbitrary food preferences and not to food shortages. Children who present clinical signs of xerophthalmia consume fewer carotene-rich vegetables than normal children with healthy eyes, but they also consume less of practically everything else. In Indonesia, 92 percent of children in whom xerophthalmia had resulted in blindness in one or both eyes were severely malnourished, weighing less than 70 percent of their expected weight-for-height. At the xerophthalmia clinic at Madurai, India, all children showed signs of protein-calorie malnutrition, with 80 percent weighing less than 60 percent of normal weight-for-height.

The "curse" therefore is not that rice is the staple but that xerophthalmic children eat practically nothing but rice to the exclusion of more expensive but more nutritious foods such as meat, fish, and dairy products. Contrary to McLaren's assertion, therefore, it is a shortage of food that produces the high incidence of xerophthalmia because the consumption of animal foods would prevent both malnutrition and xerophthalmia. If one tries to reverse this logic and argues that it is a failure to eat more green, leafy vegetables that causes the blindness, one gets into a sick joke. Xerophthalmia is associated with an extremely high rate of mortality. But xerophthalmic children do not die from xerophthalmia; they die from protein-calorie malnutrition (or from respiratory or gastrointestinal infections to which protein-calorie malnutrition makes them vulnerable). Although there is some contrary evidence, it is conceivable that by dosing malnourished children with vitamin A or by getting them to eat quantities of green, leafy vegetables, their eyesight could be preserved close to the hour of death; but their mortality rate would remain unchanged. The contrary evidence is that children with mild symptoms of xerophthalmia have a higher rate of mortality than children whose eyes are normal, regardless of their overall nutritional status as judged by height-for-weight measurements. This could mean that mild vitamin A deficiency predisposes children to experience fatal episodes of respiratory or gastrointestinal infections. Or it could simply mean that children who more readily display ocular symptoms of vitamin A deficiency are also more vulnerable to gastrointestinal and respiratory diseases. But even those experts who hold that Vitamin A deficiency increases mortality rates independently of general nutritional status admit that "the possibility also exists that diarrhea and respiratory disease increase the risk of xerophthalmia, thereby establishing a vicious cycle."

Actually, the more severe the protein-calorie malnutrition, the more difficult it becomes to prevent or cure xerophthalmia simply by increasing the intake of carotene or vitamin A. Clinical evidence indicates that in children receiving therapeutic doses of vitamin A, recovery from xerophthalmic impairment is delayed or transitory unless they are also treated for protein-calorie malnutrition. British xerophthalmic specialist A. Pirie, writing in the *Proceedings of the Nutrition Society*, states: "correction of protein-energy malnutrition is essential to assure a sustained chemical cure and repeated massive vitamin A therapy is advisable until that occurs."

With these grim details in focus, a significantly different picture of the avoidance of green, leafy vegetables by Third World children begins to emerge. I shall not argue that avoidance represents an optimization of practical costs and benefits, since I am not prepared to weigh the costs of dying prematurely with xerophthalmia against the cost of dying prematurely without xerophthalmia. But it seems likely that the aversion to dark green, leafy vegetables represents an attempt to satisfy the malnourished child's most urgent calorie-protein needs first. If, as a result of poverty, the only choice available is to eat rice or green, leafy vegetables, it is rice that represents by far the better bargain. Life of sorts can be sustained on rice alone. The disadvantaged child's number one nutritional priority must be to eat large quantities of it—as much as can possibly be crammed into a small stomach. And this may be more than family finances can provide. In a sense, therefore, the child may not be eating too much rice, but too little, given the absence of alternative foods. But would it not be better at any level of rice consumption to eat green, leafy vegetables? Not necessarily. What the clinical evidence about the relationship between protein-calorie malnutrition and the treatment of xerophthalmia suggests is that in severely malnourished children, rather massive quantities of green, leafy vegetables may be needed—much more than the thirty grams per day recommended for the normally nourished and healthy child. If large quantities of green, leafy vegetables are needed to have any effect, questions about costs of production and land use arise. Is there really enough surplus agricultural land and labor to provide large quantities of these foods?

Finally, I find myself wondering what would happen if, under parental pressure, toddlers aged two or three were to give up their aversion to dark green, leafy vegetables. Bearing in mind the excruciating choices which peasant families are forced to make in the allocation of food, would there not be a tendency to give the less economically productive members more green, leafy vegetables and less rice? If so, it may not be irrational to spurn green, leafy vegetables. Who can blame hungry weanling children for not wanting to be fed on leaves—next to water and grass, the least efficient source of proteins and calories available to humankind? To blame a toddler's rejection of green, leafy vegetables on a silly aversion to greens is to fly in the face of the fact that Asian and Southeast Asian diets contain considerable quantities of dark green, leafy vegetables (as I pointed out in the chapter on lactophobes and lactophiles). Indeed, studies carried out in Indonesia show that "leafy vegetables rich in beta-carotene were already consumed on a regular basis by families with and without xerophthalmia." If anything, the poorer the family, the more greens they eat and the less rice. So there is no certainty that by advising the poorest families to feed more greens to their toddlers, and by doing nothing else, any substantial improvement in overall child morbidity and mortality rates would be achieved.

As I said, failure to identify the rational causes of apparently irrational foodways can lead to ineffective or dangerous remedies. Conviced that xerophthalmia was largely the result of bad thoughts, the World Health Organization went so far as to declare in 1976 that "if the consumption of green leafy vegetables and suitable fresh fruits by young children could be substantially increased, there is every reason to believe that the problem will be solved." Fortunately, most nutritionists are aware that the prevention and treatment of xerophthalmia must be part of broader programs aimed at increasing protein-calorie consumption as well as at increasing the consumption of vitamin A.

●　●　●

While affluence has made it unnecessary for most developed countries to weigh the costs and benefits of starving adults versus starving children, it has certainly not diminished the importance of cost-benefit reckoning in the determination of what we eat. If anything, with the rise of transnational corporations that produce and sell food on the world market, our foodways are being constrained by an ever more precise but one-sided form of cost-benefit reckoning. To an increasing extent what is good to eat is what is good to sell. Moreover, affluence has been shown to have its own unanticipated restraints in the form of foodways that are dangerous because there is too much to eat rather than too little. We now realize that the "on" switches of human appetite are far more sensitive than the "off" switches. This genetic defect is a standing invitation to the food industry to overnourish its customers. But the cost in terms of obesity and cardiovascular disorders have already led to a widening aversion to high-fat, high-cholesterol animal foods. Neither overnutrition nor the reaction it has produced can be understood apart from the complex interaction of practical restraints and opportunities with their different and often inversely related bottom lines for consumers, farmers, politicians, and corporations. As I pointed out at the beginning of this book, optimization is not optimization for everybody. That is why this is not the moment in history to advance the idea that foodways are dominated by arbitrary symbols. To eat better we must know more about the practical causes and consequences of our changing foodways. We must know more about food as nourishment, and we must know more about food as profit. Only then we will really be able to know food as thought.

REFERENCES

See Bibliography pp. 258–74 for full citations.

CHAPTER ONE
GOOD TO THINK
OR GOOD TO EAT?

page 14, line 18
Abrams 1983
page 15, line 4
Fischler 1981:60
page 15, line 9
Soler 1979:129
page 15, line 12
Welsch 1981:369

CHAPTER TWO
MEAT HUNGER

page 19, line 8
Kifner 1985
page 19, line 20
Economist 1981
page 20, line 18
Kozlowski 1981
page 20, line 35
Economist 1980:43
page 21, line 1
Rudbeck and Meyers 1982
page 21, line 8
Crittenden 1981

page 21, line 21
Pimentel and Pimentel 1979:52;
Pimentel et al. 1975
page 23, line 3
Chase 1982
page 23, line 24
Nair 1983
page 24, line 20
Whyte 1974:62
page 24, line 36
Crittenden 1981
page 25, line 8
Perissé et al. 1969
page 25, line 13
Barr 1981
page 25, line 15
Omwale 1979:7–8
page 25, line 18
Nair 1983; Schofield 1979:90–91
page 26, line 5
Siskind 1973:84
page 26, line 13
Gross 1975:532
page 26, line 13
Lee 1979:451
page 26, line 34
Gross 1975:532
page 27, line 1
Dentan 1968:34

page 27, line 5
Good 1982
page 27, line 30
Marshall 1976:57
page 28, line 25
Harris 1984
page 30, line 3
Redford, da Fonseca, Lacher n.d.
page 30, line 13
Harding 1975
page 30, line 24
William Hamilton 1983
page 30, line 32
Teleki 1981
page 30, line 35
Wrangham 1977
page 34, line 16
McLaren 1974
page 35, line 2
Scrimshaw 1977
page 35, line 36
Dolphin 1982
page 37, line 33
McNeil 1984
page 38, line 3
Milton 1983
page 38, line 20
Maga 1982; Cheryan 1980; Harland and Prosky 1979; Reinhold et al. 1976
page 39, line 12
"Lipid Research Clinics Coronary Primary Prevention Trial Results" 1984
page 39, line 28
Abrams 1980:64
page 40, line 6
McCarron et al. 1984; Kolata 1984
page 40, line 13
Kolata 1985
page 40, line 16
National Research Council 1982:5–18
page 40, line 27
Ibid.: 11–13
page 41, line 3
Kolata 1985a

page 41, line 13
Reed 1980:294
page 41, line 26
Speth 1983:155
page 42, line 1
Eaton and Konner 1985:285
page 42, line 13
Speth 1983:144ff
page 42, line 36
Stefansson 1944:234
page 44, line 2
Bunch 1985:1
page 44, line 22
Eaton and Konner 1985:283
page 45, line 17
National Research Council 1982

CHAPTER THREE
THE RIDDLE OF
THE SACRED COW

page 48, line 15
Lewis 1955:105
page 48, line 29
Gandhi 1954:3–4
page 49, line 30
Batra 1981:8–9
page 50, line 9
Malik 1979:484
page 50, line 20
Yang 1980
page 52, line 17
Mitra 1881: 34–35
page 52, line 20
Bose 1961:109
page 52, line 36
Bondi 1982:203
page 54, line 32
Lodrick 1981
page 55, line 11
Kosambi 1975:136
page 57, line 25
Subrahmanyam and Ryan 1975; Binswanger 1977
page 58, line 4
Chakravarti 1985:36

page 59, line 32
Vaidyanathan, Nair, and Harris 1982
page 61, line 12
Heston 1971
page 63, line 6
Lodrick 1981:199
page 63, line 26
Dolberg 1982
page 64, line 10
Chakravarti 1985:34
page 64, line 32
DeWalt 1985
page 65, line 28
Gauthier-Pilters and Dagg 1981:110

CHAPTER FOUR
THE ABOMINABLE PIG

page 67, line 4
Bondi 1982:209
page 67, line 13
Towne and Wentworth 1950:7
page 68, line 7
Cohn 1936:19
page 68, line 18
Maimonides 1876:370–71
page 69, line 22
Ibid.:370
page 70, line 7
Cohn 1936:17–18
page 70, line 10
Block 1980; Klein n.d.
page 71, line 3
Benenson 1980:12–15
page 71, line 36
Douglas 1966
page 72, line 28
Grzimek 1984
page 73, line 18
Pond and Haupt 1978:276
page 74, line 6
Mount 1968:140
page 74, line 14
Ibid.:220

page 74, line 15
Pond and Maner 1984
page 75, line 17
Clutton-Brock 1981:72
page 75, line 29
Epstein 1971, vol. 2:349–50; Ducos 1968; Friedman 1985
page 76, line 7
Coon 1951
page 76, line 21
Whyte 1961
page 79, line 16
West 1971
page 80, line 8
Kenneth Russell 1985
page 80, line 13
Bulliet 1975
page 80, line 31
Glubb 1964
page 83, line 23
Herodotus 1947
page 83, line 32
Darby et al. 1977
page 84, line 7
Ibid.:185
page 84, line 14
Ibid.:185
page 84, line 12
Simoons 1961:18; Epstein 1971:354; Hawkes 1973:101
page 85, line 17
Coon 1951
page 86, line 29
Simoons 1961:40

CHAPTER FIVE
HIPPOPHAGY

page 88, line 18
Rossier 1982
page 89, line 1
Root 1974
page 90, line 29
Zarins 1976; Sherratt 1981; Olsen 1984

page 92, line 13
Hintz 1977
page 93, line 2
Kust 1983
page 93, line 10
Brereton 1976; White 1964; Simpson 1951; Law 1980
page 94, line 26
Hehn 1976:60
page 95, line 23
Brereton 1976:29
page 95, line 33
Creasy 1969:85–89
page 96, line 1
Bachrach 1970
page 96, line 7
Markov 1979:136
page 96, line 28
Migne 1850: 578
page 97, line 18
Van Bath 1963:68
page 97, line 28
Brereton 1976:71; Duby 1974:167
page 98, line 3
Braudel 1973:252–55
page 98, line 17
Gade 1976
page 98, line 22
Simoons 1961
page 98, line 25
Gade 1976
page 98, line 34
Braudel 1973:133; cf. Goody 1982:134–35
page 99, line 19
Van Bath 1963:289–91
page 99, line 26
Ibid.: 22; 64
page 100, line 12
Braudel 1973:257
page 100, line 14
Gade 1976:2
page 100, line 27
Bernheim and Rousseau 1908
page 101, line 3
Larrey 1812–17

page 101, line 23
Root 1974:84
page 103, line 19
Ross 1983:102
page 103, line 27
O'Donovan 1940:183
page 103, line 31
Ross 1980:189
page 104, line 29
Breeders Gazette 1919
page 105, line 5
Wentworth 1917
page 105, line 16
Hooker 1981:300
page 105, line 23
Ensminger 1977:vii
page 105, line 26
Corn n.d.:3
page 106, line 31
Personal communications from Ron Corn and Stanley M. Teeter
page 106, line 35
Buck 1981
page 108, line 17
Military Market 1982

CHAPTER SIX
HOLY BEEF, U.S.A.

page 109, line 8
Gallo 1983:5
page 109, line 10
Gallo and Blalock, 1981:23
page 110, line 1
Sahlins 1976:171
page 110, line 22
Thompson 1942:20
page 110, line 23
Hooker 1981:18ff
page 111, line 25
Wilson 1973
page 112, line 14
Ross 1983
page 113, line 28
Bondi 1982

page 114, line 31
Towne and Wentworth 1950:181
page 114, line 35
Henlen 1959
page 115, line 15
Cole 1938
page 115, line 19
Root and Rochemont 1976:122
page 115, line 25
Ibid.:125
page 116, line 7
Hooker 1981:57
page 116, line 10
Ibid.:112–13
page 116, line 14
Gates 1960:216
page 116, line 20
Ibid.:216–17
page 116, line 28
Root and Rochemont 1976:112
page 116, line 33
Gates 1960:231
page 117, line 31
Root and Rochemont 1976:204
page 118, line 7
Towne and Wentworth 1955
page 118, line 32
Armour 1906; Russel 1905
page 119, line 5
Ross 1980:191
page 119, line 23
U.S. Department of Agriculture 1983:12
page 120, line 35
Kolata 1985b
page 121, line 30
Hooker 1981:329
page 122, line 15
Luxemberg 1985:216; Shipp 1985
page 122, line 35
Pabst 1979; Blyskal 1982; Williams 1984
page 124, line 21
Office of the Federal Register 1984
page 128, line 6
Kleinfield 1984

CHAPTER SEVEN
LACTOPHILES AND
LACTOPHOBES

page 130, line 6
Lowie 1966:57
page 131, line 32
New York Times 1962
page 132, line 35
Bayless and Rosensweig 1966; Quatrecases et al. 1965
page 135, line 18
Ahmed 1975
page 135, line 17
Federal Trade Commission 1979:488
page 135, line 31
Ibid.:511
page 136, line 9
Ibid.:558
page 136, line 26
Phillips 1981
page 136, line 33
Lisker et al. 1980
page 136, line 35
Johnson et al. 1977
page 137, line 10
Simoons 1981
page 138, line 16
Wen et al. 1973
page 140, line 20
Molnar 1983:162ff; Malkenson and Keane 1983
page 140, line 26
Newcomer et al. 1978:219
page 140, line 29
Flatz and Rotthauwe 1977:236
page 141, line 6
Debongnie et al. 1979
page 141, line 20
Cochet et al. 1983
page 141, line 32
Federal Trade Commission 1979:512–13
page 143, line 15
MacLaughlin and Holick 1983

page 143, line 36
Durham 1986
page 144, line 24
Malkenson and Keane 1983
page 144, line 33
Ariel 1981
page 145, line 12
Ibid.
page 146, line 35
Sherratt 1981; 1983
page 147, line 2
Kenneth Russell, personal communication; Dennel 1982
page 148, line 2
Kolars et al. 1984; Savaiano et al. 1984
page 148, line 33
Ferro-Luzzi 1980b:253
page 149, line 1
Jaffrey 1973
page 151, line 14
Cross 1977
page 152, line 30
Dahl and Hjort 1976:159ff

CHAPTER EIGHT
SMALL THINGS

page 155, line 34
McGrew 1977:278
page 156, line 31
Bodenheimer 1951
page 157, line 12
Essig 1934
page 157, line 14
Bates 1960; Ruddle 1973; Hitchcock 1962
page 157, line 32
Dufour 1979
page 158, line 10
Chang 1977:13
page 158, line 20
Bodenheimer 1951:271
page 158, line 29
Ibid.:257

page 158, line 35
Spence 1977:267
page 159, line 28
Bristowe 1932 cited in Bodenheimer 1951:254
page 160, line 15
Bodenheimer 1951:40
page 160, line 20
Myers 1982; Remington 1946; Bourne 1953
page 161, line 4
Bodenheimer 1951:39
page 162, line 2
Holt 1885
page 162, line 6
Oliveira et al. 1976
page 162, line 9
Pennington and Church 1980
page 162, line 14
DeFoliart 1975; Redford and Dorea 1984
page 162, line 19
Reed 1980:162; Oliveira et al. 1976
page 163, line 21
Gorham 1979:215
page 165, line 24
Charnov 1976; Smith 1983; Winterhalder and Smith 1981
page 167, line 18
Hawkes, Hill, and O'Connell 1982
page 170, line 9
Conley 1969

CHAPTER NINE
DOGS, CATS, DINGOES,
AND OTHER "PETS"

page 176, line 14
Cooper 1983:174
page 177, line 9
Fisher 1983
page 177, line 12
Mead 1977:111
page 178, line 4
Evans-Pritchard 1940:28

page 178, line 11
Ibid.:26
page 180, line 15
Newsweek 1983
page 180, line 32
Luomala 1961
page 180, line 35
Savachinsky 1975
page 181, line 27
Luomala 1961:228
page 183, line 1
Ibid.:209
page 183, line 13
Ibid.:207
page 183, line 19
Ibid.
page 183, line 24
Ibid.:202
page 184, line 19
Savachinsky 1975:474
page 185, line 14
Driver and Coffin 1975
page 185, line 32
Driver 1961:34
page 186, line 6
Carroll 1984
page 186, line 29
Lowie 1938:303–307
page 187, line 21
Cited in Annette Hamilton
1972:289
page 187, line 23
Ibid.
page 187, line 27
Meggitt 1965
page 188, line 3
Isobel White 1972:201
page 189, line 9
Annette Hamilton 1972:
288
page 189, line 26
Macintosh 1975:99
page 189, line 30
Corbett and Newsome 1975
page 190, line 3
Webster's Third New International Dictionary

page 192, line 30
Quigley, Vogel, and Anderson
1983:270
page 193, line 12
Salmon and Salmon 1983:255–66
page 193, line 22
Drake 1981:57
page 194, line 15
Harlow and Harlow 1962:136
page 194, line 31
Fox 1981:29
page 195, line 24
Wall Street Journal 1985
page 196, line 20
Katcher 1981:53
page 196, line 24
Horn and Meer 1984
page 197, line 25
Katcher 1981; Quigley et al. 1983

CHAPTER TEN
PEOPLE EATING

page 200, line 12
Rivera 1960:44–46
page 201, line 14
Zeries 1960:126
page 201, line 29
Metraux 1947:22–24
page 202, line 7
Rivera 1960:46
page 202, line 35
Gajdusek 1977
page 203, line 18
Sorenson and Gajdusek 1969
page 203, line 25
Steadman and Merbs 1982
page 203, line 30
Lindenbaum 1979
page 203, line 35
Reed and Gajdusek 1969:340
page 206, line 23
Staden 1929:155–62
page 206, line 28
Arens 1979

page 207, line 2
Forsyth 1985
page 208, line 6
Staden 1929:21
page 209, line 3
Cited in Forsyth 1983:155
page 209, line 22
Ibid.:159
page 209, line 33
Ibid.:163
page 210, line 11
Ibid.:164
page 211, line 5
Ibid.:166
page 211, line 24
Cited in Abler 1980:314
page 211, line 30
Ibid.
page 212, line 4
Thwaites 1896:1901,
34:33
page 212, line 27
Ibid., 13:61
page 213, line 30
Ibid.:67
page 214, line 10
Ibid.:79
page 214, line 16
Arens 1979:129
page 216, line 31
Abler 1980:315
page 217, line 7
Cited in Abler 1980:313
page 217, line 16
Vayda 1960:70
page 217, line 29
Ibid.:72
page 219, line 29
Montaigne 1927:210
page 223, line 19
Erskine 1853:260
page 223, line 33
Sahlins 1983:81
page 224, line 4
Thompson 1908:358
page 224, line 12
Sahlins 1983:80

page 224, line 30
Earle 1977
page 225, line 10
Sahlins 1958
page 226, line 19
Bernal Diaz 1956:215
page 226, line 21
Sahagun 1951:24
page 226, line 2
Tapia 1971:583
page 226, line 32
Ortiz de Montellano 1983:404
page 226, line 36
Tapia 1971:583
page 227, line 11
Sherburne Cook 1946
page 227, line 17
Berdan 1982:114
page 227, line 34
Motolinia 1951:116
page 229, line 31
Sahlins 1978:45
page 230, line 29
Berdan 1982:24
page 232, line 2
Drennan 1984
page 233, line 23
Ortiz de Montellano 1978:614

CHAPTER ELEVEN
BETTER TO EAT

page 235, line 11
Bennet 1967:251
page 235, line 15
Harns 1967
page 237, line 5
Wood 1979:154
page 237, line 15
Ferro-Luzzi 1980a
page 238, line 17
Ibid.:107
page 238, line 28
Ibid.: 109
page 238, line 31
Ibid.:110

page 238, line 32
Ibid.:109
page 239, line 12
Christine Wilson 1980
page 240, line 6
Ibid.:72
page 241, line 21
Gulati 1981:27–28
page 242, line 7
Nichter and Nichter 1983:238
page 243, line 7
Dewalt and Pelto 1977:82
page 243, line 21
Tielsch and Sommer 1984:194
page 244, line 23
McLaren 1976:28

page 244, line 36
Pirie 1983:57–58
page 245, line 14
Kahn, Hague, and Kahn 1984
page 245, line 19
Tielsch and Sommer 1984:194–95;
Sommer and Muhilal 1982
page 245, line 32
Sommer et al. 1984:1094
page 246, line 8
Pirie 1983:58
page 247, line 15
Tielsch and Sommer 1984:199
page 247, line 26
Quoted in Pirie 1983:60

BIBLIOGRAPHY
OF CITED REFERENCES

Abrams, H. Leon. 1980. "Vegetarianism: An Anthropological/Nutritional Evaluation." *Journal of Applied Nutrition* 12:53–87.

———. 1983. "Cross Cultural Survey of Preferences for Animal Protein and Animal Fat." Paper presented at Wenner-Gren Founation Symposium no. 94, 23–30 October, Cedar Key, Florida.

Abler, Thomas. 1980. "Iroquois Cannibalism: Fact Not Fiction." *Ethnohistory* 27:309–316.

Ahmed, H. F. 1975. "Irritable-Bowel Syndrome with Lactose Intolerance." *Lancet* 2:319–20.

Arens, William. 1979. *The Man-Eating Myth.* New York: Oxford University Press.

Ariel, Irving. 1981. "Theories Regarding the Etiology of Malignant Melanoma." In *Malignant Melanoma,* ed. Irving Ariel, 9–32. New York: Appleton-Century-Crofts.

Armour, J. O. 1906. *The Packers and the People.* Philadelphia: Henry Aetemus.

Bachrach, Bernard. 1970. "Charles Martel, Mounted Shock Combat, the Stirrup and Feudalism." *Studies in Medieval and Renaissance History* 7:49–75.

Barr, Terry. 1981. "The World Food Situation and Global Grain Prospects." *Science* 214:1087–95.

Bates, Marston. 1960. "Insects in the Diet." *American Scholar* 29:43–52.

Batra, S. M. 1981. *Cows and Cow-Slaughter in India.* Institute of Social Studies. Occasional Papers. The Hague.

Bayless, T. M., and N. S. Rosensweig. 1966. "A Racial Difference Incidence of Lactase Deficiency: A Survey of Milk Intolerance and

258

Lactase Deficiency in Healthy Adult Males." *Journal of the American Medical Association* 197:968–72.

Bellamy, Edward. 1917. *Looking Backward, 2000–1887*. Boston: Houghton Mifflin.

Benenson, Abram, ed. 1980. *Control of Communicable Diseases in Man*. 13th ed. Washington, D.C.: The American Public Health Association.

Bennet, John. 1967. "On the Cultural Ecology of Indian Cattle." *Current Anthropology* 8:251–52.

Berdan, Frances. 1982. *Aztecs of Central Mexico*. New York: Holt, Rinehart and Winston.

Bernal Diaz del Castillo. 1956. *The Discovery and Conquest of Mexico 1517–1521*. New York: Farrar, Straus and Giroux.

Bernheim, S., and P. Rousseau. 1908. *Le cheval aliment*. Paris: Librairie J. Rousset.

Block, Abraham. 1980. *The Biblical and Historical Background of Jewish Customs and Ceremonies*. New York: KTAV Publishing House.

Blyskal, Jeff. 1982. "The Burger Boom Slows Down." *Forbes* (11 October):45–46.

Binswanger, Hans. 1977. "The Economics of Tractors in the Indian Subcontinent." International Crops Research Institute for the Semi-Arid Tropics. Occasional Papers. Hyderabad.

Bodenheimer, F. S. 1951. *Insects as Human Food*. The Hague: W. Junk Publishers.

Bondi, A. 1982. "Nutrition and Animal Productivity." In *CRC Handbook of Agricultural Productivity*, ed. Miloslav Recheigl, 195–212. Boca Raton, FL: CRC Press.

Bose, A. N. 1961. *Social and Rural Economy of Northern India, 600 B.C.–200 A.D*. Calcutta: K. L. Mukhopadhyay.

Bourne, G. H. 1953. "The Food of the Australian Aboriginal." *Proceedings of the Nutrition Society*. 12:58–65.

Braudel, Fernand. 1972. *The Mediterranean and the Mediterranean World in the Age of Phillip II*. 2 vols. New York: Harper & Row.

———. 1973. *Capitalism and Material Life: 1400–1800*. New York: Harper & Row.

Breeders Gazette. 1919. "Horse Meat is a Fact." 76:598.

Brereton, J. M. 1976. *The Horse in War*. New York: Arco Publishing.

Bristowe, W. S. 1932. "Insects and Other Invertebrates for Human Consumption in Siam." *Transactions of the Entomological Society of London* 80:387–404.

Buck, Ernest. 1981. "Consumer Acceptance of a Flaked and Formed Horsemeat Steak Product." Report produced for the M & R Packing Company, Hartford, CT.

Bulliet, Richard. 1975. *The Camel and the Wheel*. Cambridge: Harvard University Press.

Bunch, Karen. 1985. "U.S. Food Consumption on the Rise." *National Food Review* (Winter-Spring):1–4.

Carroll, Michael. 1984. "Why We Don't Eat Dogs—Usually." Unpublished manuscript.

Chakravarti, A. K. 1985. "Cattle Development Problems and Programs in India: A Regional Analysis." *Geo Journal* 10(no. 1):21–45.

Chang, K. C., ed. 1977. *Food in Chinese Culture: Anthropological and Historical Perspective*. New Haven: Yale University Press.

Charnov, Eric. 1976. "Optimal Foraging: The Marginal Value Theorum." *Theoretical Population Biology* 9:129–36.

Chase, Charlotte. 1982. "Food Symbolism and Proletarian Unrest in Poland." Paper read at the Annual Meeting of the American Association for the Advancement of Science, 3–8 January, Washington, D.C.

Cheryan, M. 1980. "Phytic Acid Interaction in Food Systems." CRC Critical Reviews in Food Science. *Nutrition* 13:297.

Clutton-Brock, Juliet. 1981. *Domesticated Animals from Early Times*. London: British Museum of Natural History.

Cochet, Bernard, et al. 1983. "Effects of Lactose on Intestinal Calcium Absorption in Normal and Lactase-Deficient Subjects." *Gastroenterology* 84:935–40.

Cohn, Rabbi Jacob. 1936. *The Royal Table: An Outline of the Dietary Laws of Israel*. New York: Block.

Cole, Arthur. 1938. *Wholesale Commodity Prices in the United States 1700–1861*. Cambridge: Harvard University Press.

Conley, Robert. 1969. "Teeth of the Wind." *National Geographic* 136 (no. 2): 202–27.

Cook, Sherburne. 1946. "Human Sacrifice and Warfare As Factors in the Demography of Pre-Colonial Mexico." *Human Biology* 18:81–102.

Coon, Carleton. 1951. *Caravan*. New York: Henry Holt.

Cooper, Gale. 1983. *Animal People*. Boston: Houghton Mifflin.

Corbett, L., and A. Newsome. 1975. "Dingo Society and Its Maintenance: A Preliminary Analysis." In *The Wild Canids*, ed. Michael Fox, 369–79. New York: Van Nostrand Reinhold.

Corn, Ronald. n.d. *Hippophagy*. Report prepared for Ronald J. Corn, president of M and R Packing Company and Marco International. Hartford.

Creasy, Edward. 1969. *The Fifteen Decisive Battles of the World*. New York: Heritage Press.

Crittenden, Ann. 1981. "Consumption of Meat Rising in the Developing Countries." *New York Times*, 25 August :1.

Cross, B. A. 1977. "Comparative Physiology of Milk Removal." In *Comparative Aspects of Lactation*, ed. M. Peaker, 193–210. New York: Academic Press.

Cuatrecasas, A., et al. 1965. "Lactase Deficiency in the Adult: A Common Occurrence." *Lancet* 1:14–18.

Dahl, G., and A. Hjort. 1976. *Having Herds: Pastoral Herd Growth and Household Economy*. Stockholm: Stockholm Studies in Anthropology.

Darby, William, P. Ghalioungui, and L. Givetti. 1977. *Food: The Gift of Osiris*. vol. 1. New York: Academic Press.

Debongnie, J. D., et al. 1979. "Absorption of Nutrients in Lactase Deficiency." *Digestive Disease Sciences* 24:255.

Decroix, Emile-François. 1864. *L'Alimentation par la viande de cheval*. Paris: Asselin.

DeFoliart, G. R. 1975. "Insects as a Source of Protein." *Bulletin of the Entomological Society of America* 21:161–63.

Dennel, Robin. 1982. *European Economic Prehistory*. New York: Academic.

Dentan, Robert. 1968. *The Semai: A Non-Violent People of Malaya*. New York: Holt, Rinehart and Winston.

DeWalt, Billie. 1983. "The Cattle Are Eating the Forest." *Bulletin of the Atomic Scientists* 39:18–23.

———. 1985. "Mexico's Second Green Revolution." *Mexican Studies* 1:29–60.

Dewalt, Kathleen, and Gretl Pelto. 1977. "Food Use and Household Ecology in a Modernizing Mexican Community." In *Nutrition and Anthropology in Action*, ed. T. Fitzgerald, 74–93. Amsterdam: Van Gorcum.

Dolberg, Frands. 1982. *Livestock Strategies in India*. Institute of Political Science. Aarhus, Denmark.

Dolphin, David, ed. 1982. *B12*. 2 vols. New York: John Wiley.

Douglas, Mary. 1966. *Purity and Danger: An Analysis of Concepts of Pollution and Taboo*. New York: Praeger.

Drake, Katherine. 1981. "Companionship's Comparative Costs." *Money* (December):56ff.

Drennan, Robert. 1984. "Long Distance Movement of Goods in the Mesoamerican Formative and Classic." *American Antiquity* 49:27–43.

Driver, Harold. 1961. *Indians of North America*. Chicago: University of Chicago Press.

Driver, Harold, and J. Coffin. 1975. "Classification and Development of North American Indian Cultures: A Statistical Analysis of the Driver-Massey Sample." *Transactions of the American Philosophical Society* 47:165–456.

Duby, Georges. 1974. *The Early Growth of the European Economy*. Ithaca: Cornell University Press.

Ducos, P. 1968. *L'Origine des animaux domestiques en Palestine*. Bordeaux: Imprimeries Delmas.

————. 1969. "Methodology and Results of the Study of the Earliest Domesticated Animals in the Near East (Palestine)." In *The Domestication and Exploitation of Plants and Animals*, ed. P. Ucko and G. Dimbleby. Chicago: Aldine.

Dufour, Darna. 1979. "Insects in the Diet of Indians in the Northwestern Amazon." Paper read at the 48th Annual Meeting of the American Association of Physical Anthropology, April, San Francisco.

Durham, William. 1986. *Coevolution: Genes, Cultures, and Human Diversity*. Stanford: Stanford University Press.

Earle, Timothy. 1977. "A Reappraisal of Redistribution in Complex Hawaiian Chiefdoms." In *Exchange Systems in Prehistory*, ed. Timothy Earle and Jonathan Ericson, 213–32. New York: Academic Press.

Eaton, S. B., and M. Konner. 1985. "Paleolithic Nutrition: A Consideration of Its Nature and Current Implications." *New England Journal of Medicine* 312:283–89.

The Economist. 1980. 19 July :43.

The Economist. 1981. 1–7 August : 42–43.

Ensminger, M. Eugene. 1977. *Horses and Tack*. Boston: Houghton Mifflin.

Epstein, H. 1971. *The Origin of Domestic Animals in Africa*. 2 vols. New York: Africana Publishing Co.

Erskine, John. 1853. *Journal of a Cruise among the Islands of the Western Pacific*. London: Dawsons of Pall Mall.

Essig, E. O. 1934. "The Value of Insects to the California Indians." *Scientific Monthly* 38:181–86.

Evans-Pritchard, E. E. 1940. *The Nuer: A Description of the Modes of Livelihood and Political Institutions of a Nilotic People*. Oxford: Clarendon Press.

Federal Trade Commission. 1979. California Milk Producers Advisory Board, et al., Final Order, Etc. in Regard to Alleged Violation of Secs. 5 and 12 of the Federal Trade Commission Act. Docket 8988. Washington, D.C.: Federal Trade Commission Decisions.

Ferro-Luzzi, G. E. 1980a. "Food Avoidance at Puberty and Menstruation in Tamiland"; "Food Avoidances in Pregnant Women in Tamiland"; "Food Avoidances during the Peuperium and Lactation in Tamiland." In *Food, Ecology and Culture: Readings in the Anthropology of Dietary Practices*, ed. John Robson, 92–100; 101–8; 109–17. New York: Gordon and Breach.

———. 1980b. "Commentary: Lactose Malabsorption Reconsidered." *Ecology of Food and Nutrition* 9:247–256.

Fischler, Claude. 1981. "Food Preferences, Nutritional Wisdom and Sociocultural Preferences." In *Food, Nutrition and Evolution: Food As an Environmental Factor in the Genesis of Human Variability*, ed. Dwain Walcher and Norman Kretchmer, 59–67. New York: Masson Publishing.

Fisher, Maxine. 1983. "Of Pigs and Dogs: Pets as Produce in Three Societies." In *New Perspectives on Our Lives with Companion Animals*, ed. Aaron Katcher and Alan Beck, 132–37. Philadephia: University of Pennsylvania Press.

Flatz, Gebhard, and Hans Rotthauwe. 1977. "The Human Lactase Polymorphism: Physiology and Genetics of Lactase Absorption and Malabsorption." In *Progress in Medical Genetics*, ed. A. G. Steinberg, et al., 205–49. Philadelphia.

Forsyth, Donald. 1983. "The Beginnings of Brazilian Anthropology: Jesuits and Tupinamba Cannibalism." *Journal of Anthropological Research* 39:147–78.

———. 1985. "Three Cheers for Hans Staden: The Case for Brazilian Cannibalism." *Ethnohistory* 32:17–36.

Fox, Michael. 1981. "Relationship Between Human and Non-Human Animals." In *Interrelations Between People and Pets*, ed. Bruce Fogle, 23–40. Springfield, IL: Charles C. Thomas.

Friedman, Thomas. 1985. "In Israel New Fight over Pork Sales Turns Pigs into Endangered Species." *New York Times*, July 20, p. 2.

Gade, Daniel. 1976. "Horsemeat as Human Food in France." *Ecology of Food and Nutrition* 5:1–11.

Gajdusek, D. Carleton. 1977. "Unconventional Viruses and the Origin and Disappearance of Kuru." *Science* 197:943–60.

Gallo, Anthony. 1983. "Food Consumption Patterns: Concentration and Frequency." *National Food Review* (Spring): 5–7.

Gallo, Anthony, and William Boehm. 1979. "What Influences Demand for Red Meat?" *National Food Review* (Summer): 24–27.

Gallo, Anthony, and James Blalock. 1981. "Foods Not Eaten by Americans." *National Food Review* (Summer): 22–24.

Gandhi, Mohandas. 1954. *How To Serve the Cow*. Ahmadabad: Navajvan Publishing House.

Gates, Paul. 1960. *The Farmer's Age: Agriculture: Economic History of the United States*. vol. 3. New York: Holt, Rinehart and Winston.

Gauthier-Pilters, Hilde, and Anne Dagg. 1981. *The Camel: Its Evolution to Man*. Chicago: University of Chicago Press.

Geoffroy Saint-Hilaire, Isidore. 1856. *Lettres sur les substances alimen-*

taires et particulièrement sur la viande de cheval. Paris: Librairie de Victor Masson.

Glubb, Sir John. 1964. *Great Arab Conquests*. Englewood Cliffs, N.J.: Prentice Hall.

Good, Kenneth. 1982. "Limiting Factors in Amazonian Ecology." Paper read at the Annual Meeting of the American Anthropological Association, Washington, D.C.

Goody, Jack. 1982. *Cooking, Cuisine, and Class: A Study in Comparative Sociology*. New York: Cambridge University Press.

Gorham, J. Richard. 1979. "The Significance for Human Health of Insects in Food." *Annual Review of Entomology* 24:209–24.

Gross, Daniel. 1975. "Protein Capture and Cultural Development in the Amazon Basin." *American Anthropologist* 77:526–49.

Grzimek, Bernhard. 1984. *Animal Life Encyclopedia*. New York: Van Nostrand Reinhold.

Gulati, Leela. 1981. *Profiles in Female Poverty: A Study of Five Poor Working Women in Kerala*. Delhi: Hindustan Publishing.

Hamilton, Annette. 1972. "Aboriginal Man's Best Friend?" *Mankind* 8:287–95.

Hamilton, William. 1983. "Omnivorous Primate Diets and Their Relevance to Contemporary Human Dietary Overconsumption of Meat and Other Goodies." Paper read at Wenner-Gren Foundation Symposium no. 94, 23–30 October, Cedar Key, FL.

Harding, Robert. 1975. "Meat Eating and Hunting in Baboons." In *Socioecology and Psychology of Primates*, ed. R. H. Tuttle, 245–257. The Hague: Mouton.

Harland, B. F., and L. Prosky. 1979. "Development of Dietary Fiber Values for Foods." *Cereal Foods World* 24:387.

Harlow, Harry, and M. Harlow. 1962. "Social Deprivation in Monkeys." *Scientific American* 207(5):137–46.

Harner, Michael. 1977. "The Ecological Basis for Aztec Sacrifice." *American Ethnologist* 4:117–35.

Harris, Marvin. 1967. "Reply to John Bennet." *Current Anthropology* 8:252–53.

———. 1977. *Cannibals and Kings*. New York: Random House.

———. 1984. "Animal Capture and Yanomano Warfare: Retrospect and New Evidence." *Journal of Anthropological Research* 40:183–201.

Hawkes, Kristen, Kim Hill, and J. O'Connell. 1982. "Why Hunters Gather, Optimal Foraging and the Aché of Eastern Paraguay." *American Ethnologist* 9:379–98.

Hawkes, Jaquetta. 1973. *The First Great Civilizations*. New York: Alfred Knopf.

Hehn, Victor. 1976. *Cultivated Plants and Domesticated Animals in*

Their Migration from Asia to Europe. Amsterdam: John Benjamins.

Henlen, Paul. 1959. *Cattle Kingdoms in the Ohio Valley.* Lexington: University of Kentucky Press.

Herodotus. 1947. *The Persian Wars.* New York: Modern Library.

Heston, Alan. 1971. "An Approach to the Sacred Cow of India." *Current Anthropology* 12:191–210.

Hintz, Harold. 1977. "Digestive Physiology." In *The Horse,* ed. J. W. Evans, 241–58. San Francisco: W. H. Freeman.

Hitchcock, Stephen W. 1962. "Insects and Indians of the Americas." *Bulletin of the Entomological Society of America* 8:181–87.

Holt, Vincent M. 1885. *Why Not Eat Insects?* Reprinted in 1969. London: E. W. Classey.

Hooker, Richard. 1981. *Food and Drink in America.* New York: Bobbs-Merrill.

Horn, Jack, and Jeff Meer. 1984. "The Pleasure of Their Company." *Psychology Today* (August):52ff.

Jaffrey, Madhur. 1973. *An Invitation to Indian Cooking.* New York: Alfred Knopf.

Johnson, J. D. et al. 1978. "Lactose Malabsorption among Adult Indians of the Great Basin and American Southwest." *American Journal of Clinical Nutrition* 31:381–87.

Kahn, M. U., E. Hague, and M. R. Kahn. 1984. "Nutritional Ocular Diseases and Their Association with Diarrhoea in Matlob, Bangladesh." *British Journal of Nutrition* 52:1–9.

Katcher, Aaron. 1981. "Interaction Between People and Their Pets: Form and Function." In *Interrelations between People and Pets,* ed. Bruce Fogel, 41–67. Springfield, IL: Charles C. Thomas.

Kifner, John. 1985. "Poles Fairly Calm over Price Rise." *New York Times,* 14 February.

Klein, Isaac. n.d. *A Guide to Jewish Religious Practice.* New York: The Jewish Theological Seminary of America.

Kleinfield, N. R. 1984. "America Goes Chicken Crazy." *New York Times,* 9 December: Section 3.

Kolars, J.C., et al. 1984. "Yogurt—An Autodigesting Source of Lactose." *New England Journal of Medicine* 310:1–3.

Kolata, Gina. 1984. "Does a Lack of Calcium Cause Hypertension?" *Science* 225:705–6.

———. 1985a. "Heart Panel's Conclusions Questioned." *Science* 227:40–41.

———. 1985b. "Testing for Trichinosis." *Science* 227:621; 624.

Kosambi, Damodar. 1975. *An Introduction to the Study of Indian History.* Bombay: Popular Prakashan.

Kozlowski, Zygmunt. 1981. "Special Focus: Food Consumption Problems in Poland." *Food Policy* 6:47–52.

Kroc, Ray. 1977. *Grinding It Out: The Making of McDonald's*. Chicago: Henry Regnery.

Kust, Matthew. 1983. *Man and Horse in History*. Alexandria, Va.: Plutarch Press.

Larrey, Dominique. 1812–17. *Mémoires de chirugie militaire et campagnes*. Paris: J. Smith.

Law, Robin. 1980. *The Horse in West African History*. Oxford: Oxford University Press.

Lee, Richard. 1979. *The !Kung San: Men, Women, and Work in a Foraging Society*. New York: Cambridge University Press.

Lewis, W. A. 1955. *The Theory of Economic Growth*. Homewood, Il.: R. D. Irwin.

Lindenbaum, Shirley. 1974. *Kuru Sorcery: Disease and Danger in the New Guinea Highlands*. Palo Alto, Calif.: Mayfield.

———1984. "Lipid Research Clinics Coronary Primary Prevential Trial Results." *Journal of the American Medical Association* 251:351–74.

Lisker, R., et al. 1980. "Double Blind Study of Milk Lactose Intolerance in a Group of Rural and Urban Children. *American Journal of Clinical Nutrition* 33:1049–53.

Lodrick, Deryck. 1981. *Sacred Cows, Sacred Places*. Berkeley: University of California Press.

Lowie, Robert. 1938. "Subsistence." In *General Anthropology,* ed. Franz Boas, 282–326. New York: Heath.

———1966. *Culture and Ethnology*. New York: Basic Books.

Luomala, Katherine. 1961. "The Native Dog in the Polynesian System of Values." In *Essays in Honor of Paul Radin,* ed. Stanley Diamond, 190–239. Waltham: Brandeis University.

Luxemberg, Stanley. 1985. *Roadside Empires: How the Chains Franchised America*. New York: Viking Penguin.

Macintosh, N. W. G. 1975. "The Origin of the Dingo: An Enigma." In *The Wild Canids,* ed. Michael Fox, 87–106. New York: Van Nostrand Reinhold.

MacLaughlin, Julia, and M. Holick. 1983. "Photobiology of Vitamin D_3 in the Skin." In *Biochemistry and Physiology of the Skin,* ed. Lowell Goldsmith, 734–54. New York: Oxford University Press.

Maga, J. A. 1982. "Phytate: Its Chemistry, Occurrence, Food Interactions, Nutritional Significance, and Methods of Analysis." *Journal of Agricultural Food Chemistry* 30:1.

Malkenson, F., and J. Keane. 1983. "Radiobiology of the Skin." In *Biochemistry and Physiology of the Skin,* ed. Lowell Goldsmith, 769–814. New York: Oxford University Press.

Maimonides, Moses. 1876. *The Guide for the Perplexed*. Translated by M. Friedlander. London: Pardes.

Malik, S. L. 1979. "Comment on 'Questions in the Sacred-Cow Controversy' by F. J. Simoons." *Current Anthropology* 22:484.

Markov, Walter. 1979. *Battles of World History*. New York: Hippocrene Books.

Marshall, Lorna. 1976. "Sharing, Talking, and Giving: Relief of Social Tensions among the !Kung." In *Kalahari Hunter-Gatherers: Studies of the !Kung San and Their Neighbors*, ed. Richard Lee and Irven Devore, 349–72. Cambridge: Harvard University Press.

McCarron, David, et al. 1984. "Hypertension and Calcium." *Science* 226:386–89.

McGrew, William. 1977. "Socialization and Object Manipulation of Wild Chimpanzees." In *Primate Bio-Social Development*, ed. Susan Chevalier-Skolinkoff and Frank Poirier, 261–88. New York: Garland.

McLaren, Donald. 1974. "The Great Protein Fiasco." *Lancet* (no. 2):93–96.

————1976. "Historical Perspective of Nutrition in the Community." In *Nutrition in the Community*, ed. Donald McLaren, 25–34. New York: Wiley.

McNeil, N. I. 1984. "The Contribution of the Large Intestine to Energy Supplies in Man." *American Journal of Clinical Nutrition* 39:338–342.

Mead, Margaret. 1977. *Letters from the Field: 1925–1972*. New York: Harper & Row.

Meggit, M. J. 1965. "The Association between Australian Aborigines and Dingoes." "In *Man, Culture, and Animals*, ed. A. Leeds and A. P. Vayda, 7–26. Washington, D.C.: The American Association for the Advancement of Science.

Metraux, Alfred. 1947. "Mourning Rites and Burial Forms of the South American Indians." *American Indigana* 7:7–44.

Migne, J. P., ed. 1850. *Patrologiae*. Vol. 89:578.

Military Market. 1982. August:11.

Milton, Katherine. 1983. "The Role of Food Processing Factors in Primate Food Choice: An Examination of Some Determinants of Dietary Variation Among Non-Human Primates and Implications for the Hominid Diet." Paper read at Wenner-Gren Foundation Symposium no. 94, 23–30 October, Cedar Key, FL.

Mitra, Rajendra. 1881. *Indo-Aryans*. vol. 1. Calcutta: W. Newman and Co.

Molnar, Stephen. 1983. *Human Variation: Races, Types, and Ethnic Groups*. 2d ed. Englewood Cliffs, N.J.: Prentice Hall.

Montaigne, Michel Eyquem de. 1927. *The Essays of Montaigne*. New York: Oxford University Press.

Motolinia, Toribio. 1951. *History of the Indians of New Spain*. Washington, D.C.: Academy of American Franciscan History.

Mount, Lawrence. 1968. *The Climatic Physiology of the Pig*. London: Edward Arnold.

Myers, Norman. 1982. "Homo Insectivorus." *Science Digest* (May):14–15.

Nair, Narayanan. 1983. "Animal Protein Consumption and the Sacred Cow Complex in India." Paper read at Wenner-Gren Foundation Symposium 94, 23–30 October, Cedar Key, FL.

National Research Council. 1982. *Diet, Nutrition, and Cancer*. Washington, D.C.: National Research Council.

Newcomer, Albert, et al. 1978. "Lactase Deficiency: Prevalence in Osteoporosis." *Annals of Internal Medicine* 89:218–20.

Newsweek. 1983. 12 December:60.

New York Times. 1962. 7 January.

Nichter, Mark, and Mimi Nichter. 1983. "The Ethnophysiology and Folk Dietetics of Pregnancy: A Case Study from South India." *Human Organization* 42:235–46.

O'Donovan, J. 1940. *The Economic History of Livestock in Ireland*. Dublin: Cork University Press.

Office in the Federal Register. 1984. *Code of Regulations: Animals and Animal Products*. Washington, D.C.: National Archives and Records Service, General Services Administration.

Oliveira, J. F. Santos, et al. 1976. "The Nutritive Value of Four Species of Insects Consumed in Angola." *Ecology of Food and Nutrition* 5:91–97.

Olsen, Stanley. 1984. "The Early Domestication of the Horse in North China." *Archaeology* (January–February): 62–63; 77.

Omwale. 1979. "The Meat Myth and Caribbean Food Planning." Institute of Social and Economic Research, University of the West Indies. Working paper 25. Jamaica.

Ortiz de Montellano, B. R. 1978. "Aztec Cannibalism: An Ecological Necessity?" *Science* 200:611–17.

———1983. "Counting Skulls: Comment on the Aztec Cannibalism Theory of Harner-Harris." *American Anthropologist* 85:403–6.

Pabst, Henry. 1979. "The Hamburger Phenomenon." Proceedings of the 32d Annual Meat Conference. Chicago: National Livestock and Meat Board.

Pennington, Jean, and Helen Church. 1980. *Food Values of Portions Commonly Used*. New York: Harper & Row.

Perissé, J., F. Sizaret, and P. François. 1969. "The Effects of Income on the Structure of Diet." *Nutrition Newsletter* 7.

Phillips, S.F. 1981. "Lactose Malabsorption and Gastrointestinal Function: Its Effect on Gastrointestinal Transit and Absorption of Other Nutrients." In *Lactose Digestion: Clinical and Nutritional Implications*, ed. David Paige and Theodore Bayless, 51–57. Baltimore: Johns Hopkins University Press.

Pimentel, David, et al. 1975. "Energy and Land Constraints in Food Protein Production." *Science* 190:754–61.

Pimentel, David, and M. Pimentel. 1979. *Food, Energy and Society*. New York: John Wiley.

Pirie, A. 1983. "Vitamin A Deficiency and Child Blindness in the Developing World." *Proceedings of the Nutrition Society* 42:53–64.

Pond, G. Wilson, and Jerome Maner. 1984. *Swine Production and Nutrition*. Westport, Conn.: AVI.

Pond, Wilson, and K. Haupt. 1978. *The Biology of the Pig*. Ithaca: Comstock Publishing Associates.

Quigley, J., L. Vogel, and R. Anderson. 1983. "A Study of Perception and Attitudes towards Pet Ownership." In *New Perspectives on Our Lives with Companion Animals*, ed. Aaron Katcher and Alan Bach, 266–75. Philadelphia: University of Pennsylvania Press.

Redford, Kent, and José Dorea. 1984. "The Nutritional Value of Invertebrates with Emphasis on Ants and Termites as Food for Mammals." *Journal of the Zoological Society of London* 203:385–95.

Redford, Kent, G. Bouchardet da Fonseca, and T. E. Lacher, Jr. n.d. "The Relationship Between Frugivory and Insectivory in Primates." Mimeo.

Reed, Patsy. 1980. *Nutrition: An Applied Science*. San Francisco: West Publishing.

Reed, Lucy, and D. Carleton Gajdusek. 1969. "Nutrition in the Kuru Region." *Acta Tropica* 26:331–45.

Reinhold, J. G., B. Faradji, P. Abadi, and F. Ismail-Beigi. 1976. "Decreased Absorption of Calcium, Magnesium, Zinc, and Phosphorus by Humans Due to Increased Fiber and Phosphorus Consumption as Wheat Bread." *Journal of Nutrition* 106:493–503.

Remington, Charles L. 1946. "Insects as Food in Japan." *Entomological News* 57 (no. 5): 119–21.

Rivera, Diego. 1960. *My Art, My Life: An Autobiography*. With Gladys March. New York: The Citadel Press.

Root, Waverly. 1974. "They Eat Horses, Don't They?" *Esquire* 81 (January): 82–85.

Root, Waverly, and Richard de Rochemont. 1976. *Eating in America*. New York: William Morrow.

Ross, Eric. 1980. "Patterns of Diet and Forces of Production: An Economic and Ecological History of the Ascendancy of Beef in the United States Diet." In *Beyond the Myths of Culture: Essays in Cultural Materialism*, ed. Eric Ross, 181–225. New York: Academic.

————1983. "The Riddle of the Scottish Pig." *BioScience* 33:99–106.

Rossier, Emanuel. 1982. *Viande chevaline*. Paris: Cereopa.

Rudbeck, J., and P. Meyers. 1982. "Feed Grains: The Sluggish Demand Means Stepped-Up Competition." *Foreign Agriculture* (January): 10–11.

Ruddle, Kenneth. 1973. "The Human Use of Insects: Examples from the Yukpa." *Biotrpica* 5:94–101.

Russel, Charles. 1905. *The Greatest Trust in the World*. New York: Ridgway-Thayer.

Russell, Kenneth. 1985. "The Differential Adoption of Post-Pleistocene Subsistence Strategies in the Near East." Doctoral dissertation, University of Utah.

Sahagun, Bernardino de. 1951. *The General History of the Things of New Spain: Florentine Codex*. Book 2. Santa Fe, New Mexico. School of American Research. Salt Lake City, Utah: University of Utah Press.

Sahlins, Marshall. 1958. *Social Stratification in Polynesia*. Seattle: University of Washington Press.

————1976. *Culture and Practical Reason*. Chicago: University of Chicago Press.

————1978. "Culture As Protein and Profit." *New York Review of Books* (23 November): 45–53.

————1983. "Raw Women, Cooked Men and other Great Things of the Fiji Islands." In *The Ethnography of Cannibalism*, ed. Paula Brown and Donald Tugin, 72–93. Society for Psychological Anthropology. Washington, D.C.: American Anthropological Association.

Salmon, Peter, and Ingrid Salmon. 1983. "Who Owns Who? Psychological Research into the Human-Pet Bond in Australia." In *New Perspectives on Our Lives with Companion Animals*, ed. Aaron Katcher and Alan Beck, 243–65. Phialdephia: University of Pennsylvania Press.

Savachinsky, Joel. 1975. "The Dog and the Hare: Canine Culture in an Athabaskan Band." In *Proceedings of the Northern Athabaskan Conference*, ed. A. Clark, vol. 2, 462–515. Ottowa: National Museum of Canada.

Savaiano, D., et al. 1984. "Lactose Malabsorption from Yogurt, Sweet Acidophilus Milk, and Cultured Milk in Lactase-Deficient Individuals." *The American Journal of Clinical Nutrition* 40:1219–23.

Schofield, Sue. 1979. *Development and the Problems of Village Nutrition*. Montclair, N.J.: Allenheld, Osmund.

Scrimshaw, Nevin. 1977. "Through a Glass Darkly: Discerning the Practical Implications of Human Dietary Protein-Energy Interrelationships." *Nutrition Reviews* 35:321–37.

Sherratt, Andrew. 1981. "Plough and Pastoralism: Aspects of Secondary Products Revolution." In *Pattern of the Past: Studies in Honor of David Clarke*, ed. I. Hodder, G. Isaac, and N. Hammond, 261–305. Cambridge: Cambridge University Press.

————1983. "The Secondary Exploitation of Animals in the Old World." *World Archaeology* 15:90–104.

Shipp, E. R. 1985. "The McBurger Stand That Started It All." *New York Times*, 27 February: 14.

Simoons, Frederick. 1961. *Eat Not This Flesh*. Madison: University of Wisconsin Press.

————1981. "Geographic Patterns of Primary Adult Lactose Malabsorption: A Further Interpretation of Evidence for the Old World." In *Lactose Digestion: Clinical and Nutritional Implications*, ed. David Paige and T. Bayless, 23–48. Baltimore: Johns Hopkins Press.

Simpson, George G. 1951. *Horses: The Story of the Horse Family in the Modern World and through Sixty Million Years of History*. New York: Oxford University Press.

Siskind, Janet. 1973. *To Hunt in the Morning*. New York: Oxford University Press.

Smith, Eric. 1983. "Anthropological Implications of Optimal Foraging Theory: A Critical Review." *Current Anthropology* 24:625–51.

Soler, Jean. 1979. "The Semiotics of Food in the Bible." In *Food and Drink in History: Selections from the Annales, Economiks, Civilisations*, ed. Robert Foster and Orest Ranum, 126–38. Baltimore: Penguin.

Sommer, Alfred. 1984. "Increased Risk of Respiratory Disease and Diarrhea in Children with Preexisting Mild Vitamin A Deficiency." *American Journal of Clinical Nutrition* 40:1090–95.

Sommer, A., and Muhilal. 1982. "Nutritional Factors in Corneal Xerophthalmia and Keratomalacia." *Archives of Ophthalmology* 100:399–411.

Sorenson, E., and D. Carlton Gajdusek. 1969. "Nutrition in the Kuru Region." *Acta Tropica* 26:281–330.

Spence, Jonathan. 1977. "Chi Ing." In *Food in Chinese Culture: Anthropological and Historical Perspectives*, ed. K. C. Chang, 261–294. New Haven: Yale University Press.

Speth, John. 1983. *Bison Kills and Bone Counts*. Chicago: University of Chicago Press.

Staden, Hans. 1929. *The True History of His Captivity 1557*. New York: Robert McBride and Co.

Steadman, Lyle, and Charles Merbs. 1982. "Kuru and Cannibalism?" *American Anthropologist* 84:611–27.

Stefansson, Vilhajalmur. 1944. *Arctic Manual*. New York: Macmillan.

Subrahmanyam, K. V., and J. G. Ryan. 1975. "Livestock as a Source of Power in Indian Agriculture: A Brief Review." International Crops Research Institute for the Semi-Arid Tropics. Occasional Paper no. 12. Hyderabad.

Tapia, Andrew de. 1971. *Relación Hecha por el Señor Andrés de Tapia sobre la Conquista de México*. In *Colección de Documentos Para la Historia de México*, ed. J. G. Icozbalceta, vol. 2, 554–94. Liechtenstein: Nendelu. Kraus reprint.

Teleki, Geza. 1981. "The Omnivorous Diet and Eclectic Feeding Habits of Chimpanzees in Gombe National Park, Tanzania." In *Omnivorous Primates: Gathering and Hunting in Human Evolution*, ed. Geza Teleki and R. O. Harding, 303–43. New York: Columbia University Press.

Thompson, Basil. 1908. *The Fijians: A Study of the Decay of Custom*. London: Heinemann.

Thompson, J. 1942. *The History of Livestock Raising in the United States 1607–1860*. Washington, D.C.: United States Department of Agriculture.

Thwaites, R. G., ed. 1896–1901. *The Jesuit Relations and Allied Documents: Travels and Explorations of the Jesuit Missionaries in New France*. 83 vols. Cleveland: Burrows Brothers.

Tielsch, James, and A. Sommer. 1984. "The Epidemiology of Vitamin A Deficiency and Xerophthalmia." *Annual Review of Nutrition* 4:183–205.

Towne, R. W., and E. Wentworth. 1950. *Pigs: From Cave to Corn Belt*. Norman: University of Oklahoma Press.

———1955. *Cattle and Men*. Norman: University of Oklahoma Press.

U.S. Department of Agriculture. 1981. Policy Memo, 27 March. "Labelings of Combinations of Ground Beef or Hamburger and Soy Products." Washington, D.C.: U.S. Department of Agriculture, Food Safety and Quality Service.

———1983. *Food Consumption, Prices and Expenditures 1962–82*. Washington, D.C.: United States Department of Agriculture, Economic Research Service, Statistical Bulletin 702.

Upadhye, A. N. 1975. "Tantrism." In *A Cultural History of India*, ed. A. L. Basham, 100–110. Oxford: Clarendon Press.

Vaidyanathan, A., K. N. Nair, and M. Harris. 1982. "Bovine Sex and Species Ratios in India." *Current Anthropology* 23:365–73.

Van Bath, B. H. Slicher. 1963. *The Agrarian History of Western Europe: A.D. 500–1850*. London: Edward Arnold.

Vayda, A. P. 1960. *Maori Warfare*. Polynesian Society Maori Monographs, No. 2. Wellington: Polynesian Society.

Wall Street Journal. 1985. 14 January: 14.

Wen, C. P., et al. 1973. "Lactose Feeding in Lactose-Intolerant Monkeys." *American Journal of Clinical Nutrition* 26:1224–28.

Welsch, Roger. 1981. "The Interdependence of Foodways and Architecture: A Foodways Contrast on the American Plains." In *Food in Perspective: Proceedings of the Third International Conference on Ethnological Food Research*, Cardiff, Wales, 1977, ed. Alexander Fenton and T. Owens, 365–76. Edinburgh: John Donald.

Wentworth, G. E. 1917. "Shall We Eat Horses." *Breeders Gazette* 72:911.

West, James King. 1971. *Introduction to the Old Testament*. New York: Macmillan.

White, Isobel. 1972. "Hunting Dogs at Yalata." *Mankind* 8:201–5.

White, Lynn. 1964. *Medieval Technology and Social Change*. New York: Oxford University Press.

Whyte, Robert O. 1961. "Evolution of Land Use in South-Western Asia." In *A History of Land Use in Arid Regions*, ed. L. D. Stamp. UNESCO Arid Zone Research 17.

———1974. *Rural Nutrition in Monsoon Asia*. New York: Oxford University Press.

Wilson, Anne. 1973. *Food and Drink in Britain: From the Stone Age to Recent Times*. London: Constable.

Wilson, Christine. 1980. "Food Taboos of Childbirth: the Malay Example." In *Food, Ecology and Culture: Readings in the Anthropology of Dietary Practices*, ed. John Robson, 67–74. Palo Alto, Calif.: Mayfair.

Winterhalder, Bruce and Eric Smith, eds. 1981. *Hunter-Gatherer Foraging Strategies: Ethnographic and Archaeological Analysis*. Chicago: University of Chicago Press.

Wood, Corinne. 1979. *Human Sickness and Health: A Biocultural View*. Palo Alto, Calif.: Mayfield.

Wrangham, R. W. 1977. "Feeding Behavior in Chimpanzees in Gombe National Park, Tanzania." In *Primate Ecology: Studies of Feeding and Ranging Behavior in Lemurs, Monkeys and Apes*, ed. T. H. Clutton-Brock, 503–38. New York: Academic Press.

Yang, Arnand. 1980. "Sacred Symbol and Sacred Space in Rural India: Community Mobilization in the 'Anti–Cow Killing' Riot of 1893." *Comparative Studies in Society and History* 22:576–96.

Zarins, Juris. 1976. "The Domestication of Equidae in Third Millennium B.C. Mesopotamia." Ph.D. dissertation, University of Chicago.

Zerries, Otto. 1960. "En Endocanibalismo en la America del Sur." *Revista de Museo Paulista* 12:125–75.

INDEX

Outstanding Books from the Touchstone Library

☐ **Why Nothing Works**
The Anthropology of Daily Life
(Originally published as *America Now*)
By Marvin Harris

A brilliant exploration of why Detroit recalls
thousands of cars yearly; why toasters burn out
just after warranties expire—in other words, why
nothing works. With his keen anthropologist's
eye, Harris links our problems to the vast
bureaucracies that now direct our lives.
63577-8 $7.95

☐ **The Forest People**
By Colin Turnbull

Turnbull's classic study of the BaMbuti Pygmies
of the Congo has taken a preeminent place
alongside the works of Margaret Mead and Franz
Boaz in setting the standard for all ethnographic
writing.
64099-2 $9.95

☐ **The Family of Man**
*Created by Edward Steichen
for the Museum of Modern Art
Prologue by Carl Sandburg*

One of the most celebrated photography books
ever published. Here are 503 classic
photographs from around the world, drawn from
the landmark Museum of Modern Art exhibition.
Includes the work of Henri Cartier-Bresson,
Irving Penn, Alfred Eisenstaedt, Dorothea
Lange, Margaret Bourke-White and many other
international masters.
Paper   55411-5 $12.95
Cloth   55412-3 $19.95

☐ **Popul Vuh**
The Definitive Edition of the Mayan Book of the
Dawn of Life and the Glories of Gods and Kings
Translated by Dennis Tedlock

The first unabridged English edition of one of the
most extraordinary documents of the human
imagination—and *the* most important text in the
native languages of the Americas. With
introduction and commentaries.
61771-0 $9.95

☐ **The Mountain People**
By Colin Turnbull

In what Margaret Mead called a "beautiful and
terrifying book," Turnbull movingly presents the
story of a tribe of hunters whose society has
deteriorated in the face of rapidly diminishing
resources.
64098-4 $9.95

☐ **Touch the Earth**
A Self-Portrait of Indian Existence
*Compiled by T.C. McLuhan
Photographs by Edward S. Curtis*

American Indian culture is described through the
words of the Indians themselves. The fifty-three
sepia photographs taken by Curtis in the early
part of this century are almost the last visual
record of a people and their way of life.
22275-9 $8.95